Abridged
CONSUMER ECONOMICS
Eleventh Edition

Dr. Eugene D. Wyllie

School of Business
Indiana University

Dr. Nancy A. Lang

Assistant Professor and Director
Center for Economic Education
College of Business
Northern Kentucky University

Dr. D. Hayden Green

Business Education Department
Oak Park and River Forest High School
Oak Park, Illinois

Dr. Roman F. Warmke

Late Professor and Director
Center for Economic Education
College of Education
Ohio University

Published by
SOUTH-WESTERN PUBLISHING CO.

CINCINNATI   WEST CHICAGO, IL   CARROLLTON, TX   LIVERMORE, CA

Preface

The Eleventh Edition of *Consumer Economics* provides an overview of the roles of the individual, business, government, and foreign trade in the American economy. The individual economic roles of earning income, consuming, and performing as a citizen (voter) are carefully examined. Special emphasis is placed on the consumer activities of buying, saving, borrowing, investing, and insuring.

Consumer Economics, Eleventh Edition, has evolved from the successful use of preceding editions for nearly a half century. Countless suggestions have contributed to the development of this book into its present form. This book has kept pace with changing social, governmental, and business activities and trends. As a result of studying *Consumer Economics*, Eleventh Edition, you will be able to (1) operate more intelligently and efficiently as a member of our society and (2) understand our economic system and the relationships among the individual, business, labor, government, and foreign trade.

Specifically, *Consumer Economics*, Eleventh Edition, will enable you to:

1. explain the roles of consumers, investors, business, government, and international trade in the American economy;
2. explain the effect of business, labor, and government activities on individual decision making;
3. discuss the role of money and banking in our economy;
4. explain the basic economic principles that one must know in order to participate as a citizen (voter) in issues of local, state, and national importance;
5. identify the essentials of efficient management of your economic affairs;
6. describe how the consumer as a worker contributes to production in the American economy;

7. explain how the problems of unemployment and inflation affect the consumer;
8. identify the many federal, state, local, and private agencies providing consumer protection;
9. identify your legal rights and responsibilities as a consumer;
10. explain how to spend income and use credit wisely;
11. describe the many kinds of insurance available to the consumer and why they are important;
12. explain the important economic factors to consider when choosing a place to live;
13. explain the costs of owning a car and the procedures to follow in buying a new or used car.

Economic theory is not overemphasized in this book. A practical, non-theoretical writing style is used throughout. For instance, the student not only learns the economic function of money and credit but also learns how to manage money and credit in making daily consumer decisions. Principles and facts are given only to provide the background for a thorough analysis of the issues facing consumers in our economic society.

The authors are especially indebted to the countless students, teachers, economists, business people, labor leaders, government officials, and others who made this edition possible.

Eugene D. Wyllie
Nancy A. Lang
D. Hayden Green

Contents

PART FIVE   TRANSPORTATION AND SHELTER

PART SIX   INSURANCE

PART 1
Fundamental Economic Concepts

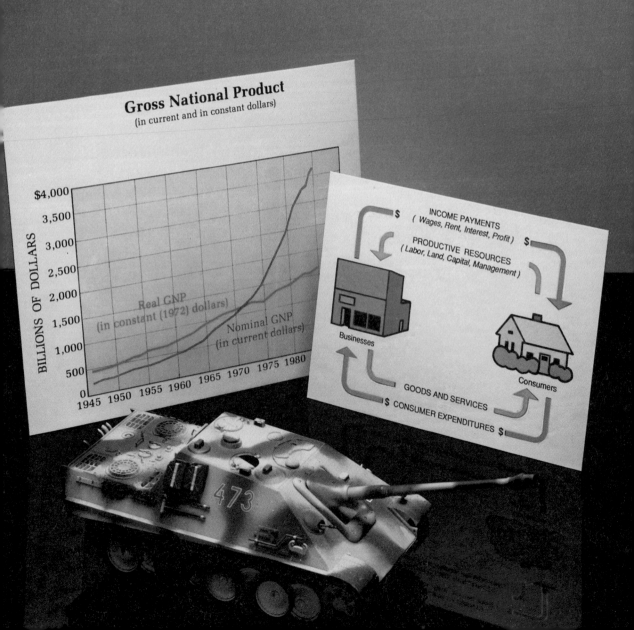

1

The Economic Setting

We constantly try to satisfy our wants and needs as individuals and as a society. We set goals and make choices in order to reach these goals. Economics is basically the study of how we make these choices.

After studying this chapter, you will be able to:

1. explain what is meant by economics, economic goods and services, economic wants and needs, and opportunity costs; and
2. list and explain six economic goals of American society.

WHAT ECONOMICS IS ALL ABOUT

Economics examines how people satisfy their unlimited wants and needs for goods and services with limited resources. More specifically, *economics* is the study of a process that involves choice making as people try to get the most satisfaction possible when they buy goods and services. The place where this choice-making process occurs is called the economy.

If you are like most people, you cannot buy all the goods and services you would like. Therefore, you must make choices. Most individuals and all nations are faced with the problem of making these choices. If a person or a nation is not able to have all the goods and services wanted or desired, *economic scarcity* exists.

Illus. 1–1

If you are like most people, you cannot buy all the goods and services you would like. Therefore, you must make choices.

Economic Goods and Services

An *economic good* is any material (tangible) object that people use to satisfy their wants or needs. The object must be scarce enough that people are willing to pay money for it. Almost everything you own is an economic good; for example, the clothes that you are wearing or the breakfast that you had this morning are economic goods.

The medical advice of a doctor, the winning run produced by a professional baseball player, and the ride provided by a taxi driver are not material objects, but they do satisfy wants or needs. These activities are classified as economic services. An *economic service* is any intangible product that people use to satisfy their wants or needs.

Economic Wants and Needs

Economic wants are the goods and services we buy for pleasure or comfort, such as cosmetics, sports equipment, and designer clothes. We may want many other intangible things, such as the love and affection of our family, the respect and admiration of our friends, and recognition for our achievements. These cannot be valued in terms of money, however, and therefore they are not economic wants.

Economic needs are such basics as food, clothing, and shelter. The distinction between economic needs and economic wants is sometimes difficult to make. What might be considered a want by one person could be considered a need by another. A car might represent a need for your parents who depend upon it for transportation to work. Your desire for a car is probably a want considering the other sources of transportation available to you.

Your wants usually change over a period of time. These changes might be the result of getting older, increased education, increased income, or a change in the place where you live. There are many sides to even your most basic needs and wants. For example, if you are hungry, you will eat almost anything. At other times, you are more selective about the food you eat.

How People Satisfy Economic Wants and Needs

Most people obtain money by working. This money is then used to buy goods and services to satisfy needs and wants. Sometimes people do not spend all the money they earn, but save some to buy things they want or need at a later date.

Some people do not have to work because they already have enough money to satisfy their economic wants and needs. Most of us, however, need the money we earn from our work to buy goods and services. Naturally, we want our work to be enjoyable and to provide satisfaction as well as money.

Opportunity Costs

Individuals are constantly making choices among the things they want. For example, you may want to go to a movie and you may want to go bowling. Assume that you only have enough money available at the time to do one or the other.

You must decide which way you are going to spend your money. The *real* or *opportunity cost* of what you choose is the value of your next best alternative or what you give up when you make your decision. In this case, the opportunity cost of going bowling is not going to the movie. The opportunity cost of going to the movie is not going bowling. Even if there were no monetary cost for the movie or for bowling, there would still be an opportunity cost since you cannot do both at the same time.

NATIONAL ECONOMIC GOALS

As individuals we cannot satisfy all of our economic wants. Therefore, we must make choices. The same is true for the nation. As a group we decide what those choices will be. Through the years we have established certain national economic goals with which most people agree. Though individuals may differ on the order of importance, we agree as a nation that we should strive for the following:

1. economic freedom,
2. economic efficiency,
3. economic growth,
4. economic stability,
5. economic opportunity,
6. economic security.

Economic Freedom

When people are free to make choices, they must decide what they want and then they must set their goals. As we said before, the real or opportunity cost of any choice is what people must give up to gain what they want. For example, you might have to decide whether to spend money for a vacation or for more education; to buy shoes or a suit; to make a down payment on a house or to buy a new car. To make wise decisions, you must think carefully about the value of each choice. Individuals have the *economic freedom* to make their own choices when satisfying their economic needs and wants. Economic freedom is discussed in more detail in Chapter 3 where we analyze personal economic goals.

Illus. 1–2
The real or opportunity cost of what you choose is what you give up when you make your decision. The opportunity cost of taking a vacation may be not continuing your education.

Economic Efficiency

Economic efficiency means making the best use of your limited resources—land, labor, capital (tools and machinery), and management. For example, a farmer can use land to produce either corn or wheat. The farmer must also determine the right amount of lime and fertilizer to use, the crop rotation schedule, and other conservation practices necessary to yield the greatest profit over a period of time. The combination of resources that produces the most or the best products is considered to be the most efficient economic mix.

Economic Growth

Most people expect to be better off than their parents, and for the most part, this is a reasonable goal. As a result of increases in our technology, our capital supply (tools and equipment), and our education, we have been able to produce more goods and services for each person. We generally accept the notion that the amount of goods and services we are able to buy will increase. This is *economic growth*. Chapter 30 is devoted to this economic goal.

Economic Stability

This goal represents a desire for a high level of employment without inflation or deflation. *Inflation* exists when there is a rise in the average level of prices for goods and services in the economy without a corresponding increase in the production of goods and services. During inflation the dollar loses much of its value. Inflation is hard on people with fixed incomes—for example, retired people—and on people who loan money. *Deflation* exists when the average price level falls. Deflation is equally undesirable in that it brings about increased unemployment and a waste of economic resources. Americans want neither inflation nor deflation; we want *economic stability*, which is few ups and downs in business activity. These fluctuations in the business cycle will be discussed in Chapter 31.

Economic Opportunity

Wealth consists of tangible goods that have monetary value because they are useful, desirable, and relatively scarce. Our wealth is made up of the things we own at a given time. Most people acquire wealth by working to earn an income. Other forms of income include: interest on savings; rent from an apartment building; or payments such as social security or private pensions, which are called transfer payments. A *transfer payment* is income received from government, business, or individuals for which no goods or services were produced.

Most people want to acquire more wealth—they want to own more land, buildings, and personal possessions. This wealth is usually acquired by working to earn an income and by investing successfully. Everyone has the right to earn an income or to invest to acquire wealth. This is known as *economic opportunity*.

Economic Security

People want always to be able to buy the economic goods and services to meet, at least, their basic needs. This is called *economic security*. Programs designed to create economic security include: care for the aged (such as Medicare and social security); support for the unavoidably unemployed (such as unemployment insurance); and aid for depressed areas (such as urban redevelopment). These programs will be treated in more detail in Chapter 22. Not everyone agrees on the types of economic security that should be provided in the United States, but nearly everyone supports some form of economic security.

Illus. 1–3

Everyone has the right to earn an income. This is known as economic opportunity.

FACTS EVERYONE SHOULD KNOW ABOUT THE BASIC ECONOMIC PROBLEM

1. Economics is the study of how people satisfy their unlimited wants and needs for goods and services with limited resources.
2. The existence of scarcity requires that individuals and the nation make choices.
3. An economic good is a tangible product; an economic service is any intangible product.
4. Opportunity cost is the value of the next best alternative foregone.
5. As a nation we have the following broad economic goals:
   a. economic freedom,
   b. economic efficiency,
   c. economic growth,
   d. economic stability,
   e. economic opportunity, and
   f. economic security.

VOCABULARY BUILDER

deflation
economic good
economic needs
economics
economic scarcity
economic service

economic wants
inflation
real or opportunity cost
transfer payment
wealth

REVIEW QUESTIONS

1. What are tangible products? What are intangible products?
2. Why must we usually make choices in what we buy?
3. What is an individual's freedom to make economic choices called?
4. What is making the best use of limited resources called?
5. What is the goal of economic growth?

6. What is the smoothing out of the ups and downs of business activities called?
7. What economic goal refers to the ability to acquire wealth?
8. What is economic security?

DISCUSSION QUESTIONS

1. If an item is available at no cost, it is not an economic good. How might this item become an economic good in a different situation?
2. How might one item be an economic need for one person but an economic want for another?
3. How and why do our wants sometimes change and increase?
4. How might two people agree on the same economic goals but differ on priorities of these goals? Use specific examples to illustrate your answer.
5. Is a person with a high income always wealthy? Without reference to specific people, give examples.
6. How does opportunity cost differ from actual or accounting cost?

Economics in Action

In Chapter 1, you learned that economics is basically a study of the process by which we make choices—individually and collectively—to satisfy our wants and needs. In this chapter we shall look at this process in more detail.

After studying this chapter, you will be able to:

1. list and explain three major types of economic systems;
2. describe our economy by explaining resource allocation, factors of production, and flows; and
3. list and explain the four basic characteristics of the American economy.

HOW ECONOMIC SYSTEMS ARE ORGANIZED

There are three types of economic systems:

1. Traditional economy
2. Command or directed economy
3. Market economy

Traditional Economy

In a *traditional economy* economic life is determined by such things as habit, custom, and religious tradition. In this system, economic roles are carried on from generation to generation.

For example, if your ancestors were carpenters, you will be a carpenter. In the economies of the distant past, economic decisions were based on tradition. In primitive societies today, economic decisions are still based on what has been done in the past.

Illus. 2–1

In a traditional economy, economic roles are carried on from generation to generation. You do what your ancestors did for a living.

Command or Directed Economy

Under a *command* or *directed economy*, the basic economic decisions are made by a central authority that consists of either a person or a group. The central authority decides, for example, how much of the production will be devoted to consumer goods and services. It also decides how much will be devoted to the production of tools and machinery used to produce additional goods. Under this system the individual consumer has little influence over the kinds of goods and services produced. In a command economy people have a limited voice in economic decison making.

Market Economy

A market economy is familiar to all of us, but is probably the most difficult to describe in a brief summary. A *market economy* is essentially a system where consumers vote (through buying or not buying particular goods or services) to determine what and how much will be produced. If a particular good or service is priced too high or is not wanted by potential customers, its production is stopped or cut back since it is not profitable. Likewise, if a particular good or service is extremely popular with consumers, more producers will enter the market. It is a system where people are free to determine for themselves what goods and services will be produced. Most of our discussions in this textbook are devoted to the market economy.

Mixed Economies

There is probably no pure economic system. A market economy may have elements of a command (directed) economy. For example, the sale of certain goods is restricted (rationed) during wartime because of limited supplies. The main characteristic of an economic system should be considered when applying the label of traditional, command, or market economy. Every economy tends to be a *mixed economy*. That is, each system has some elements of the traditional, some elements of the command, and some elements of the market economy.

ECONOMIC SYSTEMS EXAMINED

No matter what type of economy you examine, economics can be divided into three parts:

1. How limited resources are shared or allocated (distributed) among the members of the society. This is called *resource allocation.*
2. How resources are provided to business by consumers for which the consumers receive payments.
3. How the flow of goods and services and the corresponding flow of money function. This is illustrated in the circular flow.

Resource Allocation

Since human wants are greater than the resources available to fulfill them, goods and services must be allocated. Trying to make the most efficient use of available resources is called *economizing*. Every economy must determine what goods and services to produce and how to distribute those goods and services among the people.

These two broad decisions can be subdivided further into four problems of resource allocation faced by all economies:

1. *What* should be produced?
2. *How should* the goods and services be produced?
3. *How much* should be produced?
4. *How* should production be shared?

The study of economics involves an analysis of these four questions.

Factors of Production

The productive resources provided by consumers to businesses include the use of labor, land, capital, and management. These productive resources are called *factors of production*. In return for the use of these factors of production, businesses make income payments in the form of wages and salaries for labor, rent for owners of land, interest for owners of capital, and profit for management.

Labor (Human Resources). Labor in its broadest sense includes all physical effort, mental effort, and use of technical skills. In the United States people generally have a great deal of freedom to choose the type of work they want to do, the geographic area in which they want to work, and the kind of business activity in which they want to be engaged.

Land (Natural Resources). Natural resources are materials supplied by nature. Human beings did not create them, although people may have had to work to extract them from the earth or put them in a usable form. Tangible economic goods, such as foods, fabrics, machines, and houses, all had their origin in the earth; hence, they come from natural resources. Fabrics, for example, may be made either from natural fibers such as wool or cotton or from synthetic fibers such as dacron or rayon. But regardless of the type of fiber, the materials from which the fibers originated were natural resources. These resources comprise the basic elements for the production of tangible goods. One of our greatest economic problems is the conservation and wise use of natural resources.

Capital (Tools and Equipment). In an economic sense, capital refers to any buildings, equipment, or other physical property (other than raw materials) used in a business. Goods used for productive purposes in a business are known as capital goods. One of the most important capital goods is machinery.

Management (Entrepreneurship). Management is the key to a successful business operation. Even if we had the most modern buildings and equipment and the most intelligent and

Illus. 2-2

In the United States people generally have a great deal of freedom to choose the type of work they want to do.

industrious labor force, there could not be a successful business without good organization and management. In all businesses, plans must be made, workers hired, raw materials obtained, and equipment purchased or built. Putting all these factors together is called *entrepreneurship*, a function of management.

Circular Flow of Goods and Services and the Flow of Money

All people are *consumers*; that is, users of goods and services. Even the smallest child has certain needs and wants that must be satisfied. But some consumers are too young, too old, or too ill to be *producers*—the people who create economic goods or services. Consequently, the production of others must provide enough for the needs and wants of those who are not producers.

Businesses bid for the productive services (labor) of consumers. Labor helps to produce the goods and services that are used in our economy. In return for productive services, businesses provide consumers with income in the form of salaries or wages. The consumers, in turn, spend their income (money) for the goods and services produced. As a result, we have a circular flow of goods and services and money.

The circular flow of goods and services, and the flow of money in a market economy, are illustrated in Figure 2–1.

In Figure 2–1 the label *businesses* is used to represent all types of employment, including self-employment and employment by the government. As we examine economics in more detail, we shall study the effects of government spending and taxes, consumers' savings, operations of financial institutions such as banks, and foreign trade.

What to Produce. In our society, owners of property (such as factories, farms, or materials) are basically free to produce what they want for themselves or to produce what others want and are willing to buy. Few of us could produce all the goods and services we need. Therefore, we often work for others to earn income to buy goods and services that we need or want.

In a market economy, the individual, who has free choice, directs business production by his or her demand (through purchases). The individual provides labor, land, or capital

Figure 2-1
Circular Flow Diagram

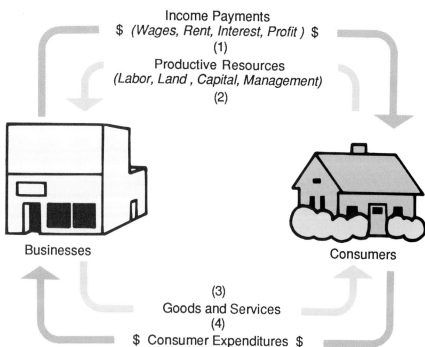

Income Payments
$ *(Wages, Rent, Interest, Profit)* $
(1)
Productive Resources
(Labor, Land , Capital, Management)
(2)

Businesses

Consumers

(3)
Goods and Services
(4)
$ Consumer Expenditures $

which the business firm uses to produce the goods and services needed to satisfy consumer demands. These goods and services are bought by consumers who provide income to the firm.

How to Produce. In a market economy, profit is the incentive for the producers to satisfy the wants of consumers. Management must always be aware of competition. In a market economy, the owners of property are free to determine how they can most efficiently use available resources.

Producers may use some of their own property, hire labor, borrow money, buy materials, rent or buy land, and buy or lease equipment to produce in the most efficient manner. In this process of production, the producers pay out income to workers, landowners, and suppliers of materials. These paid-out incomes become part of the circular flow of money.

There are many factors management must consider when trying to make production profitable. It is management's responsibility to enable the producer to sell the best product at the lowest price and still make the highest profit possible.

Management must decide how to use labor and capital to reduce costs, speed production, and improve quality. Competition with other producers forces management to satisfy the customers' desires as to design, color, and other characteristics of a product.

How Much to Produce. The amount of goods and services produced is determined by how much consumers are willing to buy at the prices offered. If people do not like the good or if the price is too high, they will not buy it and the producer will quit making it. If producers make products that are well liked and that can be sold at a profit, they will probably expand their business and produce more goods. If a competitor offers a new product that is lower in price or that consumers like better, the first producer will have difficulty selling its good.

In a market economy, consumers influence what will be produced by the way they spend their income. Of course, businesses try to influence the demand of consumers through advertising and other selling activities, but the final decision is made by the consumers. Consumers decide whether or not to buy and in what quantities and at what price. Because of the

Illus. 2-3

Businesses try to influence the demand of consumers through advertising.

competitive nature of business, if consumers cannot obtain what they want from one producer, there is usually another producer more than happy to satisfy them.

How Production is Shared. How much we share in production is determined by the relative scarcity of what we have to offer and by the productivity of our resources. A worker who is well educated usually earns more than one who is not. Efficient workers produce more goods than inefficient workers and are generally paid higher wages because they are more productive. Highly skilled managers usually receive more pay than those with less ability. Goods and services of high quality usually sell for higher prices than those of low quality. In other words, in a competitive market we pay for our resources, whether labor or materials, according to how they satisfy wants.

RESOURCE ALLOCATION PROBLEMS RELATED TO A MARKET ECONOMY

1. What to produce—the demand for goods and services as expressed by consumer spending.
2. How to produce—the use of productive resources (land, labor, capital, and management) in a production process to satisfy wants.
3. How much to produce—amount of goods and services produced as determined by consumer spending.
4. How production is shared—payment for resources according to how they satisfy consumer wants.

IMPORTANT CHARACTERISTICS IN THE COORDINATION OF OUR ECONOMY

The market economy is set apart from other economic systems because of several unique characteristics. These features include the right to private property, freedom of choice, profit motivation, and competition. A knowledge of these characteristics will help you understand the coordination of our economic system. Such knowledge provides insight into the resource allocation process, and it will help you to understand the nature of the flow of goods and services and money.

Private Property

The sources of our personal income include wages for work we do, profits from the operation of a business, interest for money we lend, rent for use of buildings or land, or transfer payments such as social security. After local, state, and federal taxes are paid, people can spend or save as much of their income as they wish.

The portion of income that people keep, regardless of whether it is kept in money, invested in securities (stocks, bonds), or held in the form of material assets (land, buildings), is known as *private property*. By saving some of their income, people and businesses can buy land, buildings, and other things. This private property may then be used to earn more income. Property ownership rights are an important characteristic of the American economy.

Let us assume for a moment that the government owned all property. This would mean that the government would have to direct the production of all economic goods needed by us to live. There would be no profit, hence little incentive to produce or improve a product. Government ownership of property, and therefore the means of production, would have us receive goods as the government chose to allocate them. The right to own property and to use it in making a profit provides Americans with an incentive to establish and operate business enterprises.

Freedom of Choice

The more than 230 million people in the United States want, need, and demand many economic goods and services. Business provides most products and services for consumers. But how does business know what goods and services consumers want? How does business know how much of each good or service to provide? How can the demands for goods and services by more than 230 million people be satisfied at prices they are able and willing to pay?

These economic questions are answered in large measure in the United States through the market system, a system based on freedom of choice. In a market system, no person, bureau, or government agency should be able to make arbitrary decisions to answer the questions for the country as a whole. How consumer needs will be satisfied is decided primarily by individual consumers, workers, and owner-managers individually and collectively. The market provides the answers to such questions as what needs for goods and services shall be satisfied, who shall produce specific goods, and who shall be employed in certain businesses. In a pure market economy, markets are self-regulated and self-controlled. The main regulating or controlling factors in a market economy are profits and competition, which are discussed later in this chapter.

In a market economy consumers have freedom of choice and their choices influence what will be produced, how much of each product will be produced, and the price that will be paid for goods and services. Producers in a market economy are free to engage in any lawful business from which they believe they can make a profit. In a market economy people may live where they wish, compete for the jobs available, and buy whatever goods and services they want and can afford.

Profit Motivation

Most people get satisfaction from accomplishments; many people enjoy helping others by making needed products or providing services; but, in the final analysis, most people work to earn an income. The income earned is used to meet their basic needs and wants, and the part that is left over may be invested in private property which may be used to produce additional income.

The part of our income that we save may be deposited in a bank or invested in a building or other property from which we hope to receive an income. We can also invest our savings in a business enterprise that we plan to operate ourselves, such as an appliance repair shop, a restaurant, or any other business that provides consumers with some goods or services that they want or need. The income remaining after the costs of running the business have been paid is called *profit*.

People would be considered unwise if they were to invest their savings in a business in which there was no chance to make a profit. Furthermore, businesses could not continue to operate long if their income was only great enough to meet costs. Corporations like Chrysler, Xerox, Texaco, and USX are no different in this respect than are business enterprises owned and operated by a single individual. They, too, must make a profit to remain in operation.

Usually, the more efficient a business is, the greater its profits will be. A business increases its chances for greater profits by offering consumers better products, lower prices, and better services than competing firms. Consumers are always looking for better products and services at lower prices. Only businesses that provide consumers with products and services that compete favorably with those offered by other business firms can stay in operation. Thus, consumers benefit from the efforts of businesses to make a greater profit by making their operations more efficient.

A portion of the profits of corporations is kept for use in the business—to pay expenses in years when business is not good, to build new buildings, and to buy and replace machines, equipment, and materials. Profits are also used to expand business activities which, in turn, create more jobs for more people.

Competition

Since a primary motive of business is to make as large a profit as possible, what prevents a business firm from demanding excessively high prices for its products and services? Why can't a business set its prices as high as it wishes?

When two or more firms offer the same or similar goods or services, they try to attract consumers by offering their products and services at prices that are either lower than or comparable to those of other firms serving the same consumers. Such businesses are said to be competitors. *Competition* is the effort of two or more businesses acting independently to attract customers. A firm may compete with its rivals in several ways. It may lower prices or give more favorable credit terms; it may improve its goods or services or create new ones that will better satisfy consumer needs; or it may change its goods and services to include features that competing goods do not have, making its goods and services more attractive to consumers.

The right to compete is important in our market economy. Everyone is free to enter a trade or business and to compete with others. Individuals may be restricted, however, by limited education and by lack of money to invest in a business. Workers are also free to move from job to job, although there may be family ties, lack of information, or other barriers that restrict such mobility. Businesses, likewise, are free to compete for workers' services.

Several federal laws have been passed to assure competition. These laws prevent businesses from agreeing upon prices to be charged for a good or service, thereby eliminating the effect of competition. An exception to the laws of competition are public utilities, such as water, electricity, telephone, and public transportation. A public utility usually has exclusive rights to provide services to a community, since one large utility company can often operate more efficiently than several smaller firms. This type of utility company is a *monopoly* because it is the only supplier of a particular service. To assure reasonable rates, these public utility monopolies are controlled by public commissions.

VOCABULARY BUILDER

competition
consumers
economizing
factors of production

monopoly
private property
producers
profit

REVIEW QUESTIONS

1. How is economic life determined in a traditional economy?
2. Who makes the basic economic decisions in a command economy?
3. Who ultimately decides what goods and services will be produced in a market economy?
4. What is the payment or return for the use of each factor of production?
5. What four problems do all economies face?
6. What is meant by the circular flow of goods and services and the circular flow of money?
7. What is the incentive for businesses to satisfy consumer wants in a market economy?
8. In a market economy what are the responsibilities of management?
9. In a market economy who determines how much of certain goods and services will be produced?

10. How are prices (for goods, services, labor, etc.) determined in a market economy?
11. How is resource allocation determined in a market economy? Explain.
12. What is the role of profit in a market economy?
13. What does business do with profits? Give examples.
14. How might profits benefit workers?
15. In a market economy, what prevents businesses from setting any price they wish for goods and services?
16. Why are some monopolies allowed in a market-oriented economy like the United States?

DISCUSSION QUESTIONS

1. What are some of the freedoms that you would lose if you lived under a government that owned all property?
2. How do you think your local stores determine what to sell and at what price?
3. How does profit determine whether or not a product will be produced? Could there be cases where products that could satisfy wants and needs would not be produced? Explain.
4. In what ways might competition help consumers?
5. Does the market system help the consumer? Why or why not?

The American Economy

To understand the activity of the total economy, one must first understand the activities and roles of the individual consumer. Similarly, to fully understand individual economic behavior, one must relate that behavior to the total economy.

After studying this chapter you will be able to:

1. identify three basic roles of the individual,
2. list and define four basic activities that the consumer performs,
3. define personal economic analysis and aggregate economic analysis, and
4. explain at least ten problems of society.

PERSONAL ECONOMIC ANALYSIS

Most individuals serve as workers, for which they receive an income. Every person is a consumer in that everyone has certain needs and wants that must be fulfilled. Most people also function as citizens, though some are more active in this role than others. Therefore, individuals can perform the roles of workers, consumers, and citizens. *Personal economic analysis* is a study of how an individual earns and uses income while functioning as a worker, a consumer, and a citizen.

Individual Roles

As workers, most individuals earn an income with which they buy economic goods and services. Some people work primarily for the satisfaction derived from their efforts. In any case, everyone must have some source of income if they are to meet even their most basic needs. For our purposes, we will consider the worker as one who receives income. The opportunity cost of working is the leisure time that one gives up in order to earn income.

As consumers, individuals try to satisfy their wants by acquiring goods and services. Savings is often given up so one can purchase goods and services. The opportunity cost is the savings one gives up for the present enjoyment of goods and services.

As citizens, individuals strive to obtain for themselves and others the benefits of public services. For example, citizens vote to pay taxes to build better roads or schools. Paying taxes reduces the amount of money an individual has to spend on goods and services such as stereos, automobiles, or entertainment. The individual's *discretionary funds*, the money left after buying necessities such as food, clothing, and shelter, are reduced. As a citizen, each person joins with other members of society to make collective decisions. The opportunity cost of collective decision making is the loss of some individual choice.

Consumer Activities

In one's role as a consumer, the individual must make decisions regarding spending, borrowing, saving, and investing. When individuals decide to spend part or all of their income, they do so to satisfy their wants by acquiring goods and services. The opportunity cost of buying a particular item is giving up the opportunity of purchasing a different item or keeping the income as savings.

When individuals decide to borrow money, they do so to consume more at the present time. The opportunity cost is to consume less later, since some future income must be used to pay back the money borrowed.

When individuals decide to save, they give up the pleasure of immediate consumption in order to consume more later or to have greater financial security. When individuals decide to invest, they sacrifice the present use of income or savings in order to increase future income.

FOUR WAYS CONSUMERS USE INCOME

1. Spending—The consumer gives up the opportunity to buy other goods or to save in order to satisfy wants now.
2. Borrowing—The consumer gives up the opportunity to consume more at a later date in order to consume more now.
3. Saving—The consumer consumes less at the present time in order to consume more at a later date or to increase financial security.
4. Investing—The consumer sacrifices the present use of income and savings in order to increase future income.

Personal Economic Freedom

As Americans we put a lot of emphasis on personal economic freedom. We want to live with as few government restrictions as possible. We want to increase our incomes and our wealth in order to have more goods and services. We want to be able to work where and for whom we please.

The way consumers cast votes (spend money) in the marketplace largely determines what goods and services will be produced. Every economic choice you make is an *economic vote*. You are serving as one of the final judges as to whether or not a good or service will remain on the market in its present form and at its present price. The manufacturer and the merchant try to determine what you will buy, but they may guess incorrectly.

As a consumer you have not only the power to determine what goods and services will be offered for sale, but also the ability to help set prices through your decisions to buy or not to buy these goods and services. Naturally, businesses try to influence your choices through advertising and marketing practices. You will have the opportunity to examine some of these practices in a later section of this book.

The way consumers cast votes (spend money) in the marketplace
determines what goods and services will be produced.

AGGREGATE ECONOMIC ANALYSIS

Aggregate economic analysis is the study of the relationships
that exist among the four major components (parts) of the
total economy:

1. consumers,
2. producers (businesses),
3. government, and
4. foreign trade.

The Gross National Product and Its Components

The total dollar value of all final goods and services produced
in a year is called the *gross national product* (GNP). The
gross national product consists of consumer expenditures (C),
plus business investments (I), plus government expenditures
(G), plus net foreign trade—exports minus imports (F). The
gross national product can be expressed in the following equation: $GNP = C + I + G + F$. The GNP represents the flow of
goods and services produced in an economy in a year. Much of

the study of economics is the analysis of the gross national product and its components.

Expenditures by each of the major components are either for producer goods and services or for consumer goods and services. *Producer* or *capital goods* are those used in the production of other goods—for example, tools, machinery, and equipment. *Consumer goods* are those consumed directly and not used in the production of additional goods—for example, food, housing, and clothing.

In aggregate (GNP) economic analysis, *savings* represents income received during the current year that is not used to buy consumer goods and services. When savings are used to buy producer goods and services, the expenditures are called *investments*.

Relationship Between Personal Economics and the Total Economy

The way individuals perform economic activities in their roles as workers, consumers, and citizens has a direct relationship to the aggregate economic activity of a nation. Personal economic activities cannot be analyzed without studying their effects on the whole system. Similarly, the economic condition of the total system affects individual economic activity.

An excellent way to analyze the relationship between individual and aggregate economic activites is to trace the effect each individual economic decision has on the equation $GNP = C + I + G + F$. For example, what happens to the GNP if an individual decides to increase his or her consumer spending? Assuming there will be no changes in the other components of the economy, consumer expenditures (C) would increase and thus stimulate an increase in the GNP. A similar analysis would indicate what happens to the GNP when an individual borrows money, saves a greater share of income, invests more funds, or influences governmental expenditures by the way in which he or she votes. Additional analysis might show:

1. how individual savings could lead to increased investment,
2. how government taxation and spending would influence the GNP, and/or
3. how consumer decisions regarding the purchase of foreign products might influence the GNP.

Everyone needs to have a basic understanding of our economic system. Every person's actions affect the total economy, and the condition of the total economy influences the actions of individuals. Almost every individual uses economic institutions on a daily basis. For that reason alone, one needs to have an understanding of economics. Also, nearly every political issue has an economic implication. A person without a knowledge of economics would find it difficult to function effectively as a citizen.

SOME ECONOMIC PROBLEMS OF MODERN SOCIETY

The United States has only 6 percent of the world's population but receives one-third of the world's total income. In contrast, the poorest half of the world receives only 9 percent of the total world income. This does not mean that we can be satisfied with either our level of living or our standard of living.

Our *level of living* refers to the quantity of goods and services that we are able to buy. A *standard of living* is a goal people have in satisfying their needs and wants and is highly personal. For example, a knowledge of literature or art might be important to one person. To another person, travel might be important. The point is that each person has a different standard of living and these standards usually cannot be measured in terms of money.

We must constantly try to improve both the level of living and the standard of living in the United States as well as share a concern for people of other nations. Some of the problems that we have experienced in the United States in recent years are discussed briefly on the following pages. Our discussion gives special attention to those areas involving the consumer of today.

Consumer Protection

As our economy becomes more complicated, the need for consumer protection increases. Consumer protection can be viewed in three ways. First, the consumer needs to become more informed. Second, responsible business people need to plan together to eliminate, or at least reduce, misleading advertising and consumer exploitation. Third, the government needs to provide legislation to protect consumer interests. Today, all three of these approaches are used.

An awareness of the need for consumer protection has existed for a long time. However, organized effort and concern on the part of consumers became more widespread during and following the late 1960s. The present concern for consumer protection is different from the approaches used in the past. The consumer education movement of the 1980s is more comprehensive and future oriented. Consumer protection in the 1980s starts with the premise that personal economic decision

Illus. 3-2

As our economy becomes more complicated, the need for consumer protection increases.

making must be examined in the context of the total society. Just being a good buyer is not sufficient. Even when the consumer learns more about borrowing, saving, and investing, consumer education is still incomplete.

Today's consumer must also understand the other individual roles of earning an income and performing as a citizen.

Poverty

Even in a country as wealthy as the United States, some people have an inadequate level of living. They are not able to have a reasonable diet, proper education, or adequate housing. People who live in poverty add little to the economic development of a nation. Therefore, attempting to eliminate poverty is not only humane but also makes good economic sense.

Unemployment and Underemployment

Closely related to poverty is the problem of *unemployment.* When people are not working, they obviously are not producing goods and services. When this situation exists, fewer goods and services are produced and the level of living (and usually the standard of living) for the entire society goes down. Therefore, as a nation we want all persons who are able and willing to work to be able to find employment.

When a person is working part time and would like to work full time or when a person is employed at a job that does not take full advantage of his or her skills, *underemployment* exists. Underemployment lowers the level of living of a nation.

Inflation

Inflation exists when there is a rise in the general level of prices for goods and services without a corresponding increase in output. Under such a condition, the purchasing power of the dollar declines. A person on a fixed income has a shrinking income, since fewer goods and services can be bought with the same amount of money.

Pollution

People no longer accept the idea of simply increasing the quantity of goods and services available. They are now concerned about the quality of life as well. If growth entails polluting the air and water, there is a question as to whether such growth is good for society. The cost of controlling pollution can be placed on:

1. producers,
2. consumers,
3. the general public through actions by the government, or
4. any combination of these groups.

No matter what combination is used, the cost is frequently passed on to consumers through higher prices.

Controlling Big Business, Big Labor, and Big Government

As a country becomes more developed, business and labor also begin to grow and expand. When either businesses or labor organizations become too big, they are sometimes able to control prices simply because of their size. They have enough power to charge high prices or to obtain inflationary wage contracts that would be impossible to obtain if they were smaller or less powerful. The government controls and restricts certain actions of both big labor and business. However, government (local, state, and federal), through its taxing and spending activities, is both the largest producer and consumer in the economy. Individuals, through their roles as citizens, must

Illus. 3-3

If growth means polluting the air you breathe and the water you drink, you might well question whether such growth is good for society.

decide the extent that government should intervene and participate in the economic life of the nation.

Controlling Crime

A society pays for the cost of crime several times:

1. in crime prevention programs,
2. by maintaining prisons,
3. by loss of income from persons who are confined, and
4. for rehabilitation programs when an individual has been returned to society after a period of confinement.

Maintaining National Security

In many ways the cost of maintaining national security is similar to the cost of controlling crime. Money spent for a nuclear missile does, of course, create jobs and generate income. Expenses of this type, however, do not increase the productive capacities of a country. For example, the building of an irrigation dam creates future income for a nation. By contrast, a nuclear missile might actually destroy resources rather than develop them. Nevertheless, we must maintain national security even though such expenditures use some of our resources.

Discrimination

Almost every society has some form of discrimination based on race, religion, sex, age, or some other characteristic. Such forms of discrimination are an economic waste. People who are discriminated against generally do not have the opportunity to produce as many goods and services as others. Consequently, society does not have the advantage of the full potential of the contribution these people could make.

Taxation

For many years there has been much concern about unfairness in the taxation plan of the United States. Taxation practices have changed over the years, but in the opinion of some people, certain taxation practices are still unfair. Obviously, taxation is necessary if we are to pay for public services such as parks, schools, highways, national security, and many others. The problem is finding a taxation practice that is fair. Also, government taxing and spending is used to smooth out the ups and downs of business activities.

PROBLEMS OF SOCIETY

1. Consumer protection—by consumers, by business, and by government.
2. Poverty—people not having enough money to meet their minimum essential needs.
3. Unemployment and underemployment—people not having the opportunity to work to their full potential.
4. Inflation—a rising level of prices for goods and services without a corresponding increase in output.
5. Pollution—damaging the environment.
6. Controlling big business, big labor and big government—preventing any segment of the economy, including government itself, from getting so large that it can operate without concern for what is best for society.
7. Controlling crime—the cost includes prevention programs, correctional practices, income foregone by persons confined, and rehabilitation costs.
8. Maintaining national security—using resources for national security that could be used in a more productive way if the need for national defense were not present.
9. Discrimination—people not given the opportunity to make the greatest use of their potential because of race, religion, sex, age, or some other characteristic.
10. Taxation—the problem of collecting in a fair manner the money needed to pay for public goods and services.

VOCABULARY BUILDER

aggregate economic analysis	personal economic analysis
consumer goods	producer goods
discretionary funds	standard of living
economic vote	underemployment
gross national product (GNP)	unemployment
level of living	

REVIEW QUESTIONS

1. What three economic roles can an individual perform?
2. What is the opportunity cost of saving money?
3. What are the four basic economic activities that an individual performs as a consumer?
4. What is meant by personal economic freedom?
5. Why is every economic choice you make an economic vote?
6. What are the four major components of the total economy?
7. What is the relationship between personal economics and aggregate economics?
8. Why does it make economic sense to eliminate poverty?
9. In what ways does underemployment lower the level of living for a society?
10. Does a person on a fixed income suffer or benefit from inflation? Why?
11. In what ways does society pay for crime?
12. Why are expenditures for national security frequently less productive than other forms of economic expenditures?
13. Why is discrimination an economic waste?

DISCUSSION QUESTIONS

1. How important are each of the following economic roles in the American economy: worker, consumer, and citizen?
2. Why is it necessary to understand personal or consumer economic decision making in order to understand the economic activity of a nation? Discuss this question by using the formula $GNP = C + I + G + F$.
3. How do the individual consumer activities of spending, borrowing, saving, and investing influence the total economic activity of a nation?
4. How does each of the major problems of society affect the consumer?

National Income
and Its Distribution

National income represents the total income received by all who contribute to the production of goods and services of the country for one year. The purpose of this chapter is to show how national income is divided among people and why some receive more than others. This chapter deals primarily with the national economy and those who share in the income created.

After studying this chapter, you will be able to:

1. define gross national product, net national product, national income, personal income, and disposable income;
2. discuss what affects the share of total income received by each of the following: (a) owners of land or other natural resources, (b) labor and managers, (c) lenders of money, and (d) owners of business; and
3. explain why some people receive more income than others.

GROSS AND NET NATIONAL PRODUCT

Gross national product (GNP), which was briefly discussed in Chapter 3, is the total (gross) dollar value of all final goods and services produced in the economy during a given year. By final goods we mean a product or service as it is when sold to final purchasers. These goods and services are purchased by consumers, businesses, government, and foreigners. GNP includes business inventories, which are stocks of goods held by business waiting to be sold at a later time. The GNP also includes what we export (sell to other countries) but subtracts what we import (buy from other countries).

GNP does not include *intermediate goods*, which are products used in the production of final goods and services. For example, the paint you purchase to recoat the exterior of your home is a final good, whereas the paint used by a housing contractor on a new home is considered an intermediate good. If intermediate goods were included at each stage of production, the value of output in the economy would be greatly exaggerated because of double-counting.

The gross national product can be expressed in this equation: $GNP = (C + I + G + F)$. The components of GNP are explained in detail below.

1. Consumer spending (C)—This group uses two kinds of goods. One kind is known as *durable goods*, including long-lasting items such as automobiles, household appliances, and furniture. The other kind is known as *nondurable goods*, including items that are consumed quickly, such as food, clothing, and gasoline for our automobiles. Individual consumers also buy many services. These include such items as rent, private education, medical care, legal advice, and public transportation.
2. Business investments (I)—Business investors buy products such as buildings, factories, machinery, tools, and equipment. The purchases of this group are in the form of raw materials, semifinished, or finished goods used to manufacture other goods.
3. Government (G)—Local, state, and federal governments purchase a wide variety of goods and services. The items range from equipment for national defense, public buildings, roads, and dams, to pensions for veterans, health services, education, and welfare. In 1985 state and local government purchases of goods and services accounted

for about 8 percent of the GNP and federal government purchases accounted for another 12 percent.

4. Foreign trade (F)—The difference in dollars between our total exports and our total imports represents our *net exports*, and it increases our GNP. If the value of our total imports exceeds the value of our total exports, the net difference decreases our GNP.

In 1985, the percentage represented by each component of the GNP was as follows: consumer expenditures (C), 65%; business investments (I), 17%; government (G), 20%; and net foreign trade (F), -2% (imports exceed exports).

Buildings, machinery, equipment, and other capital goods lose their value over time as a result of obsolescence and wear and tear with use. This reduction in value is called *depreciation*. When depreciation is subtracted from GNP, the result is *net national product* (NNP).

GNP and NNP are measures of economic growth and productivity. These measures are especially useful when comparing different years or countries. Generally, a larger GNP is more desirable than a smaller GNP.

NATIONAL AND PERSONAL INCOME

To those who buy goods and services included in GNP, the amount spent is a cost or expenditure. To those who receive the payment for the goods or services, the amount received is income.

National income (NI) is the amount of annual earnings received from the production of goods and services. It represents the sum of all the incomes received by individuals for their contributions to the production of all goods and services. National income arises only from productive effort. This means that national income excludes such income as your weekly allowance if you do not work to earn it, interest received on bonds, and pensions.

National income is closely related to GNP and NNP. The value of national income can be obtained by subtracting indirect taxes and a few other minor items such as transfer payments from NNP. Indirect taxes, such as sales taxes, are collected by businesses for government. Because of indirect taxes, the price of a product is higher than its actual value.

Therefore, all indirect taxes embodied in the prices people pay for products must be deducted from NNP.

The national income of the United States for 1985 was $3,222.3 billion. This is the total amount earned by all individuals, such as laborers and managers, owners of plants and equipment, lenders of money, and owners who originate ideas and assume the risks of business.

As individuals we are more concerned with personal income than with national income. *Personal income* is the annual income received by persons from all sources, whether earned or not. More will be said about personal income later in this chapter.

We all know there is quite a gap between our earnings and our take-home pay. This gap is caused by the fact that we must pay taxes on our income. *Disposable personal income* is the amount of income that people have left after all local, state, and federal income tax payments have been deducted from personal income. Disposable personal income is what people have left to spend or to save.

DISTRIBUTION OF NATIONAL INCOME AMONG PRODUCERS

In industry, the results of production are divided among those who represent the factors involved in the production of goods and services. These factors, usually classified as land, labor, capital, and management, were mentioned in Chapter 2. The results of productive effort are divided into classes or categories known as rents, wages, interest, and profits. These are various forms of income. Rents go to the owners of land or other natural resources; wages go to the workers; interest goes to the lenders of money; and profits go to the owners of business or industrial enterprises.

A person may earn income by contributing to more than one of the essential aspects of the production of goods and services. For instance, Mr. Hunt owns a repair shop which he operates and a house that he rents to Mr. and Mrs. Polinski. He earns rent from the Polinskis. He has some money in a savings account and earns interest on it. From the business that he operates, he probably draws a weekly or monthly salary, thus earning wages. Since he owns the business, he earns the profits if there are any after all the expenses of operating the business have been paid. If he owns some stock in a corporation, he receives dividends as his share of the profits of that business.

Figure 4-1 illustrates the portion of national income that is received by each group of resource owners.

Figure 4-1

Approximate Distribution of the National Income in 1985

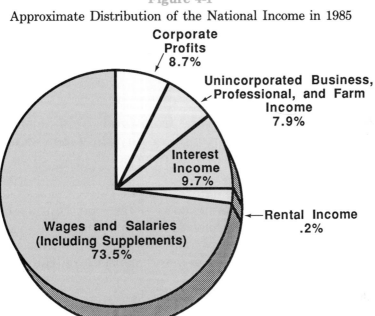

Source: Adapted from *Economic Indicators* (August, 1986).

Rent—Income Earned by Landowners

In an economic sense, *land* includes all natural resources. Farms, building sites, minerals, forests, and water are all natural resources. In many instances, people have made improvements on the land, by adding such things as buildings, permanent equipment, or dams. These improvements increase the usefulness of the land and hence its value.

Ordinarily, *rent* is the contract price received from a tenant for the temporary use of land including buildings and other improvements. In a more restricted sense, *economic rent* is that portion of income which is due solely to the land without buildings and other improvements. The more productive the land is, the greater the economic rent. In the usual sense, however, we speak of rent as income earned for the use of land and the buildings and other improvements on it.

Rent depends on the usefulness, productivity, and desirability of the property. For example, a piece of land that will produce 50 bushels of wheat per acre is theoretically worth at least twice as much as land that will produce only 25 bushels per acre. Richness of the soil, mineral deposits, and location with regard to water or transportation facilities are some of the factors that have a bearing on land value. A person who has land available for rent can obtain rent only in proportion to the productivity of the land measured in comparison with that of competing land.

Wages—Income Earned by Labor

Wages are that part of income from production belonging to those who perform either mental or physical labor. Wages are the prices paid for the labor. The price of labor in terms of money is the value of labor.

The price of labor is determined in the same way as the price of any other economic good or service. Supply of and demand for labor are the primary factors that influence wage rates. The supply consists of the working force that is available at a given time. The demand consists of the needs of employers for workers.

Illus. 4-1

In an economic sense, land includes all natural resources. Farms, minerals, and forests are all natural resources.

Supply of Labor. The supply of labor is indicated by the number of workers who are seeking employment in each kind of work at each of the wage rates offered in the occupation. If the wage rate for an occupation is low, it is usually because of a large supply of workers (such as unskilled workers). When wages are high, it is usually because the supply of labor for those jobs is limited or scarce (such as specialists in certain fields). Workers compete for the high-paying jobs, and employers compete for workers when labor is scarce.

The fact that many occupations are available for a large number of qualified persons can affect the supply of labor. The attractiveness and the working conditions of certain jobs also affect the supply. Many other factors, such as the cost of training new employees and policies of organized labor, influence the supply of labor.

Demand for Labor. The demand for labor is a *derived demand* which reflects the demand for the products of labor. If, for any reason, the demand for a product or a service declines or disappears, the demand for the labor that produces that product or service will likewise decline or disappear. Workers will therefore become unemployed unless they are able to shift to a new type of work. The creation of demand for a new product or service may result in abnormally high wages for the comparatively few workers able to produce the product or provide the service. Wages tend to decrease, however, as more persons prepare to perform the type of work that is in high demand.

Factors Affecting Labor Supply and Demand. Wage rates, above the minimum required by law, are determined by supply and demand; but many conditions may affect either factor. Demand may fall because of lack of consumer purchasing power. Supply, too, may be affected in many ways. One common method of regulating supply is through the unionization of workers and the closed shop. Unions often attempt to maintain a *closed shop* in a given business, which means that only *union members* may be hired. Thus, nonmember workers are prevented from being employed. Other factors that may affect demand and supply are the substitution of other types of labor, the substitution of machines, and licensing requirements to practice certain professions.

Wage Differences. Why does one worker get $3.50 an hour and another $35.00 an hour? Why are those who do some of the more disagreeable work of the world rather poorly paid?

Education and training are two of the most important factors causing wage differences. Natural ability is another. The supply of people who can handle the low-paying positions is greater than the supply of those who can handle the high-paying positions. If a certain kind of work demands more training and knowledge than another, an employer is willing to pay more for someone to do this work. Some individuals are willing to work in less-desirable or high-risk jobs at a higher wage. For example, those who work the night shift tend to receive higher wages than equally skilled day shift workers because fewer workers are willing to work during the less-desirable hours. Essentially, however, the wages in each group are determined according to the supply of labor in that group. The supply of labor becomes smaller as the training and knowledge required for the job becomes greater.

Illus. 4-2

Education and training are two of the most important reasons for wage differences.

Legislation Affecting Wages. The Fair Labor Standards Act, commonly known as the Federal Wage-Hour Law, regulates wages and hours of work. The act covers employees in enterprises engaged in commerce or in the production of goods for commerce. The act was originally passed in 1938 and was amended several times. Currently, the principal provisions of the act are:

1. Minimum wage rate of $3.35 an hour (1986).
2. Regular time of 40 hours a week.
3. Overtime pay provisions. Any number of hours beyond 40 a week requires an hourly overtime rate that is 1½ times the regular rate. For certain positions, time worked on Sundays or holidays requires an overtime rate that is 2 times the regular rate.
4. Wage discrimination prohibited. Basically, wage discrimination is now prohibited on the basis of race, creed, religion, sex, national origin, or age.

In general, the Fair Labor Standards Act and its amendments apply equally to men and women and homemakers as well as factory and office workers, usually regardless of the number of employees an employer has. The Fair Labor Standards Act is enforced by the U.S. Department of Labor.

Many states have their own wage or hour rates to supplement the federal regulations. Some employment is not covered by the minimum wage legislation. For example, persons receiving tips or meals need not be paid $3.35 an hour (1986). Also, some employment is exempt from the minimum wage because the worker derives educational benefit from the job. Certain other exemptions are also possible. For further information about federal minimum wage requirements, consult your local employment office.

Interest—Income Earned by Lenders

The amount paid for the use of borrowed funds is called *interest*. Another concept of interest is that it is that portion of national income traced to the use of capital, not including land. Usually interest is considered payment for the use of money borrowed. Those who lend money take a risk that the borrowers may not be able to repay the loans when they become due. If the money is not repaid, the lenders suffer a loss. Those who lend money are entitled to a reasonable return on their money as compensation for the risk.

The *interest rate* is the price that one must pay in order to obtain the use of money. The rate is quoted as a percentage; that is, as so many dollars for every $100 borrowed. For example, an interest rate of 15 percent a year means that the price of borrowing $100 for one year is $15. The rate of interest is determined by supply and demand for money in the same way that wages are determined by supply and demand for labor. However, government agencies, such as the Federal Reserve Board and the United States Treasury, also influence interest rates.

Suppose that Robert Lopez, the owner of a department store, needs to borrow $20,000 to buy a quantity of goods. He goes to an individual or a bank and inquires about the rate that is being charged on loans made at that time. If the rate quoted seems too high, he may go to another individual or bank. Frequently, the rate of interest asked by one bank may be the same as that asked by another in the same community. In some cases, however, one bank may have more money on hand to lend than another and may therefore be willing to take a lower rate of interest in order to make the loan. When large loans are being negotiated, the bargaining for rates of interest is frequently prolonged and carefully considered on a competitive basis.

When banks have plenty of money available for which there is no immediate need, they are usually eager to lend it. When few businesses wish to borrow money, there is a lack of demand for loans in relation to available supply. As a result, interest rates on loans decline. When banks already have lent most of their funds and there is an active demand for loans, interest rates rise.

The simple laws of supply and demand, however, do not work just exactly as described. When profits and prospects for profits are strong, borrowers are willing to pay higher rates of interest if necessary. Banks are willing to lend money because they can charge higher rates and because they are reasonably sure that borrowers will have the ability to repay the loans.

If money is to be borrowed for business purposes, the amount that can be paid for its use is determined by the amount of profit that can be made from business operations. If interest rates are high, businesses are less likely to borrow; but they will borrow if there is sufficient chance for a profit. The borrower's willingness depends on how great the need for the money is and whether or not alternative sources of money are available. For example, a restaurant owner estimated that the installation of new fixtures would increase profits by $90 monthly. But interest costs on the money needed to pay for the fixtures would cost $100 monthly. Therefore, the owner decided to postpone installation of new fixtures until interest rates declined.

Profit—Income Earned by Owners

Profit is the income earned by owners of businesses after a portion of income has been paid to others. Rent is paid to owners of the land, buildings, and equipment that has been leased. Wages are paid to employees. Interest is paid to those who lend money. Taxes are paid to local, state, and federal governments. Anything left after these claims have been paid is the profit of the owners of businesses. If the income in a given period is not large enough to pay the claims of rent, wages, interest, taxes, and other expenses, the loss must come out of any accumulated savings.

Competition and Profits. Competition tends to appear when someone makes a success of a business. Sooner or later, competition slows the increase in profits. Over time, the profits of a business are limited to a fair return on the investment.

If one business has a secret that will enable it to operate at a profit that is greater than the profits of competitors, it has an important advantage. If its competitors learn the secret and become as skillful, the advantage is lost.

Owners' Rights to Profits. A business must build up a money reserve to take care of times when there may be no profits. In order to build a reserve, a profit must be earned when business is good. If a firm has no reserve, bad times may cause the firm to fail. A reserve enables a business to take reasonable risks.

If a business cannot make a profit, it may be forced to discontinue operations. This, of course, would mean a loss of the goods or services in the marketplace, the disappearance of jobs for labor, and the loss of tax income for local, state, and federal governments.

DISTRIBUTION OF PERSONAL INCOME AMONG INDIVIDUALS

As individuals we are interested not only in the distribution of the total national income but also in the distribution of that part of the national income that we receive in the form of personal income.

What Is Included in Personal Income

Personal income was previously defined as the annual income received by persons from all sources, whether earned or not. It includes:

1. before-tax wages received by individuals,
2. owner's income from a business or farm,
3. rental income from properties leased,
4. dividends from corporations,
5. interest from savings accounts, bonds, and loans, and
6. transfer payments from government and business.

Personal income does not include contributions to government by employees and employers for social insurance, such as social security and unemployment insurance.

Differences in Personal Income

The total personal income varies from year to year according to the production of the nation. It is influenced by business conditions in general. If equally divided among all men, women, and children in the United States, the 1985 personal income would give each person an average income of approximately $11,817 (after taxes) or about $227 a week. The average income per person is called *per capita income.*

Income is not distributed on a per capita basis. For several reasons, individuals earn different amounts which represent different percentages of the personal income pie. That is, fewer individuals are in the top fifth of the personal income level than in the average or low income levels. Numerous factors account for the differences in income distribution among people. Personal traits and earning abilities are the most important factors that explain differences in income. Such facts as economic conditions in the geographical area in which one lives and works, education, accumulated savings, and employment opportunities also affect the amount any one person may earn.

FACTS EVERYONE NEEDS TO KNOW ABOUT THE NATIONAL INCOME AND ITS DISTRIBUTION

1. Gross national product (GNP) is the value of all final goods and services produced in the economy during a given year.
2. Annual national income consists of the total income received in a given year by all the people who contributed to the production of goods and services.
3. Total annual national income is received as earnings for contributions to production by:
    a. land owners, in the form of rent;
    b. labor and management, in the form of wages;
    c. lenders of money, in the form of interest; and
    d. owners of business, in the form of profits.
4. Managers, owners, and lenders take risks to earn income.
5. Primary causes of inequality in receiving shares in personal income are differences among people in personal traits and earning abilities.

Illus. 4-3

Such facts as general economic conditions in the geographical area in which one lives and works, education, accumulated savings, and employment opportunities also affect the amount any one person may earn.

VOCABULARY BUILDER

depreciation
derived demand
disposable personal income
durable goods
economic rent
interest
intermediate goods

land
national income (NI)
net national product (NNP)
nondurable goods
personal income
rent
wages

REVIEW QUESTIONS

1. Who are the users or purchasers of the products and services included in the GNP?
2. What regulates the cost of rent?
3. What factors affect the labor supply?
4. How are the wages of labor determined?
5. What are the principal provisions of the Fair Labor Standards Act?
6. What factors influence the rate of interest charged borrowers at a given time?
7. What accounts for the difference in income distribution among the people of the United States?

DISCUSSION QUESTIONS

1. How may the value of goods and services be an expenditure for some and an income for others?
2. An increase in the level of purchases for business investments indicates an increase in the level of growth of our economy.
   a. Under what conditions might an increase in business investments be misleading?
   b. Would you favor a regulation or law making it compulsory for everyone who receives income to invest a certain percentage in business? Why?
3. Since the passage of the original Fair Labor Standards Act, the minimum wage has been raised several times.
   a. What are the arguments in favor of raising the minimum wage and what are the arguments against?
   b. Do you believe a minimum wage per hour should be established for all workers? Why?
4. Why do some companies earn a higher rate of profit than others?

Price, Supply, and Demand

You have learned that all economic systems must answer four basic questions: what, how, how much and for whom to produce. In a market economy, buyers and sellers gather together to determine the answers to these questions. The purpose of this chapter is to help you understand the significance of prices for consumers and producers, how supply and demand operate in the market economy, and some of the economic factors that affect price changes.

After studying this chapter, you will be able to:

1. define *price system*,
2. explain the laws of supply and demand,
3. discuss the factors that affect supply and demand, and
4. explain the market clearing process.

THE PRICE SYSTEM

Both goods and services have value if they are capable of satisfying our economic needs and wants. *Economic value* is the estimate of worth or usefulness that individuals and businesses place on goods and services based on their ability to satisfy wants and needs. Goods that are free, like the air we breathe, have great value because people cannot live without them; but the free air does not have economic value because it ordinarily cannot be bought or sold. If ordinary air were so scarce that the only way a person could get it were to buy it in containers, it would have economic value. *Price* is the exchange value of goods or services stated in terms of money. For example, the price of wheat is the amount of money required to buy a bushel of wheat.

In the days of barter, people made direct exchanges of the goods and services they needed. For example, a wheat farmer might exchange some wheat for a pair of shoes. The value of wheat as compared to that of shoes depended largely on the supply and the degree of usefulness of each product. When wheat was plentiful and shoes were scarce and difficult to produce, a considerable amount of wheat was required in return for a pair of shoes. When people found that a great many others had wheat to trade but very few had shoes to trade, more people began to produce shoes. As the supply of shoes increased, more shoes were required in return for a bushel of wheat. To a large extent, under the barter system the supply of products regulated their relative value. When the demand for a product increased, it could be traded easily for other products.

The barter system was inconvenient and inefficient for both buyers and sellers. It was often difficult and time-consuming to find someone who would agree to trade their goods for yours. Barter gave way to the price system in which one's product or labor is exchanged for money and the money is used to buy goods and services. All prices are stated in terms of money. Thus, money serves not only as a medium of exchange, but also as a measure or standard of value.

ESSENTIALS OF THE PRICE SYSTEM

1. The product of one's efforts or labor is exchanged for money. The money may be saved or may be exchanged for goods or services.
2. Price is the money value placed on the product resulting from one's efforts. Price is also the money value placed on the goods and services one buys.
3. Thus, price is a common measure of the value both of the products of one's efforts and of goods and services one may desire.

Price and Demand

People try to buy the goods they want at the lowest price possible. They want to get the most for their money. Businesses often try to attract more customers by offering sale prices on selected items. Usually people think of demand as simply how much of some given product is wanted. But in economics the term *demand* refers to the amount of a good or service that buyers are willing and able to buy at different prices during a given time. In order to influence demand, buyers must be both willing and able to purchase a product. Although there are many people who would like to buy a Mercedes, they are unable to afford such an expensive automobile. For this reason they are unable to influence the demand for Mercedes.

Illus. 5-1

Businesses try to attract more customers by offering sale prices on selected items.

As an example of demand, let's assume Tammy received $10 for her birthday. She and two of her friends visit a local clothing store. Tammy sees a T-shirt with a decal of her favorite rock group that sells for $15. She decides not to buy it because it is too expensive. She comments to her friends that she would be willing and able to buy one T-shirt if it were $10. In fact, Tammy would buy two T-shirts at $5 each and three T-shirts at $3 each. This example illustrates the *law of demand* which states that as the price goes up, the quantity demanded goes down. What happens to the number of T-shirts Tammy would buy if the price goes down? The lower the price, the more T-shirts Tammy is willing to buy. People tend to buy less of a product at a high price and buy more of it at a low price.

Factors Affecting Demand. Demand can be affected by several different factors, but they can be condensed into two categories: a change in the quantity demanded and a change in demand. Consumers should understand the difference between these two changes. Let's examine them more closely.

Change in the Quantity Demanded. When the price of a product changes, there is a *change in quantity demanded.* Price is the only factor that causes quantity demanded to change. In the example above, as the price of T-shirts decreased, quantity demanded increased. Similarly, a rise in price causes the quantity of T-shirts demanded to fall. As you can see, this is consistent with the law of demand.

Change in Demand. There are other factors that affect demand in a slightly different manner. A *change in demand* occurs when buyers purchase more or less of a product at each price. There would be a change in demand if Tammy were to increase or decrease the number of T-shirts she is willing to buy at $15, $10, $5, and $3. What might cause Tammy to change her mind? Any one of four factors may cause a change in demand including the number of buyers in the marketplace, buyers' incomes, their tastes and preferences, and the price of related goods. Usually, when the demand for a product increases, the price will rise.

If the number of buyers in the market increases, the demand for a product will increase. The baby boom of the 1950's increased the population and thereby the demand for a variety of products throughout the years. Likewise, as the number of people over 65 years of age has increased so has the demand for health care facilities and retirement communities. A decrease in certain age groups within the population will cause a decreased demand in various markets.

An increase or decrease in buyers' incomes will cause a change in demand. If Tammy receives another $10 for her birthday, her income increases from $10 to $20. Now she is willing to buy one T-shirt at $15, two at $10, three at $5, and five at $3. There has been an increase in the demand for T-shirts as a result of Tammy's additional income. On the other hand, when income goes down, the demand for a product may fall. A decrease in income can occur when factories close or lay off workers or when a person leaves a full-time job to go to school.

Buyers' tastes change for a variety of reasons. Some believe that advertising changes consumer tastes and influences their decision making. Similarly, the styles worn by popular rock groups may start a new clothing fad among you and your friends. You rush to the clothing store to be among the first to purchase the clothes. This represents an increase in demand. As soon as the fad is out of fashion, the demand for the product decreases.

Related goods may be either complements or substitutes. *Complements* are two goods that are used together such as a camera and film, automobile and tires, or flashlight and batteries. When the price of a product goes down, the demand for its complement will rise. For instance, the number or quantity of automobiles demanded will increase when the price of automobiles goes down. Remember, this is a change in the quantity demanded. How will it cause a change in demand? Now that more automobiles have been purchased it is reasonable to expect more tires will be purchased. There will be an increase in the demand for tires. A *substitute* is a good that can be used in place of another good. Examples of substitutes are steak and chicken, butter and margarine, or records and cassette tapes. When the price of one good goes up too high, buyers will buy less of that good. Instead, they will make a substitution. The result is an increase in the demand for the substitute. For example, if the price of steak goes up, the quantity of steak demanded will go down. Since chicken is a substitute for steak, the demand for chicken will go up.

PRICE AND DEMAND

1. The law of demand states that as the price of a good or service rises, the quantity demanded decreases. As price decreases, quantity demanded will rise.

2. Changes in quantity demanded relate to changes in the price of a good or service. An increase in price will cause the quantity demanded to decrease. A decrease in price will cause the quantity demanded to rise.

3. Changes in demand occur when people are willing to purchase more or less of a good or service at each price. A change in the following conditions will result in a change in demand: the number of buyers, consumer incomes, tastes and preferences, and the price of related goods. Generally, an increase in the number of buyers, consumer incomes, and consumer preferences will result in an increase in demand. A decrease in these factors will result in a decrease in demand.

4. When the price of a product goes down, demand for its complement will rise. As the price of a product increases, demand for its complement will decrease.

5. When the price of a product goes down, demand for its substitute will go down. An increase in price will cause demand for its substitute to rise.

Illus. 5-2

An increase in price will cause the demand for a product's substitute to rise. When the cost of steak increases, chicken might be bought instead.

Price and Supply

The amount of goods and services offered for sale is governed considerably by price. If the price is favorable to producers, they will offer large quantities of their products for sale. If the price is not favorable, they will reduce the quantities offered. The amount of a good or service that sellers are willing and able to offer for sale at different prices during a given time is called *supply*. A farmer may be willing to sell 10,000 bushels of wheat if the price is $5 a bushel. At a price of $3, the farmer may be willing to sell only 5,000 bushels.

As an example of supply, let's suppose you have surveyed your neighborhood and determined that there is a market for a small car wash business. How many cars would you be willing to wash if the price of each car wash were $6? If it were $5? If it were $4? If it were $3? If it were $2? You would probably be willing to wash more of your neighbors' cars at $6 than at $2. The *law of supply* states that as the price of a good or service rises, sellers will offer more of the product for sale. Let's say you would wash five cars at $6, four at $5, three at $4, two at $3, and one at $2. It is no surprise that you are willing to provide your car-washing service at higher prices. No business wishes to produce unless it receives enough money to cover costs and make a profit. Your costs are likely to include soap, a pail, sponges, towels, window cleaner, a garden hose, and a vacuum. The higher the price, the more profit sellers can expect. If the price is too low, the sellers cannot cover production costs.

Factors Affecting Supply. It is important to treat changes involving supply in a manner similar to those involving demand. Factors which affect supply can be put into the same two categories as factors affecting demand: change in quantity supplied and change in supply.

Change in Quantity Supplied. In the example above, you discovered that based on the law of supply you would be willing to wash more cars at higher prices. A change in price affects the quantity of a good or service producers are willing to sell. This is called a *change in quantity supplied*. When the price of a car wash was lowered from $4 to $2, the number of cars you were willing to wash decreased from three to one. This represents a decrease in quantity supplied. A rise in price from $4 to $6 resulted in an increase in the quantity supplied to five cars.

Change in Supply. Producers consider factors other than price as shown above. An increase or decrease in the supply of a good or service at each price is a *change in supply*. Look at the original supply of car washes. A change in supply would occur if you were willing to wash more cars or fewer cars at each price. There would be an increase in supply if you raised the number of cars to six at $6, five at $5, four at $4, three at $3, and two at $2. A decrease in supply would occur if you agreed to wash only four at $6, three at $5, two at $4, one at $3, and none at $2.

The four factors that can cause an increase or decrease in supply are the number of sellers, the price of the factors of production, the price of related goods, and the state of technology. If supply increases, price tends to decrease. If supply decreases, price tends to increase.

When more sellers enter the market, the supply rises. For example, a very profitable business will attract some of your neighbors into the car wash market. The larger number of sellers represents an increase in supply. If for some reason your neighbors find it is no longer profitable, they will leave the market. Thus, there will be a decrease in supply because there are fewer sellers providing the service. Natural causes such as freeze damage to crops can reduce supply. Rain has the potential of reducing the number of cars you are willing and able to wash.

The costs of land, labor, and capital are subject to change. For example, a rise in the cost of soap will increase the cost of production for car washes. You want to make a profit, so you will now supply less of the more-expensive service at each price. There will be a decrease in supply. If the cost of production declines, there will be an increase in supply.

The price of related goods tends to govern production and, therefore, supply. For instance, if the price of wheat goes up while the price of corn remains the same, many farmers will shift to the production of wheat. Then the production or supply of wheat will increase and the supply of corn will decrease.

The world is experiencing rapid advances in technology and innovation. The production of automobiles in today's factories is vastly different from the days of Henry Ford. The

assembly line allowed Ford to increase the production of automobiles and therefore increased the supply of Model T's. The
improved use of computer technology continues to make it
easier to produce more of a good in the same amount of time
so that the supply of that good may increase.

PRICE AND SUPPLY

1. The law of supply states that more of a good or
    service will be offered for sale at a higher price than at
    a lower price.
2. Changes in quantity supplied relate to changes in
    product price. As the price of a product increases,
    quantity supplied increases. A decrease in price will
    cause a decrease in quantity supplied.
3. Changes in supply occur when the producers are
    willing to supply more or less of a product at each
    price. The following conditions can contribute to a
    change in supply: the number of sellers, the price of
    factors of production, the price of related goods, and
    the state of technology. Generally, an increase in the
    number of sellers and technology will cause an
    increase in supply; a decrease in the price of factors of
    production and of related goods will cause an increase
    in supply.

THE MARKET IN EQUILIBRIUM

Recall that a market is where buyers and sellers make transactions to buy and sell goods and services. Each buyer has a
demand for the product exchanged in the market and wants to
pay the lowest price possible. Recall that Tammy's demand
for T-shirts at a price of $5 each was two shirts. Her friends
also had a demand for the T-shirts. Chuck would be willing
and able to buy one shirt at $5, while Jennifer would buy
three at $5. The *market demand* is obtained by adding the
number of T-shirts demanded by each buyer in the market.
Since this T-shirt market is made up of only three individuals,
the market demand at $5 is six. Most markets for goods and
services are likely to have many more buyers.

The *market supply* is the amount of a product that all sellers in a market are willing and able to supply. Naturally, producers would like to sell their goods and services at the highest price possible. In addition to the three cars you would wash at $4 each, assume there are two of your friends willing to wash two cars each at that price. What is the market supply? If the car wash market consists of the three of you in your neighborhood, the market supply at $4 is seven cars.

In the marketplace, price guides buyers and sellers in exchanging goods and services. If buyers are unwilling to purchase a product because the price is too high, sellers receive the signal to reduce the price. On the other hand, sellers do not want to sell their products at a price that is too low. Finally, buyers and sellers will agree upon a price at which everyone is satisfied. The price at which the quantity supplied and the quantity demanded are equal is called the *market clearing price*. The market is in a state of balance or equilibrium at this price.

Market Surplus

Sometimes the price is set higher or lower than the market clearing price. If this condition exists in the market, supply and demand are not equal. When the price is set above the market price, suppliers are willing to sell more of their product, but buyers desire less of the product. A *surplus* exists in a market when the supply is greater than the demand. In order to sell their product, producers must lower the price. Buyers respond to lower prices by increasing the amount they will purchase. Once again the market resumes its balance at the market clearing price.

Market Shortage

When the price is set below the market clearing price, demand will exceed supply. This condition is called a *shortage*. Many buyers shopping for bargains will be attracted by the low price, although producers will offer only a small amount of the product for sale at that price. Producers will raise the price until supply equals demand at the market clearing price. A unique feature of the market economy is the market mechanism that guides prices down when there is a surplus and guides prices up when there is a shortage.

THE MARKET IN EQUILIBRIUM

1. In a market economy, the market clearing price is the price at which the quantity supplied equals the quantity demanded. There is no surplus and no shortage in the market.
2. A surplus exists when the quantity supplied is greater than the quantity demanded and the price is above the market clearing price. There will be adjustments in the market to eliminate the surplus by lowering the price.
3. A shortage exists when the quantity demanded is greater than the quantity supplied: the price is below the market clearing price. The shortage will be eliminated by market pressures to raise the price until it reaches the market clearing price.

ELASTICITY OF SUPPLY AND DEMAND

Elasticity is the degree to which the quantity supplied or demanded changes when the price of a good or service changes. Sometimes the response to a price change is a sizable adjustment in quantity demanded or supplied; sometimes it is very slight. Regardless of the results, this valuable information provides insight into consumer behavior and helps producers make pricing decisions.

A product is said to have an *elastic* demand or supply when a change in price will bring about considerable change in the amount of the product that will be purchased or offered for sale. Many durable goods like new refrigerators, microwave ovens, and home computers have an elastic demand. By reducing the price of durable goods, a larger number can be sold. The sale of a larger number will enable the manufacturer to produce these goods at a lower cost per unit. In many instances, the reduction in price results in more profit for the manufacturer than the higher price.

The demand or supply for a product is *inelastic* when a change in price will bring about little or no change in the quantity demanded or supplied. Goods that represent a small portion of a family's total budget, such as table salt or bread, are good examples of products with an inelastic demand. An increase in the price of salt may cause only a slight decrease in the quantity demanded. During the energy crisis of the 1970s, consumers altered their consumption of gasoline very little immediately after the first price increases. This indicated that, at least initially, there was an inelastic demand for gasoline. With an inelastic demand, the profit for producers is less at the reduced rate.

PRICE, DEMAND, AND SUPPLY

1. Elasticity is the degree of change in quantity of a product demanded or quantity supplied brought about by a change in price.
2. Demand or supply for a product is elastic when a change in its price has a sizable effect on the quantity demanded or supplied.
3. Demand or supply for a product is inelastic when a change in its price has little or no effect on the quantity demanded or supplied.

Even in the case of inelastic demand, these rules do not hold strictly true when prices get too high. Although the demand for bread is relatively inelastic, if the price of bread, in relation to the price of crackers, were to go high enough, people with limited income would stop buying bread and shift to buying crackers as a substitute. This represents *substitution* as a principle of economics.

Also, when prices are high compared to the cost of production, new producers enter the industry to take advantage of the profit to be made. Their actions eventually drive the price down to the cost of production.

ECONOMIC FACTORS RELATED TO PRICE

Demand and supply are factors that directly affect price. In addition, competition, monopoly conditions, the value of money, credit, taxes, and government regulation are factors that indirectly affect price.

Price and Competition

An essential feature of a market economy is the competition among producers of economic goods for the favor of the consumer. The rivalry is of two kinds: price competition and non-price competition. Through *price competition*, producers or distributors attempt to take business away from their competitors by offering their goods or services at lower prices than their competitors. In addition to competing for the business of the consumer on the basis of lower prices, some producers and distributors offer nonprice incentives, such as higher quality of goods, latest styles, inventions and innovations, and installation and maintenance services. These nonprice inducements to attract consumers are collectively referred to as *nonprice competition.*

Price competition tends to force prices down to the lowest possible level that will still permit full coverage of the costs of production plus a reasonable profit for the industry as a whole. More efficient firms will make a better profit; less efficient firms will make a lower profit or might suffer a loss.

Competition is one means of protection for the consumer, for it helps to minimize prices, promote efficiency, and assure buyers that they can obtain what they want at the time they want it. Fundamentally we operate on the basis of a competitive system; but as will be discussed later, we also have some regulated monopolies and occasionally price controls, which set the maximum prices allowed on various goods.

Under free competition, no producer can persistently sell goods at prices that are much higher than those of competitors. If producers make excessive profit—in other words, if they charge prices that are relatively high—their customers will buy from competitors that sell at lower prices. New competitors may also enter the field. As a result of this competition, the high prices that were formerly charged will be reduced.

Efficient businesses may make more profit than inefficient ones. Inefficient producers who cannot succeed in keeping costs low find it impossible to compete with efficient producers. When inefficient producers try to lower prices to compete with efficient producers, they fail to make a profit and have to quit business. Through competition, buyers tend to get goods at the lowest prices at which the goods can be produced.

The economic principle of substitution is also an important factor in the competitive system. If the price of cotton goes high enough relative to artificial fabrics, there is likely to be a shift to artificial fabrics.

PRICE AND COMPETITION

1. Free competition among producers of a commodity assures efficiency in production, high-quality products, and lower prices to the consumer.
2. Free competition among retailers and wholesalers of a commodity causes the consumer price to fall towards the cost of production plus a reasonable profit.

Price and Monopoly

In a few instances, a producer free from competition may have absolute power to determine the selling price of a certain product or service. The control of the supply by one seller (monopolist) is known as a monopoly. As there is no competition, the seller often limits production to keep prices artificially high. The seller also tries to create and maintain demand in order to get the prices asked. In a monopoly, prices are not necessarily determined by the cost of production; rather, as has been explained, they may be determined by the monopolist in order to yield the highest profit.

Telephone companies are an interesting example of monopoly, or at least partial monopoly. If one telephone company has a monopoly on telephone service in a particular city, it has control over the supply of that service. In the absence of any local control, the telephone company could set its own rates. A rise in the rates might cause some people to discontinue telephone service. If the rates were to continue to rise, the telephone company might lose so many customers that it would not be able to make a profit. State governments, however, reserve the right to regulate the rates, or prices, charged by such companies.

PRICE AND MONOPOLY

1. In monopolies not regulated by government, supply and price are manipulated in relation to demand to yield the maximum profit.
2. Government regulation, rather than supply and demand, determines price for some monopolies such as public utilities.

Price and Money

Money is our medium of exchange. It also serves to establish the relative values of goods. The value of money is determined by the amount of goods that a dollar will purchase. When the value of a dollar is low, the dollar will not buy as much as when its value is high. In other words, money is cheap if it buys little, and it is dear if it buys much. When money changes in value, prices in general change.

Two factors that affect the price level are the quantity of money and the rapidity with which money is used. The amount of money in the United States is less than the total value of goods being exchanged at a particular time. It is estimated that the total quantity of money in the United States changes hands from 20 to 40 times a year. The quantity has been increased substantially during the history of the United States by the issue of new paper money and credit money. When there is an increase in the money available to buy goods and this money is used rapidly, prices tend to rise. A more rapid turnover of money (or credit) has the same effect as increasing the money supply.

Illus. 5-3

When there is an increase in the money available to buy goods and this money is used rapidly, prices tend to rise. A more rapid turnover of money (or credit) has the same effect as increasing the money supply.

As a simple example, let us consider an island on which there is a certain amount of money and a relatively elastic demand for certain goods. The people who have money will soon establish the values of goods. If the total supply of money is suddenly doubled, however, everyone is in the same relative position. Each person has twice as much money as formerly but cannot buy twice as many goods because all the people want the goods in the same proportion as before. If a person attempts to buy goods with the same amount of money formerly used, that person will find that other people are willing to pay more because they have more money. He or she will therefore have to pay just as much as anyone else. Prices in terms of money will rise because of the increase in the supply of money. In other words, increasing the supply of money has caused inflation of commodity prices.

Price and Credit

Increases and decreases in the use of *credit*, or the promise to pay for purchases at a later date, affect price in much the same way as increases and decreases in the supply of money. Since credit expands the use of money, it serves to increase the rapidity with which money is used. If a person has $100 to spend and borrows $100, he or she has a total purchasing power of $200. If, at the same time, the supply of products and services remain unchanged, prices will increase because there is an increased amount of money and credit with which to buy products and services. When money and credit are increased, however, the supply of products and services may also increase. If the quantity of money continues to increase faster than the supply of goods and services, prices will continue to rise. When credit decreases, prices tend to decrease.

Price and Taxes

Generally, high taxes on producers and distributors tend to increase prices, for taxes constitute part of the cost of producing any article or rendering any service. If a high tax is levied on a building, it must be included in computing the rent of the building. If a sales tax is levied on any item, such as gasoline, clothing, or drugs, it is a part of the cost of the product regardless of the person against whom it has been assessed. Part or all of the taxes are usually passed on to the consumer, either directly or indirectly. Therefore, the levying of a tax against a particular product will usually cause a rise in the price of that product.

Federal, state, and local taxes levied on the incomes of individuals reduce the purchasing power of consumers. This tends to decrease the demand for goods and services and therefore tends to lower prices.

Price and Government

The preceding discussion of prices has assumed that there is no control of prices. However, prices are controlled to a certain extent by government, by business, by farmers, and by workers. Organized groups representing various aspects of production, distribution, and consumption attempt to obtain government protection or regulation on their behalf. Labor, professional, business, and farm groups practically all seek some kind of federal legislation primarily to give them an economic advantage. Some of the legislation is undoubtedly desirable, and some is necessary. However, from the early days of the Roman Empire to the present, attempts to control price and to regulate income have created many other problems.

As citizens, we vote in local, state, and national elections on economic issues. It is important that we understand clearly the issues having to do with prices, subsidies, and government ownership of industry so that we may have a basis for intelligent voting.

The federal government also owns and operates some industries. Sometimes it sets the prices of its commodities or services at less than cost and sometimes at more than cost. Among the industries owned by the federal government in which prices are controlled are the postal system, Amtrak, and the Tennessee Valley Authority. In addition to federal ownership of industry, some states engage in production and distribution. States and municipalities own and operate many industrial and commercial enterprises, most of which have some of the characteristics of monopolies. In many government-owned enterprises, prices are set without reference to costs. Deficits are paid from funds derived from taxation.

The rates for services provided by public utilities (not government owned) are usually regulated or controlled by the state or the federal government. For example, telephone and electric rates are regulated by the government.

FACTS EVERYONE SHOULD KNOW ABOUT VALUES AND PRICES

1. The price system is the process by which people exchange labor or products for the goods and services they need through the medium of money.
2. As the supply of goods increases, the price tends to be lowered.
3. The greater the demand for goods in relation to the supply, the higher prices tend to be.
4. The price of a commodity influences consumption.
5. Competition tends to force a reasonable relationship between the cost to produce and the price asked.
6. When money is plentiful and credit relatively easy to obtain, prices tend to be high.
7. Taxes on producers tend to increase the cost of goods and therefore increase prices. Taxes on consumers reduce purchasing power and therefore tend to decrease consumption.
8. Some prices are partially or completely controlled by governments.

VOCABULARY BUILDER

complements
demand
elastic demand
inelastic demand
market clearing price

shortage
substitute
supply
surplus

REVIEW QUESTIONS

1. When does a good or service have economic value?
2. How does price relate to economic value?
3. What determines economic value in the barter system?
4. What is the relationship between price and money?
5. What is the difference between a change in quantity demanded and a change in demand?
6. What is the relationship between the law of supply and changes in quantity supplied?

7. How will the price of a product be affected if a surplus exists in the market?
8. What type of goods are likely to have an elastic demand?
9. What effect does credit have on prices?
10. How do taxes affect prices?

DISCUSSION QUESTIONS

1. How does the price system work in a market economy?
2. The consumption of frozen orange juice in the United States has increased rather rapidly within the last twenty years. Why do you think the increase has taken place?
3. Indicate if the items below will cause an increase/ decrease in the quantity demanded or an increase/ decrease in demand for jeans. Explain.
    a. The price of corduroy pants is reduced.
    b. Tony loses his part-time job at the hardware store.
    c. The Jeans Depot lowers the price of their designer jeans.
    d. The Diaz family goes shopping for school clothes in August.
4. a. What would be the effect on prices if the supply of a commodity (such as pencils) increases but the demand for it remains approximately the same? Why?
    b. What would be the effect on prices if the demand for a commodity increases but the supply remains approximately the same?
5. If you were a retailer, would you prefer to sell products with an elastic demand or to sell products with an inelastic demand? Why?
6. The history of most newly introduced products, such as the television and the automobile, shows that the products first sold at high prices, although they were not nearly so good as they were later. How do you account for the reduction in price?
7. Is there a need for regulation of public utility rates? Why?
8. What are some examples of prices of consumer goods and services that you think should be regulated by government? State the reasons for your point of view.

PART 1

Special Activities

1. The opportunity cost of buying and eating a pizza might be the record album you decided not to buy. Sometimes the opportunity cost involves merely a substitution of time. For example, you could not watch a television program and play tennis at the same time. (Assume that it will not cost you anything directly for either watching television or playing tennis.) Choosing either time or actual goods and services, give examples of what the opportunity cost might be for each of the following:
   a. Going to a movie
   b. Buying a camera
   c. Mowing a lawn for pay
   d. Sleeping late on a Saturday or Sunday morning
   In each case, compare the benefits of the action taken with the possible opportunity cost involved.

2. Six national economic goals were presented in Chapter 1. Rate these goals according to your feelings about their importance and explain why you rated them as you did. Compare your list and your reasoning with that of other members of the class. Your teacher may call on you to participate in a panel discussion or debate in order to defend your position on the ranking of the goals.

3. Using the flow diagram presented in Chapter 2, trace the effect of each of the following conditions on the total economy:
   a. A reduction in spending for the space program
   b. Increased spending by private business to reduce water and air pollution
   c. A drastic decrease in the number of cigarette smokers

4. Make a list of personal economic decisions that you have made in the past week or two about spending, borrowing, saving, or investing. Trace each of these decisions through the formula $GNP = C + I + G + F$ to show how your individual economic decisions might have affected the total economy. Explain how the conditions that exist in the total economy influenced your personal economic decisions.

5. On an outline map of the United States, enter the per capita (per person) personal income for each state for the latest available year. Obtain the figures from the latest issue of the *Statistical Abstract of the United States*. Study the map to locate areas of the country that tend to have a higher or lower income distribution pattern than the average. Provide your interpretation of the data.

6. In this part, you have learned that when the price of a product increases, the number of units that people are willing to buy will ordinarily decrease. In an attempt to deal more thoroughly with this idea, prepare three lists of items:

   a. Things people will buy with almost no regard for price
   b. Things people will tend not to buy if prices are sharply increased
   c. Things people will stop buying if substantial price increases go into effect

   Study the three lists you have prepared and, in general terms, describe or characterize the items in each list. What conclusions can you reach regarding the relationships between prices, demand for various products, and the nature of people's wants or needs?

COMMUNITY PROJECTS

1. Interview one of your parents (or a family member), a businessperson, and a government official. Ask each person if he or she must economize and why. Write a report of no more than one page for each interview. In a class discussion, compare your findings with other class members. (See Community Project 2 before you start this project.)

2. As part of the interview in Project 1, ask each person to explain the effects on the individual and the economy

when a person selects a job that will not make the most of his or her abilities. Write a one-page report of each response and compare your findings by discussing them with other class members.

3. In Chapter 2 you learned that there are several important economic institutions in the American economy. It is sometimes said that most people do not know enough about our economic system and how it operates. To find out what people know and believe about the American economy, ask the following people what the essential features and characteristics of the American economy are:
    a. Three students who are not taking this course
    b. Three teachers in your school
    c. Three neighbors in the community who work in stores or factories
    d. Three persons who own or manage a business enterprise
    Write a report in outline form, omitting the names of the persons you interviewed, in which you summarize what each of the four groups has said about the American economy. Your teacher may ask you to share your findings with other class members through class discussion.

4. Almost daily some mention is made of GNP in the newspapers. Popular news magazines frequently carry in-depth reports about GNP figures. Locate at least three current articles either from newspapers or magazines that refer to the GNP. Based on what you read in these articles, prepare a brief report indicating why GNP information is important to a community and to individuals.

5. Choose a product that you would like to sell. Determine a range of five prices that you could charge for your product and arrange them in descending order. Conduct a market survey in your class or neighborhood to determine the demand for your product. Ask each person how many units of your product they would be willing to buy at each price. Tally the responses and place your results in two columns:

    Price per unit   Quantity demanded

    Report your results and draw conclusions on the relationship between price and quantity demanded.

PART 2
The Consumer and the Marketplace

6
Consumer Protection

Many of our economic problems involve dealings with other people, and many of these dealings involve legal relations. There are laws that guide and protect us in our everyday dealings. This chapter discusses some common legal problems and the rights of consumers.

After studying this chapter, you will be able to:

1. list the essential elements of a contract;
2. explain when a contract must be in writing;
3. explain the nature and purpose of warranties;
4. identify your legal rights and obligations for goods purchased from door-to-door salespeople, for unordered merchandise, and for goods entrusted to others;
5. explain why you need legal advice; and
6. describe the process for suing a person or business in a small claims court.

CONTRACTS

Laws are not exactly the same in all states. However, under the Uniform Commercial Code (law), which has been adopted by all of the states except Louisiana, the laws relating to sales contracts are essentially the same. The discussions in this chapter follow the code.

A *contract* is an agreement between two or more competent parties that creates an obligation enforceable by law. If one of the parties does not carry out his or her part of the agreement, the other party may resort to court action.

When you buy goods on account in a store, you make a contract with the store to pay the cost of the merchandise. If you leave shoes in a repair shop to be repaired, a contract is made on the part of the repairer to repair the shoes and on your part to pay the prescribed charges. When you rent a house, you enter into a contract to pay the rent and the owner is obligated to let you have possession of the property. Many other situations that involve contracts exist in everyday life. Buying auto insurance, buying a school yearbook, shipping merchandise, or accepting a job offer all involve contracts.

The basis of a contract is an agreement between the parties. But not all agreements are contracts because some agreements do not have all the essentials of contracts. For example, Ann Meyer agrees to go camping with Joan Newberg; but if Newberg changes her mind and decides not to go, she is not breaking a contract. On the other hand, if Meyer and Newberg make arrangements to go on a camping trip together and arrange for a professional guide to provide them with equipment, food, and lodging, they have entered into a contract with the guide. They are both responsible to the guide for carrying out the contract or for settling it in some satisfactory manner if they change their minds. It is also quite possible that a court would decide that there was a contract if both or either had made certain preparations and spent any money for mutual benefit.

Element 1: Offer and Acceptance (Mutual Assent)

In every contract there is an *offer* and an *acceptance*. For example, one person offers a one-acre tract of land for sale at a price of $10,000. Another person accepts the offer, therefore promising to pay the price asked. There was *mutual assent* between the two parties: one made the offer, the other accepted the offer.

Under the principles of law, it is not considered that there is mutual assent unless both parties have freely, intentionally, and apparently assented to the same thing.

Offer. The essential characteristics of an offer are:

1. the proposal must be definite,
2. the proposal must be made with the intention that the *offeror* (person making the offer) be bound by it, and
3. the proposal must be communicated by word or actions to the *offeree* (one to whom it is made).

If you were to offer to work for an employer for "all that you are worth," the offer would be too indefinite to be the basis of an enforceable agreement. If an offer is made in obvious or apparent jest, or in disgust or anger, it is not a real offer. If someone in jest says that he or she would give a thousand dollars to see the expression on a friend's face when opening a comic birthday greeting, the offer is not real. Or if the engine in your new automobile will not start, it would not be a real offer if in disgust you say, "I would take $5 for it."

Most advertisements are not legal offers. They merely invite the prospective customer to buy or to make an offer to buy. If you walk into a store and find goods on display with a price marked on them, you might think the goods are offered for sale at that price; but the law holds that price tags on merchandise merely indicate a willingness to consider an offer made by a buyer on those terms.

Acceptance. An offer for the purchase of goods may be accepted in any way that is reasonable. For example, the seller may ship the goods or may promise to do so promptly.

As in the case of an offer, the acceptance must be indicated by some word or act. For instance, you cannot be bound against your will by an offeror who states in his offer, "If I do not hear from you by ten o'clock, October 10, I shall consider that you have accepted this offer." The acceptance must also be made by the party to whom the offer was made. If someone has made an offer to you and you tell a friend about it, the person who made the offer does not have to recognize an acceptance by your friend. The acceptance may be in the form of a definite promise that completes the mutual agreement, or it may be made in the form of some act.

For example, Miss Hill bought a microwave oven, had it sent to her home, and used it for two weeks. When the store asked for payment, she insisted on returning the oven although she had no complaint about its performance. She insisted that she had never accepted it because she had not paid for it. Courts would undoubtedly hold that there was an offer and an acceptance. On the other hand, if she had ordered it sent to her on approval (subject to a buyer's acceptance or refusal), an acceptance would not have been indicated until she had signified her approval or had kept the oven an unreasonable length of time without expressing dissatisfaction or a willingness to return it.

A definite and reasonable expression of acceptance is legal and binding if it is within a reasonable time. It may also include additional conditions not in the original offer.

As a general rule, when offers are made by letter with the acceptance to be made by mail, the offer is considered to be accepted when the acceptance is deposited in the mail. Likewise, if the acceptance is to be made by telegram, the agreement is considered to be completed when the message is given to the telegraph company.

ACCEPTANCE IS INDICATED BY:

1. Specific indication that the buyer accepts the goods.
2. Use of the goods (unless the goods were not ordered).
3. Keeping the goods for an unreasonable length of time.

Element 2: Competent Parties

The question of competence of parties determines who is legally qualified to make contracts. Anyone who is not otherwise prevented by law from making enforceable agreements may make a contract. Intoxicated persons and insane persons are not competent to contract. The reason for voiding the contracts entered into by these persons is obvious: they are not considered capable of exercising their own judgment.

In many cases, *minors* (those who are not of legal age) are not competent to contract and may not be required by law to carry out agreements. There are, however, some exceptions to this rule, such as contracting for necessaries. When a minor makes an agreement with an adult, the adult is required to fulfill the contract if it is legal; but if the minor chooses to *rescind* (cancel) the contract, he or she can, in most cases, escape responsibility. When minors reach the minimum age at which they may make a contract, they are said to have attained the *age of majority*.

AGE OF MAJORITY
(Minimum legal age to make a contract)

In the past any person under 21 years of age was considered to be a minor under common law. Minority ended on the day before the 21st birthday. In recent years, however, the 21 years of age has been reduced to 18 years in two thirds of the states and to 19 years in a few states. The "day before the birthday" rule is generally still followed. Some states provide for the termination of minority upon marriage, and some states specify that the minority of girls shall terminate sooner than that of boys.

Usually, contracts made by a minor are *voidable* (that is, they may be broken) by the minor. He or she may break them while still a minor or within a reasonable time after coming of age. If a minor reaffirms the agreement after coming of age, it becomes a binding contract. The voidability of a contract applies generally whether it has been fully performed or only partially performed.

For example, the Stanley Hardware Store accepted a properly signed order for a bicycle for $60 from Bob Garcia, age 12. When the bicycle arrived from the factory, the price had risen and the dealer insisted on getting $75 for the bicycle or canceling the contract. The dealer argued that the original agreement was not binding because Bob Garcia was a minor and was, therefore, incompetent to contract. This agreement, however, is binding on the dealer; but Bob, because he is a minor, could cancel the contract if he wished.

A minor who acquires reasonable necessaries is obligated to pay the reasonable value of the purchases. A merchant who furnishes such things as jewelry, tobacco, or sporting equipment to an ordinary minor usually cannot collect payment. But one who furnishes necessary clothes or food can collect if the amounts charged are reasonable and the goods are needed and are actually delivered. On the other hand, if all these necessaries of life are provided by the parents, any contract made by the child to obtain them is voidable. A contract by a poor child to buy expensive clothing would be voidable also.

SOME EXAMPLES OF COMPETENT PARTIES

1. A person who cannot read is bound by a contract if it has been read to him or her and is understood by him or her before signing.
2. A person who cannot read or write but who signs a contract with an "X" or other symbol is bound by the contract if it has been read to him or her and is understood by him or her.
3. Generally, a person who has made a contract while a minor may deny or accept the contract when coming of age, but failure to deny it generally makes the contract binding.

Element 3: Legal Purpose

The purpose for which a contract is made must not be contrary to law or to the interests of society. In other words, the subject of the bargain must be legal. This is referred to as *legal bargain*. In most cases, when the purpose of the contract is not legal, there is not even a contract. Neither party can be held under the agreement.

Examples of illegal bargains are those involving agreements to steal or to accept stolen goods. Anyone buying stolen goods does not get a valid claim to the goods. The goods must be returned to the rightful owner if ownership can be proved. All agreements to wager or gamble are illegal except in the cases of certain states in which betting on horse and dog racing has been legalized. For instance, if you make a bet with somebody, you have not made a legal contract. However, in a state where betting on horse races is legal, your placing of a bet is a legal contract.

Element 4: Consideration

A contract usually is an agreement whereby one person agrees to do something and another person agrees to do something else in return. What one party agrees to do in return for that which was promised by the other is known as *consideration*. For example, an automobile dealer and you may enter into a contract. You promise to pay for the automobile and the dealer promises to transfer ownership of it to you in return.

Every legal contract must have consideration. For example, Diane Sears, a wealthy member of Carolina Hills Country Club, offered to give her old set of golf clubs to a caddy at the end of the golf season. She changed her mind and did not give them to the caddy. The caddy insisted that a contract had been made. Ms. Sears insisted that there was no consideration on the part of the caddy in the nature of goods, money, services, or promises. If the caddy can prove that the clubs were promised in return for caddy service or any other favor to Ms. Sears, there probably is a contract. In the absence of such proof, there is no contract; it is simply a promise to make a gift. A gift without a consideration is not regarded as a contract.

Ordinarily, the promise made in an agreement is not enforceable unless something of value is received for the promise. The value may consist of goods, money, services, refraining from doing something that one has a right to do, or giving up a privilege.

Element 5: Proper Legal Form

To qualify as legal contracts, certain agreements must be made in the form specified by law. Most contracts, however, are informal and very simple. Every day you enter into informal contracts. It may be as simple as placing on your tray in the school cafeteria the food you have selected and accepting the offer by paying the amount the cashier requests. Other contracts, such as the purchase of real estate, must be formal.

Oral and Written Contracts. There are two types of contracts, *oral* and *written*. Ordinarily, oral evidence of a sale of personal property (movable property such as stocks and bonds, furniture, an automobile, jewelry, livestock, and agricultural crops) for under $500 is sufficient. An oral agreement to sell personal property for more than $500 is not enforceable. For example, Klein entered into an oral agreement with a friend to buy the friend's motorcycle for $650. A few days later Klein notified his friend that he did not want to buy the motorcycle. Since there was no written contract, Klein's friend cannot make Klein fulfill the contract.

Many contracts do not have to be in writing because the offer, acceptance, payment, and delivery of goods all occur within a few seconds or a few minutes. Contracts for medical and dental services need not be in writing, regardless of the amount involved. Contracts for labor and materials generally need not be in writing.

A contract should be written instead of oral when there is any chance of misunderstanding or disagreement between the parties or when a written contract is required by law. For example, Mr. and Mrs. Caruso bought a house from the East-side Realty Company for $70,000 on an oral agreement. This is not an enforceable contract because the law requires agreements of this kind to be in writing. Figure 6-1 is an example of a written contract.

Illus. 6-1

Most contracts are informal and very simple.

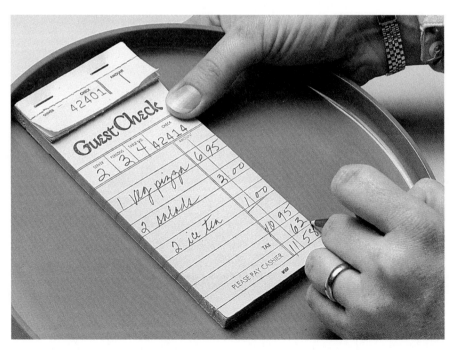

Figure 6-1
A Contract

THIS AGREEMENT is made on May 10, 1988, between James A. Wiley, 3144 Beechwood Drive, Columbus, Ohio, the party of the first part, and Diana L. Segal, 5967 Rosetree Lane, Columbus, Ohio, the party of the second part.

The party of the first part agrees to install 4 aluminum triple-track storm windows in the home of the party of the second part at 5967 Rosetree Lane, Columbus, Ohio, by June 10, 1988, in accordance with the specifications attached hereto. In consideration of which the party of the second part agrees to pay the party of the first part $585.75 upon the satisfactory completion of the work.

James A. Wiley

Diana L. Segal

THE ESSENTIALS OF A WRITTEN CONTRACT

1. The date and the place of the agreement.
2. The names and the identification of the parties entering into the agreement.
3. A statement of the agreement covered by the contract.
4. A statement of the money, the services, or the goods given in consideration of the agreement.
5. The signatures of *both* parties or the signature of legal agents.
6. In the case of some contracts, witnesses are required. In such cases the witnesses must sign in accordance with the provisions of the law.

A *bill of sale* is a written contract which provides evidence of ownership. It may be as informal as a sales slip from a department store or as formal as a document which describes the item, identifies the buyer, and includes the signature of the seller. A bill of sale is required in most states for the transfer of ownership of such items as automobiles or refrigerators. It is usually necessary to register the bill of sale with the proper county authority so that the ownership of the property can be established.

FOR YOUR PROTECTION

1. Read the entire contract *before* you sign.
2. Ask for an explanation of parts you do not understand.
3. Make sure the contract states all conditions and promises as you understand them.
4. Do not accept your copy without the signature of the other party on the contract.
5. Keep your copy of the contract in a safe place.

Express and Implied Contracts. An *express contract* is one that arises out of an agreement expressed by oral or written words. If you agree orally to buy a video recorder at a specified price and the dealer agrees to sell it to you at that price, you have made an express contract that is legally binding. An *implied contract* is one that is made through an agreement implied by the acts or the conduct of the parties involved. If you pick up an article in a store and hand the required amount of money to the salesperson, who wraps the article and hands it to you, you have made an implied contract.

Defective Agreements

An agreement may not be enforceable because it is found to be defective. Misrepresentation, use of undue influence, concealment of vital facts, or use of threats or force in obtaining agreement may make an agreement *defective*.

Agreements that are not enforceable may be classified as void or voidable. When an agreement is *void*, it has no legal force or effect. In other words, neither party can enforce the agreement. A *voidable contract* is one that may be broken (rescinded) by one or both of the parties. Such an agreement becomes an enforceable agreement if the party or parties having the option to reject the agreement choose not to do so.

Ordinarily, a mistake made by one party, such as quoting the wrong price, does not make the contract void or voidable. Mistakes that make a contract void include mutual mistakes as to the existence of the subject matter or a mistake as to the identity of the parties. For instance, a woman agreed to sell a certain vase at a definite price, but later it was found that the vase had been stolen before the agreement was made. The agreement was void because of a mistake as to the existence of the subject matter.

EXAMPLES OF VOIDABLE AGREEMENTS

1. If there is fraud in the form of misrepresentation or concealment of vital facts.
2. If a person makes an agreement as a result of threat or the use of violence.
3. If there has been undue and unfair influence and pressure to the extent that one person has not reached the agreement through the free exercise of his or her own judgment.

YOUR RIGHTS AS A CONSUMER

Never sign a blank contract or one with part of the figures or conditions left to be filled in. If someone hurries you or suggests that you sign the contract with the rest of the information to be filled in later, your suspicion should be aroused.

Do not sign a contract with the understanding that supplementary agreements will be made later. Be sure that all agreements are in the contract. In the absence of substantial proof with regard to oral agreements or supplementary written agreements, only the agreements stipulated in the contract are enforceable.

Warranties

The promises a seller makes before or after the sale that an article will operate in a specific way or that it has a specific quality are statements on which the buyer has a legal right to rely. These promises or representations are called *warranties*.

Express and Implied Warranties. An *express warranty* is an assurance of quality or a promise of performance by the seller. It may be oral or written, and it usually is given before or at the time of sale. An express warranty may be a general statement, such as "This rebuilt television set is as good as new"; or it may be limited to some particular fact about the goods, such as "This set will get Channel 19 without an outdoor antenna."

An *implied warranty* is an obligation imposed by law. In many cases, the law requires sellers to provide certain minimum standards of quality and performance even if no actual promises are made at the time of sale. The buyer has a right to expect that the article purchased will serve the purpose for which it is sold, although there is no definite statement that it will. For example, if you buy an air conditioner, you have a right to expect that it will operate. If it does not operate, you have a legal recourse. If you go into a restaurant and order food, there is an implied warranty that the food is fit to eat. If you become poisoned, the restaurant owner is liable. If it can be proved that the manufacturer or processor of the food was responsible because of improper processing or handling of the food, that party may also be held liable for any resulting damages.

"Trade puffs" or "trade talk" are not warranties and should not be relied upon by the buyer. A *trade puff* is a general claim, such as "This is the best merchandise you can buy," "This is the most popular item on the market," or "This suit is very becoming to you."

Full and Limited Warranties. For products selling for more than $15, the warranty must state whether it is *full* or *limited*. A warranty is full if there are no specific limitations on your rights under implied warranty. In other words, the product is totally guaranteed, including materials and workmanship, for the length of time specified (six months, a year, two years). If the product does not perform as expected, because of poor workmanship or faulty materials, the manufacturer will replace or repair the product. A limited warranty must state what the limitations are. For example, the limited one-year warranty on an electric wristwatch may read "battery not covered." This means the battery will not be replaced by the manufacturer if it should cease to operate nine months after purchase of the wristwatch. Figure 6-2 is an example of a warranty.

The Magnuson-Moss Warranty Act of 1975 has helped make warranties less deceptive. This act rules as deceptive any written warranty that could mislead reasonable consumers through false or fraudulent statements, promises, descriptions, excessive hedging, or omission of relevant information.

Figure 6-2

A Warranty

GUARANTEE

Upon receipt of the guarantee registration card packed with this appliance, your Suntrol Automatic Toaster is guaranteed for one (1) year against electrical and mechanical defects in material and workmanship, which will be repaired or parts replaced free of charge during this period. The guarantee does not cover damage caused by misuse, negligence, or use on current or voltage other than that stamped on the appliance. This guarantee is in lieu of any other warranty either expressed or implied. If service is required, send the appliance prepaid to the nearest Suntrol Appliance Service Company branch or authorized service station. Please include a letter explaining the nature of your difficulty.

This warranty gives you specific legal rights, and you may also have other rights which vary from state to state.

Written warranties need to be made available for the buyers to see before they buy the product. This requirement allows for comparison shopping.

For products selling for more than $15 the warranty must include:

1. the names and addresses of the warrantors,
2. exactly what is covered (e.g., defects in material, parts, and workmanship) and for what length of time,
3. a step-by-step description of the consumer's procedures for getting the warranty honored,
4. legal remedies available to the consumer, and
5. the duration of the warranty.

Extended Service Warranties. In addition to the manufacturers' warranties that come with the purchase of a product, some manufacturers offer optional or added-coverage plans under which the buyer can choose to have protection for a period of time beyond the normal warranty period, usually one year. These *extended service contracts* involve a fee that can amount to several hundred dollars for an expensive product such as an automobile. If a repair is necessary or a defect

Illus. 6-2
Extended service contracts involve a fee that can amount to several hundred dollars for an expensive product such as an automobile.

becomes apparent after the normal warranty has expired, the problem will be taken care of with little or no cost to the buyer. Whether you should consider an extended service contract depends on the amount you are willing to pay for the added peace of mind, the length of time for which the contract offers peace of mind, and the number of years that you expect to keep the product.

Sales Made at Consumer's Home

In order to give consumers some protection from the evils of high-pressure selling in their homes, the Federal Trade Commission has issued a regulation giving a consumer 3 business days to void a signed contract for goods or services of $25 or more purchased in the home. The seller is required to give the buyer a contract stating the buyer's right to refuse the sale. This remedy gives the buyer a chance to think things over after the salesperson has gone and to decide whether the purchase is wanted after all. It is a reasonably good remedy for the consumer against fly-by-night salespeople, provided the consumer knows the remedy is available and has not paid in full.

Unordered Merchandise

Some firms and organizations make a practice of sending unordered merchandise in the hope that persons receiving it will pay for it. You do not have to pay for or return unordered merchandise received in the mail. You may use it or dispose of it in any way you wish. The fact that you do not return the goods does not mean that you have accepted them. The U.S. Postal Service states: "Any unsolicited or unordered merchandise may be treated as a gift by the recipient, who has the right to retain, use, or dispose of it in any manner without any obligation whatsoever to the sender."

A practical solution to the problem of receiving unordered merchandise is to mark the package "return to sender" and place it in the mail unopened without any additional postage.

Goods Entrusted to Others

Let us say that you entrust your automobile to a garage or a parking lot for safekeeping. The garage or parking lot is responsible for its safekeeping. This is especially true if you

The United States Postal Service states that any unsolicited or
unordered merchandise may be treated as a gift by the recipient.

are given a ticket that is a receipt for your car and if you are
required to leave the keys in the car so that it can be moved.
However, if you regularly place your car in a lot and take the
keys with you, the operator of the parking lot is generally not
liable.

If you rent or borrow an article, such as a lawn mower, you
are responsible for taking reasonable care of it to prevent
damage or theft. Likewise, if you take a lawn mower to be
repaired and it is damaged in the process of being repaired,
the repairer is liable because such a person is expected to exercise reasonable care and skill. The repairer is assumed to have
the skill to do the job.

Generally, people who accept the property of others are
responsible for it. On the other hand, if neighbors bring you
some jewelry and ask you to keep it while they are away on a
vacation, you are not responsible for its loss or theft if you
take reasonable care of it.

Consulting a Lawyer

It is sound practice to go to a doctor when one is ill. Likewise, it is sound practice to consult a lawyer when one has legal problems. Some of the problems for which an individual should consult a lawyer are:

1. writing an important contract,
2. protecting or gaining one's rights, and
3. obtaining protection against lawsuits.

In selecting a lawyer, one should be careful to avoid the so-called shyster who is often too eager to take a case. It is the practice of reputable lawyers to wait for the client to request legal counsel. Only lawyers who are members of the local or state bar association should be considered. Select your lawyer with the same care that you would select your physician.

If you ask a lawyer a question, the answer will be given to you in the form of an *opinion*. Most lawyers will never state an answer definitely because the answer depends on many circumstances. What appears to be true may not be so when all the facts are known. For example, two judges in different courts, giving decisions on what may appear to be identical sets of circumstances, may give completely opposite decisions. Sometimes these decisions are reversed by higher courts.

Although many things in law appear to be definite, any statement in the field of law cannot be completely definite without knowing all the circumstances. Therefore, the statements in this chapter are general statements of law and represent additional reasons why in many cases you should consult a lawyer.

Legal Aid Societies

Because of the belief that getting justice should not depend on one's ability to pay fees and hire a lawyer, organizations called *legal aid societies* or *legal aid organizations* have been formed throughout the country. These organizations are found principally in larger cities. Sponsored by lawyers, they provide an organized method of handling cases for persons who cannot afford to obtain legal assistance.

LEGAL INFORMATION FOR CONSUMERS

1. A contract involves five elements: (a) offer and acceptance, (b) competent parties, (c) legal purpose, (d) consideration, and (e) proper legal form.
2. Some contracts must be in writing.
3. Contracts are expressed or implied.
4. Some contracts are voidable.
5. There are specific remedies if a warranty is broken.
6. Generally, when property is entrusted to another party, that party is responsible for reasonable care in safekeeping.
7. Consult a lawyer for legal advice; do not attempt to serve as your own lawyer, except in a small claims court.

Small Claims Court

Any person 18 years old or older may sue in a small claims court. If 17 or under, you must have a "friend in court" appointed to speak for you. Depending upon the state, claims ranging from $200 to $3,000 may be handled in a small claims court. Also, depending upon the state, attorneys may or may not be allowed to represent either or both the defendant (the person being sued or charged with a crime) and the plaintiff (the person who brings an action in court against another person).

The first step in using a small claims court is to file suit in the court district where the defendant lives, stating the amount of the claim. The exact name of the defendant must be correctly identified. If the defendant is an individual, do not use a nickname or abbreviated name. If the defendant is a company, check with the city clerk or county clerk to identify the company's legal name. Without the correct name identified in your suit, you may not be able to collect even if you win the case. A filing fee, usually under $10, is charged.

A summons is then served the defendant with a court order stating the trial date. A fee is also charged for serving the court order—usually under $10. Sometimes the defendant will ask to settle out of court rather than have to stand trial.

Once the trial is set, both you and the defendant are sworn in before a judge or court-appointed arbitrator (a person chosen to settle differences between two parties). Both you and the defendant give testimony and present evidence. Often the judge or arbitrator will interrupt to ask questions. In some courts, the defendant can cross-examine you, the plaintiff.

The judge or arbitrator may announce a decision in court or by letter. If you win the case, you may collect the money from the defendant. In many instances the plaintiff has to hire a lawyer to collect from the defendant. Thus, if you plan to sue an individual, it is wise to find out if the person has a job and property. If not, you may be wasting your time and money going to court.

VOCABULARY BUILDER

age of majority
bill of sale
consideration
contract
defective agreement

extended service contract
legal aid society
mutual assent
trade puff
warranty

REVIEW QUESTIONS

1. What are some of the situations in everyday life that involve contracts?
2. What are some examples of agreements that are not contracts?
3. What are the three essential characteristics of an offer?
4. What evidence may there be that a buyer has accepted the goods offered?
5. Under what conditions may a minor be held to a contract?
6. For what kinds of bargains are contracts not legal?
7. Why is the promise of a gift by a competent person not enforceable as a contract?
8. Under what conditions may a contract for a sale be oral?

9. What is the difference between an express contract and an implied contract?
10. Under what circumstances is a contract voidable?
11. Why should you never sign a blank contract or a contract containing blank spaces?
12. a. For products selling for more than $15, what must a warranty include?
    b. What is the difference between a full warranty and a limited warranty?
13. When a sale of goods or services amounting to $25 or more is made at the consumer's home, why is the buyer given 3 business days to void the contract?
14. What obligation does a person have who receives unordered merchandise in the mail?
15. a. What responsibility do you have for property you have rented or borrowed?
    b. What responsibility do you have for property entrusted to you by a neighbor for safekeeping?
16. How should you select a lawyer and what factors should you consider in selecting one?
17. What is the purpose of small claims court?

DISCUSSION QUESTIONS

1. When making a contract, what facts should you know about the competence of the other party in order to assure the enforceability of the contract?
2. What would be the effect on business if all contracts had to be in writing? if implied contracts were prohibited?
3. Jean Martin insists that she will not fulfill a contract because she did not know all the terms of the contract when she signed it. Her reason for not having read the contract carefully is that she finds it difficult to read fine print. She admits, however, that the signature is genuine. Is there anything she can do to avoid fulfilling the contract?
4. Why is it possible for two different judges to give essentially opposite rulings in apparently similar or identical cases?

7

Legal Relations
and Consumer Rights

If consumers are to be wise buyers and get the most from their income, they need information and protection. While many private and government sources supplied information and protection in the past, the rise of the consumer movement in recent years has accelerated demand for more and better aid for consumers. In this chapter you will learn about the activities of some of the agencies, laws, and services available to help consumers.

After studying this chapter, you will be able to:

1. explain the need for consumer protection,
2. explain what is meant by the "consumer bill of rights,"
3. list and explain government sources of consumer protection,
4. list and explain private sources of consumer protection,
5. write an appropriate complaint letter regarding defective merchandise or unsatisfactory service, and
6. list six consumer responsibilities.

NEED FOR CONSUMER PROTECTION

As the United States grew into a highly industrialized nation and its cities became larger, consumer problems of many kinds appeared. Poverty, poor housing conditions, unsafe working conditions, impure food, and fraudulent trade practices made more protection necessary. Throughout the years, laws protecting consumers have been passed. Beginning in the 1960s, the need for consumer protection became even more urgent when it became apparent that our natural resources were not unlimited and that pollution was threatening our very lives.

The Consumer Movement

The *consumer movement* refers to a growing consumer awareness of problems as well as a drive to achieve greater consumer protection. The consumer movement in the United States has come in three waves:

1. In the early 1900s, when there was a rapid growth of cities and industrialization.
2. In the 1930s, when the depression created great social problems and the need for wise use of limited income.
3. In the 1960s and 1970s, when consumers became aware that their survival was threatened by irresponsible use of limited natural resources, by unsafe and unhealthy products, and by pollution of water, land, and air.

Much of the consumer movement in the 1980s has focused on conservation; that is, learning how to survive in a world of limited resources. New regulation by government, by businesses themselves, and by private agencies became essential in order to improve the quality of life for all.

Consumer Bill of Rights

President John F. Kennedy, in his 1962 State of the Union Address, proposed a consumer bill of rights that included:

1. *The right to safety*—protection against the marketing of goods that are dangerous to life or health.
2. *The right to choose*—assurance of access to a variety of products and services at competitive prices.
3. *The right to be informed*—protection against fraudulent, deceitful, or grossly misleading practices and assurance of being given the facts necessary for an informed choice.
4. *The right to be heard*—assurance of representation in forming government policy and of fair, prompt treatment in enforcement of the laws.

In 1969 President Richard M. Nixon added a fifth right to the list, and in 1975 President Gerald R. Ford added the sixth.

5. *The right to redress*—assurance of right to legal correction of wrongs committed against consumers.
6. *The right to consumer education*—provision of ways to learn about consumer rights and responsibilities as economic citizens.

During the consumer movement, a number of consumer protection laws have been passed that closely follow the consumer bill of rights. Among these are the Fair Packaging and Labeling Act in 1965, the National Traffic and Motor Vehicle Safety Act in 1966, the Federal Cigarette Labeling and Advertising Act in 1967, the Truth in Food Labeling Act and the Consumer Product Safety Act in 1972, the Equal Credit Opportunity Act and the Fair Credit Billing Act in 1975, the Fair Debt Collection Practices Act in 1977, and the Depository Institutions Deregulation and Monetary Control Act in 1979.

In 1964, the first special presidential advisor for consumer affairs was appointed. For the first time there was a person at the highest level of government to represent the consumer. Now the Department of Health and Human Services has much of the responsibility to advise the president on matters of consumer interest and to coordinate all federal activities in the consumer field. Other government consumer agencies have since been established.

GOVERNMENT SOURCES OF CONSUMER PROTECTION

Government agencies concerned with consumer interests exist at federal, state, and local levels. They provide standards for products and services, information about them, and protection from questionable and unethical practices on the part of sellers.

Federal Consumer Agencies

Over fifty different federal agencies provide direct or indirect services and protection to consumers—and the number is growing. The following are some of the most important:

Department of Agriculture. The primary functions of the United States Department of Agriculture involve research and experimentation dealing with scientific production of farm products, farm management, and the agricultural education of people in rural areas. Of particular value to consumers are services provided by:

1. the *Agricultural Marketing Service*, which inspects food for wholesomeness and grades it for quality;
2. the *Consumer Marketing Service*, which regulates, improves, and protects the nation's food-marketing system; and
3. the *Food and Nutrition Service*, which provides information on nutrition and food programs such as the food stamp program, special milk programs, and school food services.

Department of Transportation (DOT). The Department of Transportation has power to promote safety in civilian aviation. The DOT handles complaints against airlines and investigates suspected violations of regulations. The DOT also oversees such other consumer protection matters as overbooking, baggage claims, and smoking restrictions.

Department of Commerce. The primary purpose of the United States Department of Commerce is to serve business; however, in serving business, the department also serves consumer interests. The following agencies are particularly important to consumers:

1. The *National Bureau of Standards*, which sets measurement standards and product safety standards. It is also involved in energy conservation, fire prevention and protection, and environmental protection projects.
2. The *Office of Consumer Affairs*, which encourages business firms to meet their responsibilities to consumers and provides consumer information.

Environmental Protection Agency (EPA). This agency is concerned with developing programs to protect and improve the quality of our environment. The agency focuses on air, noise, radiation, water quality, drinking water, solid waste, hazardous waste, toxic substances, and pesticides.

Consumer Product Safety Commission (CPSC). This agency, created in 1972, has vast powers to ensure product safety. It sets safety standards for all common household and recreational products (but not food, drugs, cosmetics, and motor vehicles). It has power to regulate production and sale of potentially hazardous products. It can ban dangerous products from the market, and it can require manufacturers and retailers to repair, replace, or make refunds on unsafe products.

Federal Trade Commission (FTC). The basic objective of the Federal Trade Commission, established in 1915, is to preserve the healthy competition of business in our free enterprise system. The purpose of the commission is to prevent injury by monopoly or by unfair or deceptive trade practices. The FTC has most of the responsibility for regulating deceptive and false advertising, discussed in Chapter 8.

Government Printing Office (GPO). The Government Printing Office provides thousands of government publications. Those of interest to consumers are listed in the free pamphlet *Consumer Information*, which can be acquired from the Consumer Information Center in Pueblo, Colorado.

Department of Health and Human Services. Programs administered by this department are vitally important to all of us. Of greatest importance to consumers are:

1. The *Food and Drug Administration (FDA)*, the primary purpose of which is to develop and enforce food, drug, and cosmetic standards. Its activities are directed mainly toward promoting purity, strength, and truthful and informative labeling of essential commodities. Laws enforced by the FDA are among the most important of all federal laws for protection of consumers.
2. *The Center for Devices and Radiological Health*, which protects consumers against unnecessary exposure to radiation from electronic products including microwave ovens, lasers, television sets, x-rays, and sunlamps.

Office of Consumer Affairs (OCA). This office analyzes and coordinates all federal government activities in the area of consumer protection. It is the center of the government's effort to help consumers. The OCA, which operates under the guidance of the Special Assistant to the President for Consumer Affairs, develops consumer information materials and assists other agencies in responding to consumer complaints.

State and Local Consumer Agencies

State and local governments provide information, services, inspections, and other forms of protection for consumers. Many states have passed laws and cities have passed ordinances to protect the health, safety, and rights of citizens. Common among these are regulations pertaining to sanitation, food handling, weights and measures, quality standards, safety, advertising, and trade practices.

The laws for consumer protection vary so widely among states that it is possible to give here only examples of subjects covered by laws.

SUBJECTS FOR STATE LAWS TO AID AND PROTECT CONSUMERS

Many states have consumer laws or are considering laws on subjects such as:

1. Consumer loans and credit, savings, and investments.
2. Solicitations for contributions to foundations and associations purporting to make significant contributions to society.
3. Wholesomeness, sanitation, and quality standards of foods, both for consumption at home and in public eating places.
4. Health and personal welfare through licensing of medical personnel, licensing and inspection of private and public hospitals and nursing homes, use of drugs, and licensing and control of funeral homes and cemeteries.
5. Standards for and regulation of the sale of household goods, such as bedding, upholstery, and fabrics.
6. Sanitation—water supply, sewage disposal, etc.
7. Real estate zoning and restrictions.
8. Insurance—life, liability, and casualty.
9. Private and public education.
10. Recreation—movies, pools and beaches, travel, motels, etc.
11. Standards—weights and measures, quality grades.
12. Personal care—licensing and control of barber and beauty shops.

In response to consumer demands, a growing number of state and local governments are providing consumer protection in the forms of laws, agencies, and consumer advocates to investigate complaints. City and county health, welfare, fire, and police departments may assist with consumer problems. Local newspapers often give information about where consumers can get help.

HOW GOVERNMENT AGENCIES AID AND PROTECT CONSUMERS

1. Informative and protective services for consumers are provided by three levels of government agencies—local, state, and federal.
2. Business and consumer statistics, weather reports, and other information are made available to consumers, producers, and distributors by the federal government.
3. Several agencies of the federal government conduct extensive research to discover procedures to assist consumers.
4. The federal government promotes fair competition among businesses and individuals, thus assuring better products and reasonable prices.
5. Consumers receive government protection from false and deceptive advertising.
6. Enforcement of standards and regulations insuring purity, potency, and truthful and informative labeling of food, drugs, and cosmetics protects consumers.

PRIVATE SOURCES OF CONSUMER PROTECTION

Consumers can make wise choices and avoid being influenced by misleading labeling, deceptive advertising, or questionable business practices. The wise consumer seeks information about the product or service being considered and then uses that information as a basis for a buying decision. The information obtained serves as a guide in choosing the right product or service. There are a number of private sources that provide information, standards, and protection for the consumer. Some of the most important are discussed in this section.

Consumer-Sponsored Services

Information about consumer products is sometimes difficult, if not impossible, for an individual to obtain. In some cases, the consumer does not have access to the information. In other cases, obtaining the needed information requires investigation and testing that the individual cannot do. Because of these difficulties, agencies and organizations have been established to obtain and distribute product information to consumers.

Consumer Federation of America (CFA). The CFA is a federation of national, state, and local consumer organizations with a membership of 30 million. It is dedicated to consumer action through education and legislation. The CFA publishes a directory of all local and state consumer groups.

Consumers' Research, Inc. (CR). Consumers' Research, Inc. is an independent, nonprofit organization established in 1927 for the purpose of providing the public with scientific, technical, and educational information. *Consumers' Research* magazine publishes articles on a wide variety of topics of consumer interest. Articles are written by staff writers and contributing editors. CR does no testing.

Illus. 7-1

There are a number of private sources of consumer information, standards, and protection.

Consumers Union of the United States, Inc. (CU). Consumers Union is a nonprofit corporation with the world's largest laboratory and testing facilities for consumer products. The organization tests products, provides information about them to consumers, and acts as an advocate for consumer protection. To guide buyers, Consumers Union publishes tests and ratings of products in its monthly magazine, *Consumer Reports*, and in annual reports.

Seals and Marks

There are many businesses, periodicals, stores, associations of businesses, and independent testing and certifying agencies that provide information for the guidance and protection of consumers. In many cases, the products that are tested for safety, quality, use, content, strength, or other characteristics may carry a seal or a mark. Among the most well known are:

Good Housekeeping. Since 1885 Good Housekeeping has provided consumer education and protection. Any product which bears the Good Housekeeping seal or which is advertised in the magazine (except for certain products identified in the magazine) carries Good Housekeeping's limited warranty. If any such product proves to be defective within four years from the date of purchase, Good Housekeeping will replace the product or refund the price paid for it. Since Good Housekeeping does not manufacture, sell, or service the merchandise, it is not liable under any implied warranty. Neither is the seal an express warranty for state law or any other purposes. Good Housekeeping provides only replacement or refund for defective products and no other form of damages or remedy. Figure 7-1 is the Good Housekeeping seal.

Figure 7-1
Good Housekeeping Seal

Underwriters' Laboratories, Inc. Underwriters' Laboratories tests products from many thousands of manufacturers all over the world. The mark of Underwriters' Laboratories, Inc., is not a guarantee; it signifies, however, that the product has been tested for reasonably forseeable risks to life and property, and that the product has been judged to be safe for normal use. More than 2 billion products carry the UL mark represented in Figure 7-2.

Figure 7-2
UL Mark

American Gas Association. AGA maintains laboratories to test gas appliances. AGA also encourages national standards for gas equipment. Products meeting its standards receive the AGA certification. This certification is not a guarantee. Figure 7-3 is the AGA seal.

Figure 7-3
AGA Seal

Association of Home Appliance Manufacturers. AHAM develops and updates appliance performance standards. It sponsors certification programs for these home appliances—room air conditioners, refrigerators, freezers, humidifiers, and dehumidifiers. Manufacturers can pass on to consumers the certification results for product comparison. As in the case of the UL mark and the AGA seal, the AHAM seal is not a guarantee. It signifies that a product has met the association's performance standards. Figure 7-4 is a certification seal for a room air conditioner.

Figure 7-4

AHAM Certification Seal for an Air Conditioner

Professional Associations

Some professional associations are concerned about the welfare of consumers. These associations may advocate legislation that would help the consumer, or they may prepare and distribute informational and educational materials. Some influential professional associations are:

Council on Dental Therapeutics. The Council on Dental Therapeutics was established by the American Dental Association to protect and inform the public about dental products. Most of the products studied by the council are used or prescribed directly by the dentist in the treatment of diseases of the mouth. Upon investigation, a product may be accepted by the council, which means that it meets certain standards for both its composition and the manner in which the product is advertised. A seal of acceptance may be used by the manufacturer of a product if it has been accepted by the council.

American Home Economics Association. For nearly 75 years the American Home Economics Association has been influential in promoting the education, welfare, and protection of consumers in the United States. This association helps to improve the quality of individual and family life through research, cooperative programs, education, and public information. Through the Consumer Interests Committee, the American Home Economics Association makes available a series of buying guides that are valuable to consumers.

American Medical Association. One particularly valuable function of the American Medical Association is the improvement of medical products. The responsibility for testing medical products and apparatus is assigned to special committees and councils. The association makes useful information available to medical societies and the general public.

Better Business Bureaus

Better business bureaus are nonprofit, business-supported organizations that provide information on local businesses and protect consumers. They handle more consumer contacts than all other agencies combined. Almost 150 local better business bureaus (BBBs) have joined together in a national organization called the *Council* of *Better Business Bureaus.*

BBBs are organized to protect the buying power of the consumer, eliminate misleading advertising, encourage honesty in business practices, and inform the public on how to buy intelligently. Consumers may contact the bureaus for pamphlets, buying guides, and other material to help them make the most of their buying power.

Consumers can protect themselves from unfair business practices and fraudulent schemes by consulting the local better business bureau. Consumers who have become victims of unfair practices should report such incidents to the bureau so that other citizens may be protected.

FUNCTIONS OF BETTER BUSINESS BUREAUS

1. Elimination of causes of customer complaints against business by:
    a. preventing unfair treatment,
    b. promoting fair advertising and selling practices,
    c. promoting informative advertising, and
    d. helping to settle a dispute between a business and a customer.
2. Cooperation with educators and business to provide students with sound knowledge of the functions of our economic system.
3. Provision for adult education in matters pertaining to management of personal business affairs and understanding of the American economy.

The Complaint Letter

If you do not receive satisfaction as a result of a complaint to the store where you bought merchandise, your next step is to write a letter of complaint to the manufacturer. Address the letter to the highest official in the company. *Standard & Poor's Register of Corporations, Directors and Executives,* available in most public libraries, lists over 37,000 American business firms, their officers, and addresses. If you have the name of the product but need to know the manufacturer, then consult *The Thomas Registry*. This reference, found in many public libraries, lists thousands of products and their manufacturers. A sample complaint letter is presented in Figure 7-5.

If after writing your letter you do not receive a reply or satisfaction, consult the appropriate local or state consumer agency. Your local library, mayor's office, or local newspaper hot line can provide you with the name and address of the appropriate agency to contact.

CONSUMER RESPONSIBILITIES

So far in this chapter you have been informed as to a number of consumer rights. Also, you have learned of a number of government consumer agencies, consumer-sponsored services, pro-

Figure 7-5

A Sample Complaint Letter

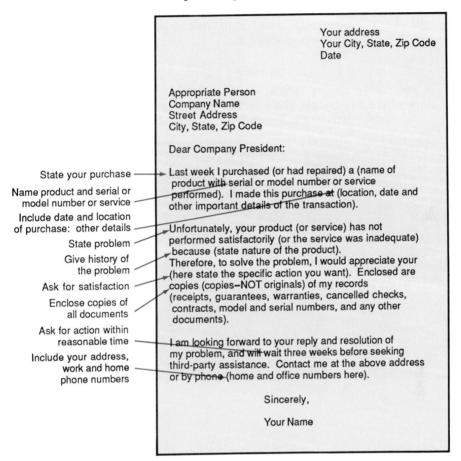

Source: *Consumer's Resource Handbook*, (Pueblo, Colorado: Consumer Information Center, 1979), 2–3.

fessional associations, and better business bureaus that provide protection to consumers.

However, along with rights go responsibilities. Like the proverb, "an ounce of prevention is worth a pound of cure," consumers must bear some responsibility for their own (and others') protection. Consumer responsibilities parallel the Presidents' bill of rights, namely:

1. Consumers must use products safely.
2. Consumers must choose goods and services carefully and wisely.
3. Consumers must make use of product information.

4. Consumers must inform proper agencies of wrongs committed in consumer dealings.
5. Consumers must exercise redress.
6. Consumers must read and ask questions about their rights and responsibilities.

Illus. 7-2

If you do not receive satisfaction as a result of the complaint to the store where you bought the merchandise, your next step is to write a letter of complaint to the manufacturer.

VOCABULARY BUILDER

Better Business Bureau
consumer movement
Consumer Product Safety
  Commission
Consumers Union of the
United States, Inc.

Environmental Protection
  Agency
Federal Trade Commission
U.S. Office of Consumer
  Affairs

REVIEW QUESTIONS

1. As the United States grew more industrialized and cities became larger, what new consumer problems appeared?
2. What is the consumer bill of rights?

3. What are the functions of the government agencies that are related to consumer interests?
4. What are the main functions of the Department of Agriculture as it relates to the consumer?
5. What are some of the major agencies under the Department of Commerce that provide services to the consumer?
6. How does the Government Printing Office assist the consumer?
7. In what way does the Department of Health and Human Services assist the consumer?
8. How do state and local agencies assist the consumer?
9. What is the Consumers Union of the United States, Inc.?
10. What are some of the more common seals designed for the protection of consumer interests?
11. When would you write a complaint letter to the manufacturer of the product you purchased?

DISCUSSION QUESTIONS

1. Why has the need for consumer protection grown over time in the United States and throughout the world?
2. What impact did the consumer bill of rights have on consumer legislation?
3. How do the grading and inspection services of the Department of Agriculture aid the consumer?
4. Why is it necessary to have state laws—as well as federal laws—that control deceptive and fraudulent advertising?
5. Some manufacturers oppose such organizations as Consumers' Research, Inc., and Consumers Union, Inc., whereas others approve of them. How do you account for the differences in attitude?
6. Why do you think some manufacturers organize an association and use a seal indicating that products of the members of that association meet certain requirements?
7. Some people assert that the scientific laboratories maintained by publishers of periodicals are operated for the benefit of manufacturers and therefore render little service to buyers. Do you think this assertion is true? Why?
8. Suppose a door-to-door salesperson calls on you. You would like to obtain information about that person's reliability and that of the company. From what source might you be able to obtain help or advice?

8

Advertising

Marketing consists of all activities that direct the flow of goods and services from producers to consumers. Advertising is one of these activities and is, therefore, an important part of our market economy. *Advertising* is any form of public announcement that makes known the existence of a good or service for the purpose of stimulating a desire for that good or service. From the advertiser's point of view, the main goal of advertising is to sell goods and services. From the consumer's point of view, the purpose of advertising is to obtain information about goods and services that are available for sale. This chapter will help you to understand the functions and practices of advertising and how they relate to consumer interests.

After studying this chapter, you will be able to:

1. explain the functions of advertising from the seller's point of view,
2. discuss the costs of advertising (who pays and how much),
3. describe how advertising can benefit consumers,
4. identify some of the major criticisms of advertising,
5. discuss kinds of advertising and types of advertising appeals,
6. describe forms of deceptive advertising,
7. analyze advertisements in order to make wise consumer choices, and
8. discuss the types of government and private regulation of advertising.

FUNCTIONS OF ADVERTISING

When our country was young, production and marketing were very simple. Most consumers produced the goods they consumed or traded with nearby acquaintances. Stores often traded goods across the counter, and very little money changed hands. The first common form of advertising was the sign used by professionals such as doctors, merchants, blacksmiths, and wigmakers.

Now we have mass production with producers and consumers widely separated. A complicated system of transportation and communication is needed to help producers reach consumers and tell them what the producer has to sell. Under our present economic system, advertising helps both consumers and producers.

Advertising From the Seller's Viewpoint

The ultimate purpose of advertising is to sell goods and services. Many functions of advertising are beneficial to consumers as well as producers and distributors. The major functions of advertising are given in the following list.

Illus. 8-1
The first form of advertising was the sign.

MAJOR FUNCTIONS OF ADVERTISING FROM THE SELLER'S VIEWPOINT

1. Stimulate consumer demand by obtaining:
   a. wider acceptance and greater use of products not yet universally used, such as home computers and video cam recorders;
   b. greater use of products already widely used, such as fruits; and
   c. acceptance of a product by consumers who have not used it.
2. Educate prospective consumers regarding:
   a. personal benefits and satisfactions to be derived from using a particular product,
   b. various uses of a product, and
   c. merits of a particular brand or make.
3. Inform consumers about new products, developments in present products, and changes in fashions and customs.
4. Maintain contact with consumers who, without advertising, may never know a product is available.
5. Stress exclusive features and important advantages of a product.
6. Build consumer preference for a particular brand of product, thus making it possible to price the product above similar brands.
7. Establish a trade name, slogan, or product image.
8. Create goodwill and develop consumer respect for the firm.
9. Obtain a list of prospective customers in order to prepare the way for sales representatives.
10. Obtain a larger share of the available business.
11. Promote the use of one class of product, such as margarine as opposed to butter.

Cost of Advertising

Advertising costs are reflected in the selling price of a product or service. Therefore, the consumer ultimately pays for advertising. It may seem unreasonable to spend $40,000 for a full-page advertisement in one issue of a national magazine or $250,000 to run a television ad one time. But these advertising media reach hundreds of thousands, even millions, of people; hence the advertising cost per unit of product sold is very small. Consumers should be interested in knowing how much of the dollar cost of their purchases represents advertising cost.

More that $87.8 billion a year is spent for advertising. This amount is 2.4 percent of the total value of all goods and services produced in the United States. About 56 percent of the total expenditure is for national advertising and about 44 percent is for local advertising. Of the $87.8 billion spent for advertising in 1984, newspapers accounted for the greatest percentage, followed by television, direct mail, radio, magazines, business and farm publications, and outdoor media, in that order. Figure 8-1 presents the percentage of the total advertising expenditures for each medium.

Figure 8-1
Percentage of Advertising Expenditures by Medium, 1984

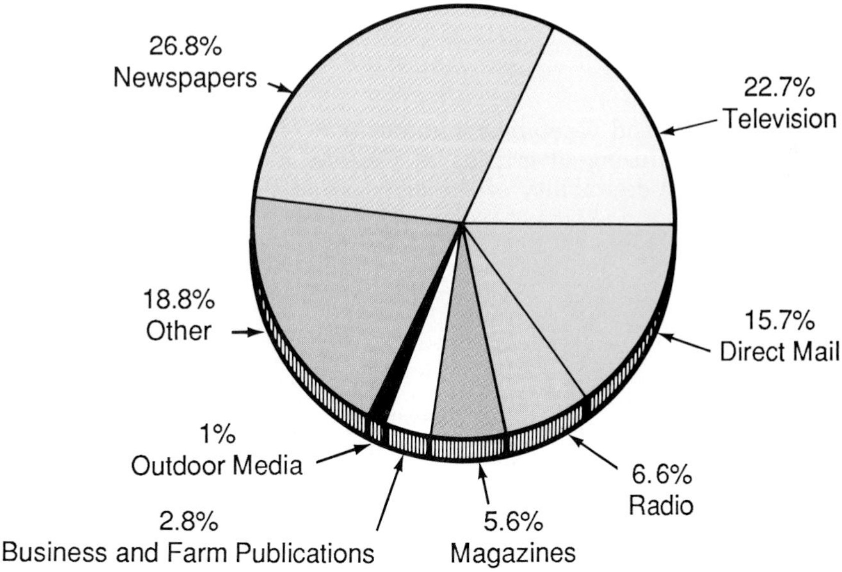

26.8%
Newspapers

22.7%
Television

18.8%
Other

15.7%
Direct Mail

1%
Outdoor Media

6.6%
Radio

2.8%
Business and Farm Publications

5.6%
Magazines

How Advertising Benefits Consumers

The influence of advertising can indirectly cause our standard of living to go up. If we become aware of new products or services that may improve our lives, we may want to buy them.

An economic want exists where there was none before. For instance, the importance of fresh fruits and vegetables in our diet was not common knowledge until producers began using advertising to educate people about the desirability of the daily use of these foods. It may be true that advertising sometimes influences us to want things we really do not need, but we are, after all, free to decide what we need and want. If consumers are informed, they will be able to make these decisions intelligently.

Educational Value. Advertising designed to change consumer behavior is an example of the educational influence of advertising. Toothpaste manufacturers, for example, attempt to get consumers to brush often and get regular dental checkups by informing them of certain tooth and gum diseases. By getting the consumer to brush often and get regular dental checkups, the manufacturer can point out the effectiveness of its toothpaste—its disease-fighting and mouth-freshening ingredients.

Illus. 8-2

Fresh fruits and vegetables were not part of our basic diet until producers began using advertising as a means of educating people about the desirability of the daily use of these foods.

Both the consumer and the toothpaste manufacturer benefit from educational advertising. The consumer, by brushing frequently, has better checkups; and the manufacturer sells more toothpaste.

Informational Value. Advertising also provides information solely for the consumers' benefit. An example of this is information regarding nutritional contents of food products. We know that heart disease is aggravated by too much salt, fat, sugar, and cholesterol in the diet. Many manufacturers of food products will, through labeling and advertising, inform the consumer as to how much of these ingredients is in each serving of their products. The manufacturers simply provide the information to the consumer to use or not.

Economic Value. No less important than the educational benefits of advertising are economic benefits. Advertising stimulates a demand for products. We would not have many of the products we enjoy if advertising did not stimulate a demand for them.

Social and Cultural Value. Finally, because advertising arouses consumer demand and penetrates deeply into American life, it can be a powerful influence on the social and cultural goals of people. For example, as our wants increase, we may demand better food, better housing, better education, better recreation, better health, and a better environment.

Advertising and Its Critics

The critics of advertising seem to fall into two camps, those who criticize advertising itself and those who criticize certain advertising techniques. The first group opposes all advertising and feels that advertising expenses are wasteful. The second group is not opposed to advertising, but it feels that much of today's advertising can, and needs to, be improved. These critics are concerned with educating consumers to demand more informative advertising. They believe that advertisers must accept high moral, social, and ethical standards. Most individual advertisers and advertising associations actively support and praise the activities of these constructive critics.

The argument that advertising should be presented in good taste may seem to have merit. A problem arises, however, when one tries to define good taste. What a person considers to be good taste is strictly an individual matter. Usually a person's judgment on this issue depends upon whether or not the person agrees with what the advertiser is suggesting. For example, some people would praise advertisements that appeal to thrift, economy, honesty, and similar qualities but reject advertising that appeals to fear, envy, and similar emotions. There is no completely satisfactory way to resolve the issue of good taste.

Probably the only way an advertiser could avoid the accusation of poor taste would be to give a strictly factual description of the product or service and make no suggestion as to why the potential consumer would be interested in buying it. Alert buyers should be their own judges of how an advertisement helps or fails to help them in their buying decisions.

THE PROS AND CONS OF ADVERTISING

Critics state that advertising:

1. promotes brand switching;
2. increases the prices of goods;
3. promotes wasteful use of a product;
4. appeals too much to emotions rather than to reason;
5. controls the media (TV, radio, newspapers, etc.);
6. is often in poor taste, filled with half-truths, or outrightly deceptive; and
7. creates undesirable wants.

Supporters of advertising answer that advertising:

1. increases total demand for products,
2. often makes lower prices possible,
3. enhances economic and individual freedom,
4. frees the media from government control,
5. can and should be improved, and
6. expands markets for new and better products.

Critics and supporters alike need to recall that advertising *has not caused* our economic system; advertising *has resulted from* it.

USE OF ADVERTISING

Advertising is everywhere—on TV and radio, in newspapers and magazines, on billboards and walls, in stores, and in our mail. Every day we are exposed to all kinds of advertising. We cannot escape it, so we should put it to the best possible use.

Kinds of Advertising

The advertising with which we are chiefly concerned is directed toward the person who buys for personal or household use, not for a business or profession. This advertising is known as *consumer advertising*.

Advertising may also be classified by its approach or intention. If the advertising is intended to stress the benefits of a certain class or type of product rather than particular brands of that product, it is known as *primary advertising*. For example, if the dairy industry uses advertising to stimulate the demand for cheese, this is primary advertising.

Selective advertising, on the other hand, attempts to persuade consumers to buy one brand rather than another. This is the kind of advertising to which consumers are most frequently exposed.

Advertising Appeals

To market goods and services successfully, the advertiser needs to understand the motives that influence human behavior. These motives are often referred to as *advertising appeals*.

Advertising is often classified in terms of rational appeals and emotional appeals. *Rational appeals* are those that supposedly center on logic by providing basic facts and information. *Emotional appeals* are those that involve the emotions and excite people to buy even if the decision to buy is not a logical one. In many advertisements, the two appeals overlap.

Psychologists today no longer make a precise distinction between rational and emotional behavior. Instead, psychologists take the approach that a person performs that behavior which is either most desirable or least threatening. This approach to human behavior is more refined than attempting to decide what behavior is rational and what is emotional. Consequently, advertisers tend to stress those appeals that would be most desirable to the potential consumer if the consumer were to purchase a particular good or service.

Deceptive Advertising

Every buyer must recognize the fact that, although the majority of advertisers are honest, some are not. Deceptive advertising hurts both consumers and businesses. Consumers are cheated, and businesses lose repeat customers.

Some dishonest advertisers use deceptive advertising appeals, claims, and schemes in spite of all efforts to stop them. Advertisers who use deceptive practices usually find them so successful that they can make big profits before any action can be taken to force them to stop. Because deceptive advertising practices appear repeatedly, consumers should know how to recognize them and be on guard against them. Some of the types of deceptive advertising found most frequently are discussed below.

One type of deceptive advertising is called *bait and switch*. A product is advertised at a cut-rate price, but no mention is made that the seller has only a few such items on sale at that price. Consequently, when customers enter the store, they are told that the item is out of stock and then an attempt is made to switch the customers to a higher-priced item. The ad is merely bait to lure the customers into the store for a switch to another item.

Fictitious pricing and *misrepresentation* are other forms of deceptive advertising. Example are: overstating the manufacturer's suggested price to convince the buyer that the advertised price is a special bargain; advertising 50 percent off the regular price when the seller has never sold the goods before; and making false or exaggerated claims about the quality and performance of a product.

Another type of deceptive advertising is the sending of *unordered products* through the mail followed by a letter demanding payment. Consumers should be aware that they are under no legal obligation to pay for unordered products sent through the mail, nor are they under any obligation to return the merchandise.

Some *contests* sponsored by advertisers might also be viewed as deceptive advertising. Often the prize given is extremely small and is simply intended to allow the advertiser a chance to make a sales pitch.

ADVERTISING'S VALUE TO CONSUMERS

A study of the following questions should indicate how useful advertising is to consumers.

1. Could you get all the information you want about the latest automobile without referring to advertisments?
2. What facts and other information about the latest developments in home appliances and equipment have you obtained through advertising?
3. What can be learned about foods from newspaper advertisements?
4. What new products have you learned about through advertising in the past two years?
5. What information about health, recreation, or sanitation have you received through advertising?
6. If all home appliances were sold without trade names or trademarks, how would you select them?
7. If canned foods did not carry labels and trademarks, how could you select canned goods wisely?
8. How do you benefit by reading the advertisements of local stores?
9. How is attendance at your school events, such as plays, athletic contests, and operettas, promoted? Is advertising involved?

Consumer Analysis of Advertising

As consumers, we are exposed daily to literally hundreds of advertising messages. Without doubt, these advertisements develop in us desires for products and services that otherwise we would not want. This, in many respects, is good for us, for it acquaints us with products and services that may make living more pleasant. It is important, however, that as consumers we not only understand the motives, methods, and practices of advertisers but also that we know how to use advertising wisely in satisfying our wants. In order to use advertising wisely, we must be able to analyze it. In Chapter 10 you will learn how advertising may be used in buying wisely. Here we shall merely present some questions consumers should ask when analyzing advertisements.

QUESTIONS TO HELP YOU ANALYZE ADVERTISEMENTS

1. Do you need the item advertised?
2. What does the product contain and how is it made?
3. How economical is the product?
4. How long will the product last?
5. How does its price compare with the prices of similar products?
6. Does the item carry any seals identifying its quality or any evidence of authoritative scientific tests?
7. What proof is used to back up the statements?
8. Are there any service or maintenance problems?
9. Are any of the advertising statements evasive or misleading?
10. Does the advertisement appeal to your intelligence or your emotions?

REGULATION OF ADVERTISING

Well-established business concerns recognize that honesty is the basis for lasting success. Of the thousands of advertisements that are printed and broadcast over the air annually, only a very small percentage are dishonest or misleading. The best safeguard for advertising honesty is the advertiser's sense of responsibility.

There are two effective types of advertising regulation. The first is government regulation through federal and state laws. The second is self-imposed regulation through standards set by the advertisers themselves. These standards are adopted by individual business firms; by advertisers' associations; and often by businesses providing advertising media, such as newspapers, magazines, radio, and television. The publishers of magazines and newspapers recognize the fact that dishonest advertising reacts unfavorably on their publications as well as on the products advertised.

Government Regulation

The major responsibility for government regulation of advertising rests with the Federal Trade Commission (FTC). It is the responsibility of this commission not only to see that advertisers follow accepted standards for honesty and reliability but also to take action against most kinds of deceptive claims in all advertising media.

The FTC is often unable to enforce regulations because a large number of cases involve lengthy and costly court battles. Sometimes much time passes before a court acts on the complaint of the FTC. However, the FTC has ruled that advertisers who are found guilty of deceptive or false advertising must correct the situation through "corrective advertising." Under the corrective advertising policy, an advertiser found guilty of false or deceptive advertising must run a corrective advertisement and indicate that the previous advertising might have been misleading.

The FTC also requires that all advertisers make available to consumers the data on which all claims for products or services are based. The consumer must be aware, however, that the FTC is able to examine only some of the more glaring complaints since the amount of advertising is huge compared to the number of people on the staff of the FTC.

In addition to regulation imposed by the FTC, most states have laws that regulate deceptive and false advertising. Many of the state laws tend to be weak and ineffective because they require proof that the advertiser intended to deceive. Also, in most cases the state laws deal only with deceptive information and not with advertising that is simply in bad taste. However, there is evidence that state laws regulating advertising are being strengthened and will be improved in the years to come. Some states have adopted the Unfair Trade Practices and Consumer Protection Law developed by the FTC, which has the potential to protect consumers if enforced. Under this law, the state attorney general has the power to control deceptive and false advertising at the state level.

Additional laws that protect the consumer were discussed in Chapter 6.

Self-Imposed Regulation

For many years business groups and professional organizations have imposed self-restriction on the advertising industry. As early as 1911 a magazine called *Printer's Ink* published what it entitled "A Model Statute" for advertisers to follow for fair advertising. This model statute proposed by *Printer's Ink* became the basis for many of the state laws that control advertising.

In 1971 the National Advertising Review Board, the American Advertising Agencies, and the Association of National Advertisers joined forces with the Council of Better Business Bureaus to establish a procedure to focus on complaints about advertising. These complaints are examined by the National Advertising Review Board. The board consists of representatives of advertisers, advertising agencies, and the general public. At present the board primarily examines claims of faulty advertising. However, the board plans to expand its activities to consider advertisements that are simply in bad taste. The first step in controlling and regulating advertising by business itself will be to use persuasion against the advertisers directly. When this does not work, the board plans to refer all deceptive advertisements to the FTC and other appropriate government regulatory agencies.

Many radio and television stations as well as newspapers and magazines screen the advertising they carry for any misleading claims and try to eliminate advertisements that are in bad taste. As might be expected, the criteria or standards used vary greatly from one business group to another. Also, trade publications frequently speak out against advertising considered to be deceptive or in bad taste. For example, a major advertising publication, *Advertising Age*, often criticizes advertisements and practices it considers to be misleading or in poor taste.

It is not surprising that many businesses are trying not to use any advertising that is deceptive or in poor taste. In recent years, advertising of this nature has been criticized severely. Many businesses realize that advertising that is deceptive or in poor taste has a tendency to damage the image of the business involved. Consequently, self-imposed restrictions on advertising by business groups are becoming more common.

VOCABULARY BUILDER

advertising   emotional appeals
bait and switch   rational appeals
consumer advertising

REVIEW QUESTIONS

1. What is the purpose of advertising from the advertiser's point of view and from the consumer's point of view?
2. Why is advertising essential in a market economy?
3. What are the major functions of advertising from the seller's viewpoint?
4. What are the major benefits of advertising for consumers?
5. What are the major criticisms of advertising?
6. How does selective advertising differ from primary advertising?
7. What are some common types of deceptive advertising?
8. What are the two types of regulation of advertising?

DISCUSSION QUESTIONS

1. In what ways does advertising stimulate consumer demand?
2. Of what social value is advertising?
3. Are the major criticisms of advertising justifiable? Discuss, from the standpoint of the possible effect upon you and other members of the class, each of the seven criticisms listed on page 116.
4. What kind of advertising appeals do you think advertisers should stress?
5. To what extent do you think that advertisements are misleading or dishonest?
6. What are some steps that you think can be taken by consumers to regulate advertisements that are in bad taste?

PART 2
Special Activities

CLASS PROJECTS

1. Your parents gave you a wristwatch for your birthday. After one week, the watch stopped running. You returned the watch to the store and received another in exchange. The second watch does not keep accurate time, even after being taken back for adjustment three times. It also stops running when you are not wearing it. The jeweler says there's nothing more he can do and will not give you another watch or refund your money. You decide you will write the manufacturer asking for a full cash refund. Write the letter.

2. Dennis Kato had the Ace Building Company build a house for him. He did some of the work himself and went to a heating company and selected a furnace, which the heating company said would heat satisfactorily. After the house was completed, Mr. Kato could not get his furnace to heat the house to a warm enough temperature to suit him in cold weather. Was there any warranty, and does Mr. Kato have any claim against the contractor or the heating company?

3. Sarah Bloom, age 15, bought a personal radio from the Acme Audio Center and asked the owner to bill her father (whom the owner knew) for the $49.95 cost of the radio. Upon receipt of the bill two weeks later, Sarah's father refused to pay and returned the radio. The owner claimed that since Sarah had used the radio, it could not be resold as new and that Sarah's father should at least pay the difference between what the radio cost new and what it would sell for used. Does the owner have a legal claim against Sarah's father or Sarah?

4. Bring to class examples of advertising that appeal to your emotions and examples of advertising that appeal to your common sense and needs. Some examples may include both types of appeals, such as toothpaste that includes brighteners (emotion) and fluoride (common sense and need). Discuss these examples in class.

5. From a newspaper or magazine, select an advertisement that appeals to you. Paste the ad on a sheet of paper, and below the ad supply information pertaining to the following:
   a. The type of appeal
   b. Useful (educational) information provided
   c. Meaningless words or statements made
   d. The type of warranty offered or guarantee made, if any
   e. Additional information that you would have liked to have seen

COMMUNITY PROJECTS

1. Prepare a list of laws and regulation in your state that in some way protect consumers. Examples to help start the list are: laws governing small loans and credit, sanitation laws, and laws for licensing and control of barbers.

2. Since small claims courts operate differently in various states, investigate the operation of small claims court in your community. Some areas you might wish to cover are:
   a. Who used this court more, consumers or small businesses?
   b. What are some tips the plaintiff should follow in preparing his or her case?
   c. What types of cases are usually brought to small claims court in your community?
   d. Is a lawyer allowed to represent either the defendant or the plaintiff in your small claims court?
   e. What is the dollar limit of claims allowed in your community?

3. Give examples of three different kinds of contracts that you, a member of your family, or a friend made within the last week and show how all five essential elements of a contract were present in each. For each contract, explain when and how the offer was made; how it was accepted; and if it could have been accepted in any other way.

4. From a copy of *Consumer Reports* select a product which had been tested. Give a short in-class report on the article, the product tested, the criteria used in testing the product, and the final results of the testing.
5. Bring to class examples of advertising that might be considered false or misleading; for example, an ad for a hair growth lotion or an ad for a portable machine that will cure arthritis. Explain why you consider these ads false or misleading. Make a bulletin board display of some of the more outrageous claims.

PART 3
Money Management

9

Managing Income

All successful people, regardless of their level of income, must do some financial planning. Basic financial planning for people at all income levels includes setting up a spending plan (budget), keeping certain records, and providing for savings and investments. People with annual incomes of $25,000 and up should go beyond the basic steps and seek expert advice from private firms specializing in complete financial and estate planning services. Even if you earn less than $25,000 annually, there are times when expert advice is needed from an attorney, an insurance advisor, or a real estate broker. Financial planning can be complex (requiring complete service from a private securities firm) or simple (requiring your own knowledge with occasional help from experts). This chapter provides some simple guidelines for individual and family financial planning.

After studying this chapter, you will be able to:

1. define a *spending plan*,
2. explain how income and expenditures (payments) can be estimated,
3. prepare a spending plan and maintain a daily cash record,
4. identify what records should be kept for financial planning and for income tax purposes,
5. describe how money can work for you, and
6. list places where savings can be put.

FINANCIAL PLANNING

In order to enjoy the highest possible level of living from one's limited income, financial planning is necessary. In this section you will learn what is required for proper financial planning.

Developing a Spending Plan

A *spending plan* (also called a budget) is a guide for spending and saving one's income. Such a guide or plan helps us get as many of the things we need and want as possible. Spending plans will seldom be the same for any two individuals or families. Since each of us (either as an individual or as a member of a family) has different wants and different life goals, each of us should set up our own spending plan.

Operating without some kind of spending plan is like going on an auto trip without a map. A spending plan involves:

1. determining immediate, short-range, and long-range goals;
2. estimating how much cash (income) will be available to spend or save; and
3. planning the expenditures (payments).

Determining Goals. This is the first step in building a spending plan or budget. One should think first of the immediate goals for the coming year. Obviously, everyone's immediate goals are to provide the basic needs of food, clothing, and shelter. In addition to these basic needs, a high school student, for example, may plan to buy a class ring, take a vacation, or buy a used car. A newly married couple may need to buy a piece of furniture or start a reserve fund for emergencies.

Short-range goals (for the next two to five years, for example) also need to be considered. A high school student may plan to save for college or to buy a new car. A newly married couple may plan to save for a down payment on a home or to buy expensive appliances such as a stove, a refrigerator, and a washer and dryer.

Long-range goals are usually planned by families and adults who have completed their education and training. Some long-range goals might include:

1. providing a college education for one's children,
2. having a debt-free home,
3. having retirement income, and
4. helping newly married sons and daughters set up housekeeping.

A short-range goal may be to purchase a class ring.

Setting goals helps one who is making a spending plan know how much money should be set aside or saved for each month and year.

Estimating Cash Available. The second step in making a spending plan is to estimate the amount of cash that will be available. This consists of cash on hand at the beginning of the spending plan period plus all income for the period. Income includes:

1. wages or salary received;
2. interest on savings;
3. earnings on investments;
4. money received from other sources such as gifts, allowances, and bonuses; and
5. money one plans to borrow.

The total of all these items is the amount of cash available for the spending-plan period.

Cash on hand includes money in your possession and in your checking account. Do not count money in savings accounts that was set aside for emergencies or some special purpose (goal). However, if you plan to spend some of your savings during the spending-plan period, you should include this amount in your estimated cash available.

When including wages or salary, list only the net amount of *take-home pay*, which is the amount available after the employer has withheld deductions for taxes and other purposes. Wages or salary may be estimated fairly well for the next year by considering the wages or salary received last year and adjusting for any expected increase or decrease.

The best way to estimate the amount of interest, earnings from investments, gifts, allowances, or bonuses is to assume that it will be the same as last year. If you know of any expected increases or decreases in such amounts, however, the adjusted amount should be used.

Money that is borrowed will be part of the cash available to spend. When the borrowed money is repaid, the payments are fixed expenditures.

Planning Expenditures. After you have figured how much available cash you will have, you need to estimate your expenditures. *Expenditures*, for the purpose of a spending plan, include payments for actual expenses (money spent for items that will be used up and never recovered) as well as for items that will last a long time and for money placed in savings. Expenditures also include payments on homes and repayments of loans.

Table 9-1 shows a method of setting up a cash spending plan on a monthly basis. This plan was adopted by a family who first kept a record for several months to see how their money was being spent. They then divided their expenditures into two groups: fixed payments and variable payments.

Fixed payments are always the same amount, whether the family pays them monthly, semiannually, or annually. Examples of fixed payments are rent or mortgage payments, insurance payments, payments on borrowed money, and charitable (including church) contributions. Note that savings are included under fixed payments. Unless a fixed amount is set aside monthly, the family would probably never save any money.

Variable payments are not constant month after month. The time of payment is usually known but the amount of the payment varies. Examples of variable payments are utility bills, medical and dental bills, and payments for clothing, personal items, and entertainment.

Note that the plan has three columns for each month: one showing the amounts spent last year, one showing the estimated amounts for this year, and one for the actual amounts spent this year. The first two columns are filled in when the spending plan is made up. The third column is filled in at the end of each month when the actual expenditures are known.

A high school student would have different expenditures than those in Table 9-1, but the spending plan would be prepared in the same way. Typical expenditures for a high school student might be for clothes, personal items, recreation, school lunches, school supplies, transportation, and gifts.

A sample cash spending plan for a high school senior appears in Table 9-2. Unlike the family plan in Table 9-1, this plan is set up on a weekly basis.

Daily Cash Record

A *daily cash record* is a form which records actual receipts and expenditures of income on a daily basis. One form of daily cash record is shown in Figure 9-1. This form provides a column for cash available and a column for each fixed payment and each variable payment listed in Table 9-1.

An entry is made in the daily cash record for money received or paid each day. Sources for daily entries include checks received, cash sales slips, grocery receipts, ticket stubs, and checkbook stubs if you use a checking account.

At the end of each month, the columns of the daily cash record are totaled. These monthly totals are then transferred to the column in the yearly cash spending plan labeled "Actual this Year." A comparison of the estimated figures with the actual figures shows how well the estimated spending plan is being followed. If too much money is being spent, it may be necessary to reduce estimated expenditures in the future.

Table 9-1

Yearly Cash Spending Plan for a Family

Cash Received and Paid	January			February		
	Actual Last Year	Estimate This Year	Actual This Year	Actual Last Year	Estimate This Year	Actual This Year
Cash available						
Cash at beginning (checkbook)	$ 500.00	$ 400.00	$ 400.00	$ 128.00	$ 150.00	$ 89.50
Net wages (take-home pay)	1,000.00	1,075.00	1,075.00	1,000.00	1,075.00	1,075.00
Interest and dividends	10.00	11.50	11.50	10.00	11.50	11.50
Borrowed money						
Total cash available	1,510.00	1,486.50	1,486.50	1,138.00	1,236.50	1,176.00
Fixed payments (expenditures)						
Rent or payment on mortgage	300.00	300.00	300.00	300.00	300.00	300.00
Life insurance	50.00	50.00	50.00			
Homeowner's insurance	275.00	290.00	285.00			
Auto insurance				150.00	170.00	170.00
Real estate taxes						
Payments on debts		40.00	40.00		25.00	25.00
Contribution to church	15.00	15.00	15.00	15.00	15.00	15.00
Savings	25.00	25.00	25.00	25.00	25.00	25.00
Total fixed payments	665.00	720.00	715.00	490.00	535.00	535.00
Variable payments (expenditures)						
Water & sewage	22.00	22.00	22.00	20.00	22.00	22.00
Telephone	15.00	15.00	15.00	15.00	15.00	21.00
Gas & electricity	200.00	210.00	200.00	150.00	175.00	180.00
Medical & dental	30.00	25.00	25.00	25.00	30.00	
Food	250.00	250.00	240.00	220.00	230.00	220.00
Clothing	50.00	50.00	35.00	35.00	35.00	
Car operation & repair	70.00	70.00	70.00	70.00	70.00	60.00
Recreation & education	50.00	50.00	50.00	40.00	40.00	25.00
Personal	30.00	30.00	25.00	25.00	30.00	29.00
Total variable payments	717.00	707.00	682.00	600.00	622.00	557.00
Summary						
Total cash available	1,510.00	1,486.50	1,486.50	1,138.00	1,236.50	1,176.00
Total payments (fixed & variable)	1,382.00	1,427.00	1,387.00	1,090.00	1,157.00	1,092.00
Cash balance at end	128.00	59.50	89.50	48.00	79.50	84.00

Figure 9-1
Daily Cash Record

Date	Explanation	Cash Available	FIXED PAYMENTS Rent	Life Insurance	Home-owners Insurance	Auto Insurance	Real Estate Taxes	Payments on Debts	Church	Savings	Other Payments	VARIABLE PAYMENTS Water & Sewage	Telephone	Gas and Electricity
Jan 1	Cash Available	400 00												
2	Life Insurance			50 00										
3	Groceries													
6	Gasoline													
7	Dental Bill													
8	Dress for Mary													
9	Interest	11 50												
10	Accident Insurance													
11	Groceries													
15	Personal Allowances													
15	Magazines													
15	Salary	537 50												
18	Homeowners Insurance				285 00									
19	Theater Tickets													
20	Gasoline													
21	Church								7 50					
22	Insurance for John													
23	Paid Dr. Smith													
24	Rent		300 00											
25	Groceries													
26	Installment Payment							40 00						
30	Salary	537 50												
31	Church								7 50					
31	Water & Sewage											22 00		
31	Savings Account									25 00				
31	Most Electric Bill													200 00
31	Groceries													
31	Telephone												15 00	
31	Totals	1486 50	300 00	60 00	285 00			40 00	15 00	25 00		22 00	15 00	200 00
Feb 1	Cash Available	89 50												
3	Life Insurance			50 00										

Table 9-2
Monthly Cash Spending Plan for a High School Student

	January 19--							
	Week One Date:		Week Two Date:		Week Three Date:		Week Four Date:	
Cash Received and Paid	Estimate this week	Actual this week	Estimate this week	Actual this week	Estimate this week	Actual this week	Estimate this week	Actual this week
Cash available								
Cash at								
beginning	$10.00	$ 9.00	$ 3.00	$ .25	$ 5.00	$14.50	$10.00	$18.75
Allowance	5.00	5.00	5.00	5.00	5.00	5.00	5.00	5.00
Part-time job	48.00	48.00	48.00	48.00	48.00	48.00	48.00	48.00
Other								
Cash gifts							10.00	10.00
Total Cash Avail.	63.00	62.00	56.00	53.25	58.00	67.50	73.00	81.75
Fixed payments								
School lunch	3.25	3.25	3.25	3.25	3.25	3.25	3.25	3.25
Transportation	10.00	10.00	10.00	10.00	10.00	12.00	10.00	10.00
Contributions	1.50	1.50	1.50	1.50	1.50	1.50	1.50	1.50
Savings	5.00	5.00	5.00	5.00	5.00	5.00	5.00	5.00
Total Fixed Payment	19.75	19.75	19.75	19.75	19.75	21.75	19.75	19.75
Variable Payments								
Hobby			2.00	3.00				
Snacks	5.00	6.00	5.00	4.00	5.00	5.50	5.00	4.50
Grooming	10.00	12.00						
Gifts					5.00	6.50		
Sports	5.00	5.00			5.00	5.00		
Movies	6.00	6.00	6.00	6.00	6.00	6.00	6.00	6.00
Clothes	10.00	10.00	5.00	3.00			25.00	24.50
Other	5.00	3.00	4.00	3.00	5.00	4.00	5.00	2.00
Total Variable Payment	41.00	42.00	22.00	19.00	26.00	27.00	41.00	37.00
Summary								
Total cash available	63.00	62.00	56.00	53.25	58.00	67.50	73.00	81.75
Total payments (fixed and variable)	60.75	61.75	41.75	38.75	45.75	48.75	60.75	56.75
Cash balance at end	2.25	.25	14.25	14.50	12.25	18.75	12.25	25.00

Another method of keeping daily cash records is to use a notebook in which a separate page is devoted to each kind of income and expenditure. From this notebook you can determine the monthly totals and insert them in the "Actual" column in your cash spending plan.

Statement of Assets and Liabilities

Occasionally, it is desirable for a family or an individual to determine how much is owned (*assets*) and how much is owed (*liabilities*). A *statement of assets and liabilities* will show what the real net worth or ownership value is.

Table 9-3 is a statement of assets and liabilities for a family. The family had to estimate the value of the household equipment, the furniture, and the automobile. By looking at their life insurance policies, they were able to determine the cash value of the policies. The value of the United States savings bonds was determined by examining a bond table.

Table 9-3

Statement of Assets and Liabilities for a Family
December 31, 19--

Cash in checking account	$ 232.00	VISA	$ 122.50
Cash in savings account	305.70	Cranley Department Store	75.00
U.S. savings bonds	250.00	First Federal Savings and	
Life insurance (cash		Loan Association (amount	
value)	391.33	still owed on house and	
Household equipment	2,500.00	lot)	25,000.00
Furniture	3,000.00	Total liabilities	25,197.50
Automobile	3,000.00	Net worth (ownership)	34,481.53
House and lot	50,000.00	Total liabilities and	
Total assets	$59,679.03	net worth	$59,679.03

(Total assets, $59,679.03 − Total liabilities, $25,197.50 = Net worth, $34,481.53)

Records Needed for Income Taxes

The records required for the cash spending plan and the statement of assets and liabilities should be saved during the year. In addition, records that will provide information in filling out income tax returns should be saved during the year.

At the end of the year, an employer is required to furnish each employee a statement (Form W-2) that shows the total amount earned and all deductions for federal, state, and city income taxes withheld. In preparing a federal income tax return, an individual is required to list the total amount earned before deductions from wages. Other types of income must also be listed, but not money from gifts or from borrowing.

A taxpayer may itemize expenses instead of taking a standard deduction. Examples of some of the deductions available by itemizing are:

1. state and local income and property taxes,
2. interest on mortgages on two residences,
3. charitable contributions,
4. a certain proportion of medical expenses if they are great enough, and
5. professional expenses (dues, journal subscriptions, and travel expenses not reimbursed by employer) beyond 2% of adjusted gross income.

Thus, it is important to have receipts (cancelled checks are acceptable) as proof of having paid these expenses. A cash spending plan and a daily cash record are not acceptable proof for income tax purposes.

Other Financial Records Needed

An inventory of valuable items, such as furniture, appliances, books, jewelry, and silverware, should be kept in case of loss by fire or theft. Dates of purchase, from whom purchased, and cost should be shown on the record.

Though deeds to property, stock certificates, bonds, and insurance policies should be kept in a safe-deposit box, a record of these items should always be kept at home for ready reference.

A SAVINGS PLAN

A savings plan requires one to set immediate, short-range, and long-range goals. It also requires one to have knowledge of where and how much of one's income should be saved.

Savings and Financial Management

In the discussion of financial planning, it was stressed that a spending plan should include regular amounts for savings. Unless savings are planned, there usually will be no savings. Unless there are savings, an individual or a family can never look forward to having the really important things that they want.

Some financial planners suggest that a basic emergency fund (equal to three to six months' take-home pay) be established by saving. Additional savings should then be accumulated to fulfill a long-range savings and investment program. Some financial advisors recommend that 10 percent of one's take-home pay should be set aside regularly for savings and investments. In the United States the national average for savings by individuals and families has been 5 percent to 7 percent; in Japan, as a contrast, the national average for individual and family savings has been 18 percent. However, Japan has no Social Security. In the United States Social Security for most Americans is compulsory saving of another 7 percent, making average savings by individuals and families 12 to 14 percent. Saving requires self-discipline. How much you save is dictated by how you feel about your future financial welfare and that of your dependents.

The savings of millions of people, when used for financing business, creates new capital, new jobs, and greater production for the benefit of all. Therefore, as people save and put their money to work where it will draw interest, they are helping their country as well as themselves.

Saving Can Be Rewarding

Setting aside a part of income regularly is known as saving. A regular savings plan is a mark of good money management. Saving can be fun if you look forward to some greater future pleasures you will acquire by giving up some of your present spending for foolish or unnecessary things. The question is whether you are willing to make a plan that will enable you to reach a desirable and pleasant goal. The decisions that you must make in planning a savings program require opportunity costs, which you studied in Chapter 1. Table 9-4 lists some of these decisions.

Setting Goals for Savings

Most people have definite goals in life, things toward which they are striving. Some of these goals are really ideals and ambitions, and some are desires for material things that will add to the comfort of living. Regardless of the kind of goals we have, money is usually a factor in achieving them. Most of us have to set aside a little at a time from our income in order to save enough to fulfill our goals.

Table 9-4

Some Decisions That Must Be Made

For immediate or short-range pleasure		For permanent value or longer-lasting happiness
Should I spend 50 cents a day on little pleasures?	or	Should I save 30 cents a day and have $100 for a summer vacation?
Should I wear the latest styles?	or	Should I wear good clothes longer?
Should I be satisfied with a limited education?	or	Should I save and go to college?
Should I spend foolishly on dates now?	or	Should I save to have money to furnish a home after marriage?
Should I buy a car now?	or	Should I buy life insurance or invest the money?
Should I drive or take a bus?	or	Should I walk and save for new clothes?
Should I buy lots of new clothes now?	or	Should I save for a down payment on a home?
Should the family spend all our income and live lavishly now?	or	Should the family plan to educate the children and prepare for old age?
Should we keep up with the Joneses?	or	Should we live our own lives and save for the future?
Should we rent a home and spend the rest?	or	Should we buy a home and invest all we can?
Should we buy now on the installment plan and pay more?	or	Should we save and pay cash?
Should we let the future take care of itself?	or	Should we make a savings, investment, and insurance program?

SOME GOALS FOR SAVING

1. Providing for emergencies, such as unemployment, hospital bills, and furnace replacement.
2. Buying insurance.
3. Furthering education.
4. Paying for a wedding.
5. Taking vacation and buying gifts.
6. Buying and furnishing a home.
7. Buying major comforts and luxuries.
8. Paying cash for major purchases instead of buying on the installment plan.
9. Starting a business.
10. Investing for future income (securities, real estate, collectibles).
11. Retiring.

A savings goal may be further education.

Making Money Work for You

Let us see how savings grow. Table 9-5 shows how much will be accumulated if $1 is deposited each week in a savings account at various rates of interest. In this table the interest is compounded quarterly. *Compound interest* is interest paid on accumulated interest as well as on the principal. Assume that a young person starts saving $1 a week in the third grade with interest at 7 percent a year, compounded quarterly. Upon graduation from high school, that person would have $757.51. The amount saved during these ten years was $520; interest amounted to $237.51.

Table 9-5

Growth Of Savings If $1 Is Deposited Weekly And Interest Is
Compounded Quarterly

Amount of Savings at End of	Annual Rate of Interest		
	5½%	6%	7%
1 year	$ 53.80	$ 53.94	$ 54.31
5 years	301.00	305.04	313.81
10 years	696.46	715.96	757.51
15 years	1,215.87	1,269.40	1,385.21
20 years	1,898.77	2,014.79	2,273.29

Had interest been compounded annually, the amount saved after 10 years plus interest would have been only $732.35. By compounding interest four times a year instead of once a year, an additional $25.16 in interest was earned. Thus, the more frequent the compounding, the more interest one earns.

Where to Put Savings

Most people save only a few dollars a month. Hence, a place is needed to put the monthly savings until enough builds up to invest in bonds, stocks, real estate, or some other form of permanent investment. In deciding on a place to put savings where they will earn income, consider these questions:

1. Will the savings be safe?
2. Will the savings earn a reasonable rate of interest?
3. Will the savings be available at any time?
4. How is interest calculated?

Financial Institutions. Commercial banks, savings banks, savings and loan associations, and credit unions all accept deposits in regular savings accounts. Interest on these accounts is usually compounded daily, monthly, or quarterly. Some institutions pay interest from the date of deposit to the date of withdrawal. Others pay interest from the first of the month if a deposit is made on or before the tenth of the month. If the deposit is made after the tenth of the month, interest won't be paid on the deposit until the beginning of the next month.

These institutions also accept time deposits (frequently ranging from ninety days to five years) at interest rates higher than regular savings accounts. A *time deposit* (also called a *certificate of deposit* or a *CD*) is a special form of savings which requires a certain amount of money to be deposited for a certain period of time. Often an interest penalty is charged for early withdrawal of the deposit.

Financial institutions, insurance companies, and brokerage firms also offer money market funds or accounts. A *money market account* is a pooling of many depositors' money into one fund for investment in short-term, interest-bearing debt instruments often issued by the federal government, major banks, and large corporations. A minimum deposit is required to open a money market account, and withdrawals from some accounts can be made by check.

U. S. Government. One of the safest and most popular methods of saving is to buy United States savings bonds. Several types of government bonds may be purchased by investors; however, the most popular among people who are saving small amounts regularly are the Series EE bonds.

Series EE bonds can be purchased in denominations of $50, $75, $100, $200, $500, $1,000, $5,000, and $10,000. The purchase price is one-half of the face value. The term to maturity is ten years. Bonds held less than five years earn interest on a fixed graduated scale, rising from 5.5 percent after one year to the guaranteed minimum of 6 percent at five years.

Another popular type of United States savings bond is the Series HH bond. The only way to acquire HH bonds is to trade a minimum of $500 worth of an older Series E or a newer Series EE bond that has reached its final maturity. Series HH bonds can be acquired in denominations of $500, $1,000, $5,000, and $10,000. They have a ten year term to maturity and pay 6 percent interest. The main difference

Illus. 9-3

One of the safest and still popular methods of saving is to buy U.S. savings bonds.

between EE bonds and HH bonds is in the method of paying interest. With Series EE bonds, interest is paid only when the bond is redeemed. With Series HH bonds, interest is paid semiannually by check.

Most of the financial institutions mentioned earlier sell United States savings bonds. A person may also use a payroll savings plan as a convenient way to invest in Series EE bonds. Under this plan, the employer deducts a small amount from each paycheck and buys a bond for the employee when a sufficient amount has been saved. Interest from savings bonds is taxed by the federal government but not by state and local governments.

Insurance Companies. In Chapters 20 and 21 you will learn more about life insurance. Most life insurance policies provide not only protection but also savings. The cash value of a policy builds up over time. Many people use such a policy as protection for the future while saving for some specific purpose.

Although life insurance annuities are discussed in Chapter 20, they are mentioned at this point as another means of saving. If one has a certain sum of money, for example $3,000, one can purchase a life insurance annuity. When the person reaches a stipulated age the money will be paid back in monthly payments with interest. Annuities can also be purchased on the installment plan. This method of saving will build up an income for retirement.

Economic Problems of Savings Programs

There is some risk in any savings or investment program. That is why it is important to put savings in a safe place.

Interest rates may change from time to time, depending on economic conditions. For example, if banks have more money than they can lend at a profit, they will reduce the interest rates they pay on deposits.

There is another economic problem involved in saving. Let us assume that you have money in a savings account on which you are drawing interest. Also assume that prices and the cost of living increase at a rate greater than the interest rate you are receiving on your savings. In such a case, the purchasing power of your savings will be decreased. In the chapter on investments you will learn how some people invest their savings to try to protect themselves against this inflationary situation.

FACTS EVERYONE SHOULD KNOW ABOUT A SAVINGS PROGRAM

1. Choices must be made between spending now or saving for substantial spending later.
2. A spending plan is desirable in any savings program.
3. Goals for saving should be established.
4. Savings of a small amount each week are worthwhile and will grow with compound interest.
5. There are several safe places to put savings where interest will be earned.

VOCABULARY BUILDER

assets
certificate of deposit
compound interest
daily cash record
expenditures

liabilities
spending plan
statement of assets and
   liabilities
take-home pay

REVIEW QUESTIONS

1. What three steps must you take in setting up a spending plan?
2. For purposes of a spending plan, what is meant by income?
3. What are some examples of fixed payments and variable payments in a family spending plan?
4. In addition to the regular spending plan, why is it necessary to keep a daily record of income and expenditures?
5. In what two ways may you keep a record of daily expenditures?
6. What are some possible assets a family renting an unfurnished house may record in a statement of assets and liabilities?
7. From a statement of assets and liabilities, how can one determine net worth or ownership?
8. Besides the information needed for a spending plan and a daily cash record, what information will be needed for income tax purposes?

9. From the point of view of economics in our society, why are the savings of people so important?

10. What are some decisions that you must make daily to determine whether to spend for immediate pleasure or to save and spend for greater values and longer-lasting happiness?

11. What are three important goals of saving?

12. What facts should be considered in selecting a place to open a savings account?

13. a. How does the price paid for a Series EE United States savings bond differ from the price paid for a Series HH bond?

    b. How does the interest paid on a Series EE bond differ from the interest paid on a Series HH bond?

DISCUSSION QUESTIONS

1. Why does information gathered from past experience help in establishing a spending plan?

2. If Mr. Murphy finds that, according to his spending plan, he is not going to have enough cash in his checking account to take care of expenses, what can he do to avoid this situation?

3. Why is it recommended that savings be classified under fixed payments in the cash spending plan?

4. Why would a carefully prepared spending plan and daily cash record not serve as proof of one's income and allowable deductions for income tax purposes?

5. If a comparison of actual expenditures with estimated expenditures in the spending plan shows that one month's expenditures for food exceed the spending plan, what would you recommend be done?

6. If income proves to be less than was originally expected, what must be done with the spending plan?

7. Suppose a young person finds it possible to save $50 a month. After a year this person has $600 and decides to use this amount as a down payment on a used automobile. It will cost $50 a month for eighteen months to complete the payments on the automobile. Is this person justified in buying the automobile?

8. If prices and the cost of living increase and we have inflation, how does this affect savings in a savings account?

Buying Wisely

Earning money is important, but how you spend it can be more important. Buying wisely means allocating one's income for:

1. necessities (food, clothing, shelter, medical care),
2. savings to cover emergencies and intermediate and long-range goals, and
3. some luxuries.

After studying this chapter, you will be able to:

1. explain why buying is considered choice making,
2. describe some general guides to buying,
3. describe how advertising helps consumers to make choices, and
4. describe differences between standards, brands, and labels.

BUYING IS CHOICE MAKING

Buying is always a matter of making choices. Choices must be made between:

1. wants and needs,
2. one product and another of the same kind,
3. two entirely different kinds of products, and
4. spending your money now or saving it.

No product is worth buying unless it is worth more to the buyer than the money spent for it. If you think carefully about every purchase you make, there will be less chance of buying unneeded and unwanted luxuries instead of filling the real needs of yourself and your family.

BEFORE YOU BUY, ASK THESE QUESTIONS:

1. Do I really need or want it? If so, why?
2. Is it worth the cost in terms of my effort to earn the money?
3. Is there a better use for the money?
4. Am I buying it to do as others do? to show off? to make someone envious? to make myself feel important?
5. What is the opportunity cost of buying this item?

Values Determine Choice

Choice making is usually determined by our *values*, those things we feel are important in our lives. For example, many people value family unity. They believe in doing things together, such as family vacations, family membership in the YMCA, and family outings on weekends and holidays. Some believe that higher education is very important; thus they will sacrifice some luxury items now so as to save money for education later.

The real needs of the average family are usually limited, but wants can be increased almost without limit. Because of high-pressure advertising and selling, easy credit, and rising levels of living, there is a tendency to want to keep up with the Joneses. We try to tell ourselves that what actually is a luxury is instead an urgent need.

Most families do not earn enough money to buy unlimited luxuries. In fact, many families cannot buy all their real needs without practicing self-control. In the average family the tendency is to follow individual selfish urges in filling emotional wants rather than practice individual self-control for the benefit of the whole family. If mother wants something, she may buy it on an emotional urge. If father wants something, he may buy it without consulting the family. If children want something, they may spend their own money without much thought or they may put pressure on mother and father to buy the things they want. If family buying is considered from the point of view of unselfish group needs, most families can get the most out of their income.

Large amounts of money can slip through the fingers of every member of the family by buying little things that merchants call *impulse items*. These are the little things that sit by the cash register and are easy to pick up for fifteen to fifty cents. Because shoppers have a little money in their pockets, they might buy these items on impulse, without thinking whether they need them.

The Decision-Making Process

Choice making involves taking several steps, whether we are buying an article of clothing or a used car. These steps are:

1. *Defining the problem.* What do I expect the product to do for me? How will it satisfy my goal?
2. *Identifying alternatives.* What choices are available to me?
3. *Stating the criteria.* How much am I willing and able to pay? What type of guarantee do I want and expect? How durable is the product?
4. *Evaluating the alternative.* How do the various alternatives compare as to service, convenience, performance, and price?
5. *Making the decision.* Which alternative will best satisfy my goals and values for the price I can afford?

GENERAL GUIDES TO BUYING

Buying wisely is important to the economic well-being of the individual and family. The general buying guides on the following pages will help you to spend your money more wisely. Don't forget, however, that a spending plan (Chapter 9) should be the first step in buying wisely.

Comparison Shopping

In the United States we have a wide variety of competing goods and services from which to choose. The smart shopper will compare products as to price, quality, and opportunity cost by checking advertisements and visiting more than one place of business. The wise shopper will avoid impulse buying, which is the opposite of comparison shopping. *Impulse buying* is buying a good or service on a sudden whim or urge without first considering cost, need, alternatives, and ability to pay.

Price, Quality, and Value

There are two extremes of thinking in regard to prices. One is that the highest priced item is the best; the other is that the lowest priced item is the best bargain. Neither viewpoint is correct. The price of an item must be related to its quality and how it satisfies your needs and wants.

For some people, beauty is important; others seek durability; still others want special features, such as a timer on a stove. The product that gives you the most value for your money is the best bargain. It could be the cheapest or the most expensive product.

Service Is Important

Price may not always be the most important consideration in buying. When buying mechanical or electrical equipment, as well as many other products, it is important to buy a product that will operate without trouble. However, when trouble occurs, you must be sure you can get good repair service.

When to Buy

In Chapter 5 you learned how prices are affected by supply and demand. When businesses have an overly large supply of a product, they usually lower prices in order to avoid having a large inventory of goods taking up valuable space. If the supply of a given product is low and the demand for it is high, businesses can raise the price of that product. When demand for a product is low (such as the end of a season for winter clothing), the prices usually fall. Thus, seasonal sales are usually an indication that supply and demand are at work lowering prices.

Timing can be an important factor in buying wisely, for prices may vary widely at different times of the year. For example, at the beginning of a season, certain goods sell at their highest prices. As the season progresses, prices are gradually lowered, since merchants hope to dispose of goods before the season's end.

Fresh fruits and vegetables usually sell at their lowest prices during the summer. As one might guess, goods that are hardest to store have wide differences in price. The prices of canned goods are lowest soon after the canning season.

During periods of generally high prices, consumers should avoid buying anything they do not really need. They should save their money and wait until prices are lower. Of course, everyone has to eat regularly. Purchases of food cannot be put off until prices fall. However, one can watch prices and buy the kinds of foods that are currently being sold at the most attractive prices.

All retail stores have special sales during which prices are lower than at any other time. Some sales include standard items that are kept in stock regularly. Other sales are clearance sales to close out styles, models, or items at the end of the season. Some are sales of special goods brought in for the sale.

In almost every community stores have seasonal sales, such as sales of housewares in March, school clothes in August, furniture in August, toys after Christmas. Consumers can find bargains and save money by waiting for sales. Table 10-1 gives some examples of seasonal sales.

Table 10-1

Seasonal Sales

WINTER	SPRING
After-Christmas sales on toys, winter clothing, and leftover Christmas stock White sales Home appliances and furniture Housewares China and glassware	Pre-Easter sales Lawn and garden supplies Winter blankets Luggage
SUMMER	FALL
Building supplies Storm windows Housewares and furniture July clearance sales Back-to-school specials and Labor Day sales	Auto batteries Women's coats Home improvements supplies Stoves and water heaters Pre-Christmas sales

Illus. 10-1
Consumers can find bargains and save money by waiting for sales.

Unit Pricing

Unit price is the price of a standard unit of an item, used for the comparison of brands and sizes. Comparing prices of similar products of unequal size (quantity) is difficult without unit pricing. For example, Which is a better buy, an 8-ounce tube of toothpaste at $1.58 (Brand A) or a 6-ounce tube of toothpaste at $1.29 (Brand B)? To calculate unit price, divide the price by the weight or volume. Thus, the 8-ounce tube costs 19 3/4 cents an ounce ($1.58 ÷ 8) and the 6-ounce tube, 21 1/2 cents an ounce ($1.29 ÷ 6).

Quantity Buying

People who buy in the smallest units pay more than those who buy in larger units. For example, an 8-ounce can might sell for 30 cents, but a 16-ounce can might sell for 50 cents—a lower unit price with the larger size. Besides buying in *larger* units, it is often possible to achieve a lower unit price by buying *more* units. For example, one unit might sell for $1; two for $1.80; three for $2.50. But buying more than is needed or a larger size than can be used without waste is not economical.

Trading Stamps and Premiums

Nothing is free in this world. Somebody pays. If you receive premiums or trading stamps, the cost of these is included in the prices you pay. It is not a good idea to buy at a certain store only because it offers premiums and stamps. You should check to see if you are paying fair prices on all items you purchase. Noting the unit price, discussed earlier, is one way of checking. To check quality, consumers may read results of tests performed by independent testing laboratories on many brands of products.

Usually trading stamps have a cash value of $\frac{1}{10}$ of a cent per stamp (10 stamps equal 1 cent). Thus, if a product with trading stamps costs 1 cent more per dollar purchase than the same product without stamps, you are paying for the stamps.

Discount Houses

In almost every community there are stores commonly called *discount houses* that try to sell goods at lower prices than anyone else. Sometimes these firms sell standard merchandise like that sold in other stores, but very often they sell unknown brands. Some of the brands may be good, but others may be of questionable quality.

Some discount houses provide delivery service and repair service on equipment, but often they do not. Many times there is an extra charge for such services. If you buy a piece of equipment from a discount house, you may find it necessary to obtain service from an independent repairer.

When buying from a discount house, you should make sure that you are getting good merchandise and that the savings in price makes up for any possible lack of service.

SPECIFIC GUIDELINES FOR BUYING

In order to make wise buying choices, consumers need information and knowledge. The specific buying guides on the following pages will help you make wise consumer choices.

Advertisements

Advertisemnts should be studied from two points of view: for information about the product, and for deceptive or misleading statements. Some advertisements are neither informative nor deceptive. They are simply evasive or general, or they merely appeal to the emotions. The intelligent consumer will look for helpful information. Learn to recognize the difference between emotional appeals and rational appeals. Learn to evaluate statements about products to distinguish facts from false or misleading information.

From a consumer's point of view, an advertisement may be considered helpful if it provides facts about quality, standards, specifications, performance, and uses. An advertisement cannot be considered helpful it it fails to provide this information and instead appeals only to the emotions.

A more detailed discussion of advertising from the point of view of the consumer was given in Chapter 8.

Brand Names

A *brand name* is a well-known name which is associated with a particular product. The purpose of a brand name is to encourage people to ask for the product by name. Without information that would permit comparison, the recognized brands of reputable producers are often more reliable than other brands. If other information is available, however, the brand of a product should not be used as the only means of comparison.

Illus. 10-2

Buying certain products by brand name will probably mean getting the same quality each time you buy.

Brand names can be important guides for a consumer. Once you have tried a certain product, you can ask for the same brand again with reasonable assurance that you will get the same quality as before. Reputable manufacturers try to maintain standards for products carrying their brand names. The manufacturer who advertises a product heavily with the idea of building a reputation for the brand usually tries to maintain a satisfactory standard.

Standards and Grades

A *standard* is a measure of quantity, weight, size, performance, and sometimes quality of a product. Imagine trying to get along without standards. A pound or a gram is a measure of weight. A foot or a meter is a measure of distance or length. A gallon or a liter is a measure of liquids. How would we buy coffee, or fabrics, or milk without these standards of quantity? How could prices be set? How could you indicate how much of a product you want?

We identify the size of a shirt by neckband size and sleeve length; shoes by length and width; and some articles, such as rings, hats, and dresses, by numbers. Some standards pertain to performance, such as the octane rating of gasoline.

With the exception of foods, there is usually one level of quality for a product. A drug, for example, either complies with the formula of the official United States Pharmacopeia, which is known as the USP standard, or it does not. There are no degrees of quality assigned to the drug. But foods often are divided into several levels of quality, each of which is known as a grade. For example, there are four grades of butter, each of which is defined by a standard. A *grade*, then, is a term applied to standards of quality when more than one quality of a particular food is available.

Labels

A *label* is a written statement attached to a product describing its main characteristics. Standards, grades, and other information of importance to consumers may be indicated on the label. Consumers should carefully read labels on merchandise to learn the characteristics of the goods they are thinking of buying.

Informative Labeling. Informative labeling can be found on many products, including appliances, clothing, food, and fabrics. In the case of fabrics, there are various terms used to indicate shrinkage. For example "preshrunk" means the fabric should not shrink more than 2 percent. Other information on fabrics and clothing may indicate the type of fiber used, weave, water repellency, finish, crease resistance, and proper method for cleaning.

Some producers have developed a more informative type of labeling that they believe is better for the consumer than the A, B, C, or other grade labeling. Labels for foods, for instance, might contain such information as:

1. style of the pack;
2. degree of maturity of the food;
3. number of units in the can, such as the number of halves of peaches;
4. quantity in terms of weight (ounces or grams or liters);
5. quantity in terms of servings;
6. size of the can;
7. description of the raw product and the method of processing; and/or
8. suggested methods of serving.

Labeling Practices. In recent years the federal government has requried some definite labeling practices that are meant to help the consumer. For example, any manufacturer who makes a nutritional claim is required by the Food and Drug Administration to disclose certain information. Such information must include size and number of servings in the container; number of calories and grams of protein, carbohydrates, and fat in each serving; and the amount (or absence) of seven required vitamins (vitamins A and C, thiamine, riboflavin, niacin, calcium, and iron) per serving. Also, the ingredient present in the largest amount by weight must be listed first. The other ingredients follow in descending order by weight. Ingredients do not have to be listed for some standardized foods such as catsup and mayonnaise. These foods must contain certain ingredients specified by the Food and Drug Administration. Figure 10-1 is an example of a nutrition label listing the minimum information required, while Figure 10-2 is a label listing optional information.

Figure 10-1
Figure 10-1
Minimum Information that Must Appear on a Nutrition Label

NUTRITION INFORMATION
(PER SERVING)

SERVING SIZE = 1oz
SERVINGS PER CONTAINER = 12

CALORIES	110
PROTEIN	2 GRAMS
CARBOHYDRATE	24 GRAMS
FAT	0 GRAMS

PERCENTAGE OF U.S. RECOMMENDED
DAILY ALLOWANCES (U.S. RDA) *

PROTEIN	2
THIAMINE	8
NIACIN	2

*Contains less than 2 percent of U.S. RDA for
Vitamin A, Vitamin C, Riboflavin, Calcium and
Iron.

Figure 10-2
Optional Listings for Cholesterol and Sodium on a Nutrition Label

NUTRITION INFORMATION

(PER SERVING)
SERVING SIZE= 8OZ.
SERVINGS PER CONTAINER= 1

CALORIES	560	FAT (PERCENT OF	
PROTEIN	23 G	CALORIES, 53%)	33 G
CARBOHYDRATE	43 G	POLYUNSAT –	
		URATED	2 G
		SATURATED	9 G
		CHOLESTEROL*	
		(20 MG/100 G)	40 MG
		SODIUM	
		(365 MG/100 G)	830 MG

PERCENTAGE OF U.S. RECOMMENDED
DAILY ALLOWANCES (U.S. RDA)

PROTEIN	35	RIBOFLAVIN	15
VITAMIN A	35	NIACIN	25
VITAMIN C		CALCIUM	2
(ASCORBIC ACID)	10	IRON	25
THIAMINE			
(VITAMIN B1)	15		

*Information on fat and cholesterol content is provided
for individuals who, on the advice of a physician, are
modifying their total dietary intake of fat and cholesterol.

Trade Names and Terms. There are many trade names and terms used in the labeling of various products. Most of these names and terms are not meant to be deceptive or misleading. Still, they are confusing unless a person knows what they mean and knows something about the differences in quality. For instance, stainless steel is a general term used to identify a steel alloy that will not tarnish as easily as ordinary steel. However, there are many qualities of stainless steel.

How to Read a Label. The buyer should read labels carefully to obtain the following information:

1. the weight or the volume of the product,
2. the grade or the quality of the product, and
3. an analysis or a description of the contents.

It is impossible to rely on grade designations without knowing what those grades mean. Much of the terminology in use means one thing to the seller but a different thing to the buyer. If buyers take a designation at its face value, they are sometimes misled into believing the goods to be of a grade higher than they actually are. Furthermore, the terminology is made confusing by the wide variation in its use. In other words, buyers and sellers do not speak the same language. When this situation exists, grade designations are of very little value.

For instance, one would suppose that the first grade of butter is the best grade, but it is actually the third grade that is best when compared with government standards. To get the best grade of butter, one has to buy the AA grade. Similarly confusing grades are used for other products.

Figure 10-3 illustrates the type of information that a consumer may find on an informative label. Consumers should learn to use such helpful labels. To do so may encourage other producers to use equally informative labels.

Many products sold in stores today, including food products, do not carry information about standards or grades; but many, particularly foods, do contain helpful information on the label. This information can be relied on to be generally truthful and accurate.

Figure 10-3

Example of Specifications and Information on a Food Label

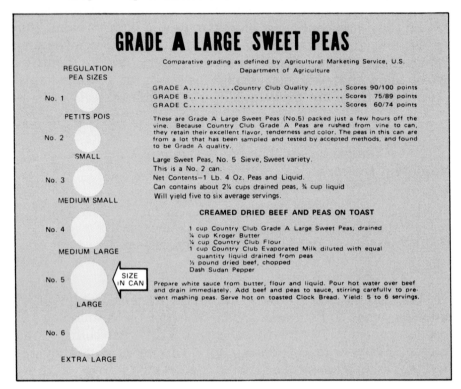

The contents listed on labels are also important, since the size of the container is frequently misleading. Deceptive containers are now illegal in interstate commerce. In examining a label, one should look for the following information:

1. specific descriptive statements,
2. facts regarding quality,
3. facts regarding quantity,
4. grades or other similar designations,
5. certificate or other mark of approval or guarantee,
6. instructions for proper use and care, and
7. warnings.

Generic Labeling

Today most supermarkets stock their shelves with no-brand products, such as canned goods, detergents and cleansers, and paper products. No-brand labeling is also called *generic labeling*. These labels are easily identified by their plain white

Buying products with generic labeling may save the customer as much
as 20%.

wrappers, single-color printing, and lack of brand name. Often
these products are not graded for uniformity. For example, a
can of sweet peas may contain several sizes, not just one uniform size. However, information pertaining to nutrition will
appear on the label. Since the producers do not have to select
and grade the products or maintain a public image, they can
sell these generic products much cheaper than brand-name
producers can. It is not uncommon to save as much as 20 percent on grocery items that carry a generic label.

brand name　　　　　　　　impulse items
discount house　　　　　　label
generic labeling　　　　　　standard
grade　　　　　　　　　　　unit pricing
impulse buying

REVIEW QUESTIONS

1. What are the five steps in the decision-making process?
2. For what types of products are service, repairs, and maintenance very important?
3. As a season progresses, why do merchants gradually reduce the prices of their seasonal merchandise?
4. What are some examples of merchandise that may be sold at high prices or at low prices, depending on the time of the year?
5. Is quantity buying always a good practice? Explain.
6. How should you determine whether you should buy where trading stamps are given?
7. What two important points should one consider when buying merchandise from a discount house?
8. Are brand names of any value in buying merchandise?
9. What type of information should one expect to obtain from an informative label?
10. How much can one save on grocery items carrying a generic label?

DISCUSSION QUESTIONS

1. How can a considerable amount of money be spent and possibly wasted by a family on the purchase of impulse items?
2. How is it possible for the highest priced item to be the best bargain? Give an example.
3. Describe a recent advertisement you saw that you feel was deceptive and not informative. What are your reasons?

4. Assume that you went into an unfamiliar grocery store to buy peas and found on the shelf two brands of peas, one of which was well known to you and the other not. What procedure would you follow in buying? Why?
5. What are some grades and descriptions of products you have seen that have meant nothing to you?
6. What are some of the arguments for and against informative labeling with fixed standards for grades?

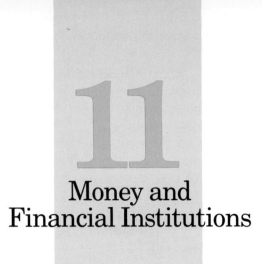

Money and
Financial Institutions

Money makes possible the orderly exchange of goods and services among producers, distributors, and consumers. Wise use of money is vital to gaining financial security. The wrong use of money can lead to serious financial problems. When we speak of money, our thoughts usually turn to banks and other financial institutions. These institutions are very important in the daily activity of a community. Most people need the services of financial institutions in order to carry on their personal or business affairs. This chapter will help you understand the functions of money and how banks and other financial institutions serve us.

After studying this chapter, you will be able to:

1. explain the four functions of money,
2. identify the kinds of money in the United States,
3. identify four major functions of financial institutions,
4. describe services offered by financial institutions which are of interest to consumers, and
5. explain what is meant by electronic banking.

MONEY

Whether in the form of coins, currency, or checks, money demands careful management regardless of how much or how little of it you have.

Nature of Money

Money is defined as anything that is generally accepted in exchange for goods, services, or payment of debts. In America, money is valuable, convenient to handle, and available in amounts as large or as small as necessary.

Functions of Money. Money is a medium of exchange. People are willing to take it as payment for their labor, the goods they sell, or the services they render. Money provides a measure of the value of labor, goods, and services. Money also serves as a means of building up the power to purchase goods and services and makes credit possible.

FUNCTIONS OF MONEY

Money serves us in four major ways:

1. *Medium of exchange.* Money lets you exchange your services (such as mowing Mr. A's lawn or working in a restaurant) for goods (such as a new jacket at the X Department Store).
2. *Measure of value.* Just as scales measure weight in pounds and ounces or kilograms and grams, money measures the value of a good in dollars and cents. The X Department Store may price a sweater at $19.95, which indicates that the store judges it to have that value to a customer. You, as a customer, may or may not agree.
3. *Store of value.* Wages or other income received may be saved or exchanged immediately for goods and services. Some of people's wages are usually saved in the form of money or bank deposits. The wages saved really are purchasing power that you have earned but not yet used. Thus, money is a store of value.
4. *Standard of future payments.* Money becomes a standard of future payment when someone buys a good and promises to pay for it in the future. For example, a consumer who purchases a home and promises to pay a certain sum each month for a 30-year period is using money as a standard of future payments.

Acceptability. The basic standard for judging the value of money is *acceptability*. Anything becomes money when it performs the functions demanded of money. In economic terminology, true wealth consists of goods capable of being bought, sold, or stored for future use. Through the use of money it is possible to build up wealth without having to collect and store goods. Except for metallic money (copper, silver, or gold), which has value in itself, money is only a claim to wealth and is acceptable to those who have things to sell. When any item used as money ceases to be acceptable in the buying and selling of goods and services, it is no longer considered to be money.

Kinds of Money

Money, you will recall, is defined as anything that people will accept in exchange for goods or services. There are three forms of money in common use in the United States: coins, currency, and checkbook money.

Coins. Money made of metal (coins) is made for convenience in paying small amounts. The U.S. Treasury has the responsibility for minting coins; the money is then issued by the Federal Reserve banks. All coins now in circulation in the United States are made of alloys (mixtures) of metals. Thus the face value of a coin is more than the value of metal of which it is made. No gold coins have been made since 1934. The last silver coin minted was the 1971 Eisenhower dollar.

Currency. The Congressional Committee on Banking and Currency has defined currency as paper (or folding) money. In the past, currency has been issued by national banks, Federal Reserve banks, and the U.S. Treasury. Today nearly all of the currency in circulation consists of Federal Reserve notes, which are issued by each of the twelve Federal Reserve banks.

Checkbook Money. Checks drawn on demand deposits (money deposited in checking accounts) are accepted by people in exchange for goods or services. Thus, according to the definition of money by the Committee on Banking and Currency, checks are money. Demand deposits account for about 70 percent of all money circulating in the country.

There are three ways in which you may build up check-book money in the form of demand deposits:

1. you may deposit coins and currency,
2. you may deposit a check that has been given to you, or
3. you may borrow and have the amount deposited to your account.

Most people receive their wages in the form of checks that they soon deposit in banks. Through the use of checking accounts, people simply write and mail checks to pay their bills. The canceled checks serve as receipts. For businesses, demand deposits are even more valuable. A business that receives many checks can quickly deposit them, which is the way most business transactions are completed. Thus the bother of handling, storing, and possibly losing large sums of money is reduced.

It is well to note here the use of the term *cash* as it relates to kinds of money. In general, *cash* is any ready money that a person or business firm actually has, including money deposited in a checking account. Therefore, the total supply of cash available for financial transactions is the sum of the paper money and coins in circulation plus the total of the balances in checking accounts.

What Backs U.S. Money?

You learned earlier that whatever is used for money must be acceptable to both the buyer and the seller. For money to be acceptable worldwide, most people feel that there should be something of real value available for exchange in case one doesn't want to buy goods and services. This item of exchange is called *backing*.

Formerly Backed by Silver or Gold. The currency of a country is said to be on a silver standard or a gold standard when the currency is backed by silver or gold dollars or bullion (uncoined silver or gold).

Before 1873, United States currency could be converted into either gold dollars or silver dollars upon request to the United States Treasury. From 1873 to 1933, the United States had a gold standard, and currency could be exchanged for gold.

In 1933, the United States went on a limited gold standard. In other words, each dollar was backed by only 25 cents in gold bullion. United States citizens could no longer exchange their currency for gold. Only foreign nations could exchange American dollars for gold. In 1973, the United States went off the gold standard completely. This means the United States no longer has to exchange gold even for American dollars held by foreign countries.

Backed by Faith and Confidence. It was stated earlier that for money to have value, it must be acceptable. Some people and nations may feel safer if money is backed by a precious metal (such as gold) that always has value. However, if you have faith and confidence in the person or the nation that issues money, you do not worry about backing.

The United States government and its people have had a long history of being a high-producing, wealthy nation. We grow more food crops per person per acre than any other nation. We produce more computers and farm machinery, for example, than any other nation. As a nation we own more cars, television sets, radios, and telephones than any other nation. We have valuable natural resources. All these things help our people and other nations to have faith and confidence in our currency. As long as we continue to manage our lives and our country in a responsible way, everyone will continue to have faith in our currency.

FINANCIAL INSTITUTIONS

Financial institutions perform many useful functions for consumers, business, and government. These functions are:

1. to receive deposits of money subject to withdrawal by the depositor either on demand or after notice has been given,
2. to make loans,
3. to pay interest, and
4. to invest some of the money on deposit.

Banks

A *bank* is a financial institution authorized by its charter (permit to do business) to perform certain financial functions. Many consumers think that all banks are alike. However, there are different kinds of banks. The various kinds of banks and their differences are described below.

Commercial Banks. A *commercial bank* is a financial institution owned by its stockholders. People become owners of a bank by buying shares of stock. The stockholders elect a board of directors to manage the bank's operations.

Commercial banks serve the day-to-day needs of both businesses and individuals. The charters of most commercial banks also permit them to receive savings deposits and to make loans. Many commercial banks today advertise themselves as *full-service banks* because they provide so many financial services for their customers. Many of these services are described later in the chapter.

Savings Banks. A *savings bank* is a financial institution that may accept savings deposits on which interest is paid to depositors. Savings banks may be stock companies or mutual companies. A *stock savings bank* is owned by stockholders who, through a board of directors, manage the bank. Profits go to the stockholders. A *mutual savings bank* is owned by the depositors and is operated mainly for their benefit. Since 1981, savings banks have also been authorized to offer interest-bearing checking accounts.

Savings and Loan Associations

A *savings and loan association* is a state or federally chartered financial institution organized to accept deposits and make loans. These institutions accept deposits, pay interest on deposits, and specialize in mortgage loans on homes, apartments, and condominium complexes. In 1981, Congress gave savings and loan associations the right to offer a wide range of additional services such as checking accounts, interest bearing checking accounts, time deposits, and personal loans. Other names for savings and loan associations are building and loan associations, cooperative banks, savings associations, thrifts, and homestead banks.

Credit Unions

Credit unions are nonprofit associations operating both as savings and lending institutions for the benefit of their members. Credit unions accept share deposits (savings deposits), make personal and mortgage loans to members, and offer special checking accounts called share drafts.

Consumer Finance Companies

Consumer finance companies are small-loan companies that lend primarily to persons of moderate means who may not have established a credit rating. These companies are regulated by state laws which govern the maximum interest rate charged on loans and the maximum amount of the loan. Unlike most financial institutions, consumer finance companies operate only to make personal loans for such things as

Illus. 11-1

Credit unions are nonprofit associations operating both as savings and lending institutions for the benefit of their members.

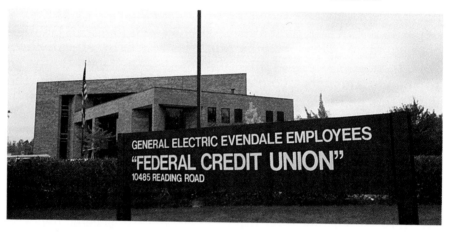

cars, household appliances, and medical bills. Consumer finance companies do not accept savings deposits nor provide checking account services.

Insurance Protection of Depositors

Protection of depositors against loss due to theft or failure of a financial institution has been provided through insurance on deposits. The Federal Deposit Insurance Corporation (FDIC), which all national banks are required to join and other banks may join if they wish, insures deposits in a given bank up to $100,000. Similarly, deposits in savings and loan associations are insured up to $100,000 for each depositor by another federal agency — the Federal Savings and Loan Insurance Corporation. Deposits up to $100,000 in federally chartered credit unions are insured by the National Credit Union Administration.

Illus. 11-2

The Federal Deposit Insurance Corporation (FDIC) insures deposits in a given bank up to $100,000.

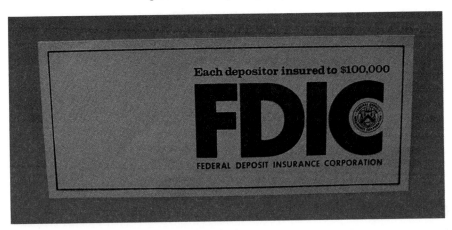

SERVICES OF FINANCIAL INSTITUTIONS

Financial institutions provide checking and savings accounts, as well as a variety of other services. Many provide 24-hour service to customers. With the use of a special plastic identification card, a customer can deposit or withdraw money after regular hours by using an automated teller.

Checking Accounts

Financial institutions accept money deposits from businesses and individuals and pay out this money when the depositors write checks on the deposits. This service is called a *checking account*, and the deposits in a checking account are called *demand deposits*. These deposits are so called because the financial institutions must pay out the money whenever the depositor demands or orders it to do so. This demand is in the form of a check. A *check* is a written order by which the depositor directs a financial institution to pay a certain amount of money to another person. The depositor who writes the check is known as the *drawer*. The person to whom the check is payable is called the *payee*. The financial institution on which the check is drawn is called the *drawee*.

About 70 percent of all money transactions (payments for goods, services, and debts) are made by checks. Money on deposit in a checking account is safe from loss or theft. Payments by checks are handy because people do not have to carry large sums of money with them at all times. Checks can be mailed more easily and cheaply in most instances than a person can walk or ride to all the places where payments have to be made.

Regular Checking Accounts. A regular checking account requires a minimum daily or monthly balance. For example, if the minimum daily balance is $300, then the account balance each day must be $300 or more. On the other hand, the minimum monthly balance simply requires the balance at the end of the month to be $300 or more. This means that your account would not have to show a $300 balance every day, making this a more favorable plan for you.

As long as the minimum balance is maintained, the depositor is given free checking. If the balance is not maintained, then a per-check and/or a monthly service fee is charged. This charge can amount to 10 to 20 cents per check and $1.50 to $5 for the monthly service fee. A regular checking account is often desirable if you write a large number (25 or more) of checks each month.

Special Checking Accounts. Sometimes called budget or economy accounts, these special checking accounts require no minimum balance. The depositor is charged a per-check fee and/or a monthly service fee. These accounts are desirable for depositors who write only a few checks each month or who find it impossible to maintain a minimum balance.

NOW Accounts. In 1981 Congress enabled savings banks, savings and loan associations, and commercial banks to offer Negotiable Order of Withdrawal (NOW) accounts. *NOW accounts* are actually interest-bearing checking accounts. These accounts pay interest on the funds in the account and they require a minimum daily balance which is usually larger than the minimum balance required for regular checking accounts. Many NOW accounts offer free check-writing service if the daily minimum balance is maintained. Some NOW accounts will not pay interest if the required minimum balance is not maintained.

Super NOW Accounts. Unlike regular NOW accounts, super NOW accounts pay interest at money market rates which are higher than passbook savings rates. Though there is no legal minimum balance required, many financial institutions set a $2,500 daily minimum balance before they pay interest at this higher rate. Checking account service is usually free if this required minimum balance is maintained. If the account balance falls below the financial institution's required minimum, interest at money market rates will not be paid; instead, interest at regular NOW account rates may be paid by some financial institutions.

Share Drafts. *Share drafts* are checks offered by credit unions. Credit union members are called shareholders. Their checks are called share drafts because a withdrawal is made on a member's shares of ownership.

Since credit unions are nonprofit institutions and are not subject to federal taxation, they can pay a higher rate of interest on deposits than other financial institutions. Usually interest is paid on whatever balance exists in the account, as most credit unions do not require a minimum dollar balance. The check-writing service is free so long as there is enough money in the account to cover the share drafts written.

Since a variety of checking account services exists, it pays to compare the available services in your community before making a decision, just as you would before buying other goods and services.

Savings Accounts

A savings account may be opened in a commercial bank, a savings bank, a savings and loan association, or a credit union. There is some difference in the interest earned among financial institutions. Obviously, the income from a savings account is greater when interest is compounded daily than when it is compounded quarterly at the same rate. Saving by depositing money in a financial institution is a conservative means of investing, but it is usually a safe means compared to other types of investments.

Regular savings accounts allow customers to deposit small amounts of money and to withdraw savings at any time. Financial institutions also accept time deposits. The savings placed in these special accounts may be recorded on forms called certificates of deposit. Or they may be recorded in a special passbook (a book in which the deposits, withdrawals, interest earned, and balance of an account are recorded) similar to the passbook provided for a regular savings account. Higher rates of interest are paid on time deposits. These special deposits, however, may not be withdrawn before the stated time without some loss of interest. The minimum deposit is often $100; the length of deposit can be from 90 days to 5 years.

Special Checks

Sometimes you may wish to make a payment to someone who will not accept your personal check. It could be an important payment in a distant city; it might be a deposit for buying a house; or it could be any one of several other situations. In such cases you may get a certified check, a cashier's check, a money order, or a traveler's check. A small fee is charged by the financial institution for issuing any of these.

Certified Checks. A *certified check* is an ordinary personal check drawn by a depositor on which the financial institution stamps or writes a certification that guarantees its payment. The amount of the check is deducted immediately from the depositor's account balance. The check then becomes an obligation of the financial institution rather than of the depositor.

For the depositor, one disadvantage of a certified check is that it will not be returned with the other canceled checks; hence the depositor will not have the endorsed check to serve as a receipt. If for any reason a certified check is returned to the drawer, it should not be destroyed. It should be redeposited in the drawer's checking account at the financial institution. Otherwise, the balance of the checking account will be short, for the amount of the check was deducted when it was certified. Another disadvantage is that the fee charged to certify a personal check is usually much larger than the fee charged to buy any of the other special checks.

Cashier's Checks. A *cashier's check* or *treasurer's check* is one that a financial institution draws on itself. It is used to pay bills owed by the financial institution. An individual may also buy a cashier's check to send money to another person. Figure 11-1 is an example of a cashier's check.

Money Orders. A *money order*, also called a *register check* or a *personal money order*, serves essentially the same function as a cashier's check. In many financial institutions, money

Figure 11-1
Cashier's Check

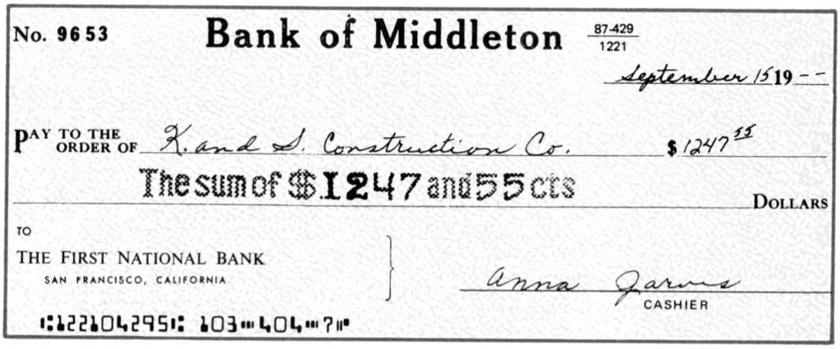

No. 9653   **Bank of Middleton**   87-429 / 1221

September 15 19 – –

PAY TO THE
ORDER OF   *K. and S. Construction Co.* $ *1247* 55

The sum of $1247 and 55 cts   DOLLARS

TO
THE FIRST NATIONAL BANK
SAN FRANCISCO, CALIFORNIA

Anna Jarvis
CASHIER

⑆1221042951⑆ 103⑈404⑈7⑆

orders are replacing the cashier's checks as a means of sending
a customer's money to another person. The name of the remit-
ter (sender) is on the money order; but it usually is not on a
cashier's check. Figure 11-2 is an example of a money order.

Traveler's Checks. People who travel do not like to carry
large amounts of cash, yet they may find it difficult to cash
personal checks. *Traveler's checks* are special forms of checks
that travelers can use in making payments. A few large banks
issue and sell their own traveler's checks, but the best known
are American Express Traveler's Checks®. These may be
purchased from the American Express Co. or from many
financial institutions. A fee is charged for each check. Traveler's checks can be purchased in amounts of $10, $20, $50,
$100, or more. At the time of purchase, each check is signed by
the buyer in the presence of the agent of the financial institu-

Figure 11-2
Money Order

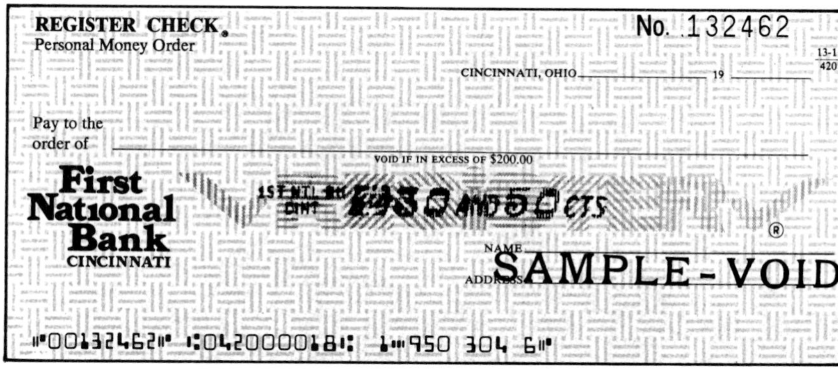

REGISTER CHECK.
Personal Money Order   No. 132462

CINCINNATI, OHIO   19   13-1 / 420

Pay to the
order of

VOID IF IN EXCESS OF $200.00

**First
National
Bank**
CINCINNATI   1ST NTL BK
CINT $180 AND 50 CTS   ®

NAME
ADDRESS   **SAMPLE – VOID**

⑈00132462⑈ ⑆042000018⑆ 1⑈950 304 6⑆

Illus. 11-3
Traveler's checks are a special form of checks that travelers can use in making payments.

tion. The check can then be cashed anywhere in the world. When it is cashed, it must be signed again in the presence of the person cashing it with a signature that matches the original signature.

Other Services

In addition to providing checking and savings accounts, issuing special checks, and granting loans, financial institutions provide other important services to customers. The granting of loans by financial institutions will be discussed in Chapter 15. Some of the other important services are discussed on the following pages.

Safe-Deposit Boxes. Safe-deposit boxes in the vaults of financial institutions are provided on a rental basis. Such boxes provide protection against burglary and fire and should be used for storing valuables that cannot safely be kept in the home or in the business office. A customer who rents a box is given a key to that box, and the financial institution has a master key. Both keys are necessary to unlock the box; neither one alone will unlock it. A financial institution cannot open a private safe-deposit box except upon the order of a court. If a customer loses a key, the bank may, in the presence of witnesses and legal representatives of the renter, have a locksmith drill the lock to open it.

Trust Functions. The trust functions of banks (and some savings and loan associations and credit unions) have proved very useful to people who wish to have their wealth managed for the benefit of others. Many wills include clauses that appoint certain trust companies or trust departments of financial institutions to administer the property left to spouses and children. *Administering* an estate (property) means either managing it for the benefit of the persons entitled to it or dividing it among these people according to law.

The trust officer of the financial institution serves, in a sense, as the business manager of an estate. The officer may also serve as a trustee for a fund that has been created to serve some special purpose. For example, a trust fund may be set up to provide an income for a charitable organization or to spend money for the care of a park, and it is the responsibility of the *trustee* to administer the finances on behalf of the organization.

Travel Service. Some financial institutions help travelers obtain foreign money and credit to be used in foreign countries. For example, if a person is traveling to Europe, the financial institution may arrange in advance to obtain foreign money for the traveler. The financial institution may also arrange for deposits to be made in foreign banks. The traveler can then go to those banks with a proper letter of identification and withdraw money as it is needed.

Drive-up Tellers. Many financial institutions provide drive-up tellers which enable you to transact business from your car. This is made possible through the use of special equipment such as a two-way voice communication system, a television camera and screen inside the financial institution, and pneumatic tubes (suction tubes that carry cash, checks, passbooks, or loan payment books from your car to the teller and back to you).

Electronic Fund Transfers (EFT)

EFTs (electronic fund transfers) use computer and electronic technology as a substitute for checks and other forms of banking. EFTs eliminate the need for costly paper transactions, checks, deposit slips, and even paper money. EFTs use cash machines, computer terminals, and push-button telephones to provide a variety of financial services.

Automatic Transfer of Funds. With automatic transfer of funds you can authorize your financial institution to take a certain sum of money each month from your savings account and put it into your checking account or vice versa. For example, if you wish to save $25 of your check each payday, you can authorize your financial institution to transfer $25 from your checking account to your savings account as soon as your paycheck is deposited.

You could also authorize an automatic transfer of funds from your savings account to your checking account whenever you write a check for an amount larger than the balance in your checking account. This transfer protects you from writing a bad check (one that will not be covered by sufficient funds in your checking account).

Automatic Payment of Bills. By using this service you can authorize your financial institution to pay certain monthly bills, such as utility bills, installment loan payments, and home mortgage payments, when they come due. This service saves you from having to write a number of checks, saves you postage, or saves you the cost of driving your car to make a payment in person. Also, since these bills are paid automatically, there is no danger of your forgetting to pay the bills on time. Thus, you can avoid having to pay a penalty.

Payment of Bills by Telephone. There may be some bills that you don't want your bank to pay automatically. For example, you may not want to pay the full amount of your VISA charge account and your department store account this month. By calling your bank and providing your EFT identification number, you can instruct your bank to make whatever size payments you desire without having to write and mail checks. Your bank will deduct the payments from your account and transfer the funds to the creditors' accounts during the phone call.

Direct Deposits to Accounts. You may authorize the government to automatically deposit your social security check in your account each month. The same type of transaction is

Illus. 11-4

By calling your bank and providing your EFT identification number, you can instruct your bank to make payments without having to write and mail checks.

used by some employers. Instead of paying each employee by check every payday, the employer authorizes its financial institution to deposit employees' paychecks in their accounts. This type of transaction has the advantages of safety and convenience. You don't have to worry that your check may be lost, stolen, or delayed in the mail. You don't have to stand in line or make out a deposit slip to deposit your paycheck.

Automated Teller Machines (ATMs). The machines may be located on the premises of the financial institution or in shopping areas. Many transactions can be performed with the use of these machines. For example, by inserting into the machine an identification card that authorizes you to use EFT services, you can order the machine to dispense cash from either your savings or checking account, or to make a loan. The machines can be used to make payments on certain loans and credit card accounts, to make deposits, to transfer funds from one account to another, or to determine the current balance in your savings or checking account.

Point-of-Sale (POS) Transfers. For years, individual banks experimentally connected merchant point-of-sale (POS) terminals (which are identical to cash registers) to their computers,

Many transactions can be performed with automated teller machines.

allowing customers to use a *debit card* to transfer funds electronically to a retailer's account. The debit card is similar to a credit card, but there is one important difference: with a debit card, the money for the purchase is immediately transferred from your bank account to the store's account.

The Checkless Society. A few years ago, people thought the checkless society—an all-electronic future—would be upon us in full force by the late 1980s. This was not to be, however. Most bank customers are afraid of anything having to do with electronics and computers. They fear breakdowns of the electronic equipment, computer errors that could tie up one's funds for days or weeks, and the loss of interest from float on interest-bearing checking accounts.

Float is the time between writing and mailing the check and the time it is debited (cashed) at the bank. Let's say a $500 check took 10 days to clear (paid by the bank). At 5½ percent interest for 10 days the drawer of the check earns 76 cents ($500 x .055 x 10/360 = 76 cents).

FACTS EVERYONE SHOULD KNOW ABOUT FINANCIAL INSTITUTIONS AND THEIR SERVICES

1. Financial institutions perform many useful services to consumers, such as providing checking account services, paying interest on savings accounts, and renting safe-deposit boxes.
2. Money deposited in banks, savings and loan associations, and credit unions is insured by the federal government.
3. Financial institutions offer a wide range of savings plans at varying interest rates, depending upon the amount deposited and the length of time until maturity.
4. Many routine financial transactions can now be performed by using automated teller machines at convenient locations 24 hours a day, 7 days a week.

VOCABULARY BUILDER

backing
cashier's check
certified check
check
commercial bank
consumer finance company
credit union
debit card

demand deposit
drawee
float
money
money order
NOW account
payee
savings and loan association
share draft

REVIEW QUESTIONS

1. What are the functions of money?
2. a. What is true wealth?
   b. If money ceases to be of value, who would be the only persons who possess wealth?

3. What backs or makes valuable the currency of the United States?
4. What are four important functions of financial institutions?
5. How do consumer finance companies differ from other financial institutions?
6. What agencies of the federal government protect customers' deposits in banks, savings and loan associations, and credit unions?
7. Why are demand deposits so called?
8. What are the advantages of a checking account?
9. In what way are special checks important to consumers?
10. In addition to checking and savings accounts, certificates of deposit, and special checks, what other services do financial institutions provide consumers?
11. What are the advantages of automatic payment of bills?
12. What kinds of financial transactions can be performed at an automated teller machine?

DISCUSSION QUESTIONS

1. When would a person not be wise to use money as a store of value?
2. In what respect is a financial institution similar to any other business?
3. In many states there are laws against overdrawing bank accounts. Do you believe these laws are justified?
4. What types of items would you recommend keeping in a safe-deposit box? Why?
5. Could there be any disadvantages to electronic banking? Explain.

Investing

In this chapter you will learn about the various choices for investing savings and about the decisions that must be made when investing.

After studying this chapter, you will be able to:

1. list eight kinds of investments available,
2. describe the differences between stocks and bonds,
3. define a mutual fund, and
4. identify sources of investment information.

KINDS OF INVESTMENTS

Although many people use the words *saving* and *investing* to mean the same thing, they are different. *Saving* means not using all that you earn in wages and salary. *Investing* means using money to make money by getting a return on your savings in the form of interest, dividends, rent, or profits. Some of the most common types of investments are discussed on the following pages.

Savings Programs

The savings programs discussed in Chapter 9 provide an easy way to save money for emergencies, major expenses such as insurance premiums, and special short-term goals. Money in savings accounts is readily available when needed, and the funds earn interest while they accumulate. However, if the rate of interest is less than the rate of inflation, the purchasing power of the savings declines.

Alternatives to regular passbook savings accounts are time deposits (CDs), money market certificates, money market accounts, United States savings bonds, and insurance annuities. These alternative plans yield higher interest than regular savings accounts, thereby combating inflation; but they require that the funds remain with the financial institution for a period of time ranging from ninety days to several years. Early withdrawal can result in loss of considerable interest.

Everyone needs funds for emergencies and short-term needs, so savings accounts are useful. After these needs are met, however, thought should be given to investing long-term savings in a way that will provide a larger rate of return and protection from inflation.

IRAs

One of the long-term goals for saving is to provide retirement income. An *IRA* (Individual Retirement Account) is a special retirement plan designed to encourage you to save for your future. Depending on your income, the amount you place in the account (up to $2,000 a year for a single person) and the interest earned yearly are not taxed until you begin withdrawing funds at age $59\frac{1}{2}$ or older. When you start withdrawing funds at retirement, you are probably in a lower tax bracket than when you were putting money into your account. Thus, the account is taxed at a more favorable rate.

The financial institutions offering IRAs use a variety of investment opportunities—money market funds, Treasury bills, mutual funds, CDs, and real estate—to earn money in order to pay interest on your individual account. Just remember, IRAs are retirement savings, not savings to buy a home or to finance a college education. Unless you are totally disabled, any money withdrawn prior to reaching age $59\frac{1}{2}$ is subject to a penalty imposed by the Internal Revenue Service. Anyone under age 70 $\frac{1}{2}$ with earned income is eligible to open an IRA.

Stocks

Ownership in a *corporation* (a business made up of a number of owners) is represented by shares of stock. When you buy stock in a corporation, you are buying a share in the ownership. If the corporation is successful, you take part in its success through *dividends* (the part of the profits of a corporation that each stockholder receives) or through an increase in the value of the stock. On the other hand, if the corporation is not successful, it may pay no dividends, the value of the stock may decrease, and you may even lose your investment.

There are two kinds of stock: common stock and preferred stock. A corporation may have both types or it may have only common stock.

Common Stock. Owners of *common stock* of a corporation are entitled to participate in the earnings and in the election of a board of directors. A corporation makes no promise or guarantee that a dividend will be paid. If a corporation does not make a sufficient profit, a dividend will not be paid, since a dividend is a share of profits.

Illus. 12-1

Ownership in a corporation is represented by shares of stock.

Preferred Stock. The owners of preferred stock also have a share in the ownership of a corporation. Usually they do not have a right to vote in the election of corporate directors. They do, however, have certain preferred claims.

Preferred stock pays dividends at a stated percentage rate whenever a dividend is declared. Owners of preferred stock receive their fixed share of profits before the common stockholders are paid any dividends.

Bonds

A *bond* is a printed promise to pay a definite amount of money (the face value of the bond) at a stated future time, with yearly interest at a stated rate. When you buy a bond, you are lending money to the government or corporation that issued the bond. A bond is only as good as the government or corporation that issues it.

Some high-grade bonds sell at a premium—that is, for more than face value (the amount printed on the bond). This lowers the yield or return. For example, a two-year $5,000 bond paying interest at 9 percent sells for $5,100; interest, however, is paid only on $5,000. Other bonds may be sold at a discount—that is, for less than face value. This has the effect of increasing the yield over the stated interest rate. For example, a two-year $5,000 bond paying interest at 8.5 percent sells for $4,900. However, interest is paid on the full $5,000.

Corporation Bonds. Corporation bonds are evidence of a debt owed by a business to investors. The business agrees to repay the sum on a certain date and under certain conditions. It also agrees to pay interest at stated intervals. Bondholders have a claim prior to stockholders on the earnings of the corporation. Table 12-1 illustrates the differences between corporation stocks and bonds.

U.S. Government Bonds. In Chapter 9 you learned about U.S. savings bonds, Series EE and HH. These bonds are not marketable. They cannot be sold by the owner to someone else. They can only be returned to the government (through a bank) for cash.

There are other types of federal government bonds, however, that are marketable and can be purchased as an investment. Often these bonds pay a higher rate of interest than the savings bonds.

Municipal Bonds. Besides federal government bonds, there are bonds issued by states, counties, cities, school districts, villages, townships, and other government agencies. These are called *municipal bonds.*

Table 12-1

Differences Between Corporation Stocks and Bonds

Factor	Stocks	Bonds
1. Relationship to business	Represents ownership.	Represents creditorship (debt).
2. Control of management	Stockholders elect the directors.	No voice in management.
3. Rate of return on investment	Fixed rate on preferred stock but not on common stock. Dividends not guaranteed: if no profits, no dividends.	Fixed interest rate is guaranteed and must be paid even if no profits.
4. Maturity (due date)	No maturity date on stocks. They may be held as long as the corporation is in business or sold at any time.	Maturity date stated and bond must be repaid at that time. It could be called (paid) before the maturity date.
5. Need	All business corporations have shares of stock to provide initial working capital (money for day-to-day operations such as wages, materials, and other expenses).	If the corporation does not need to borrow large sums, no bonds will be issued.
6. Claim against corporate assets	After all creditors (debts) have been paid, stockholders have claim against remaining corporate assets.	Have claim against corporate assets prior to claim of stockholders, since bonds represent debts.

Any government unit that issues a bond is required by law to make provision to pay the interest and the debt when it becomes due. The money for interest payments and repayment of the amount borrowed usually comes from taxation.

Interest earned on municipal bonds is exempt from federal income taxes. For that reason, many people like to buy municipal bonds even though they may not be quite as safe as federal or state bonds.

Mutual Funds

One of the principles of investment is not to place all your eggs in one basket. Many small investors, however, are not able to buy a variety of stocks or bonds. Therefore, these investors may prefer to buy shares of stock in companies known as *mutual funds*. The money received from the sale of shares in such companies is invested in a great variety of securities (primarily stocks and bonds). A person who invests in mutual funds is part owner of a company that owns several different types of securities. Instead of investing $1,000 in one particular corporation, it is possible for an investor to buy $1,000 worth of shares in a mutual fund, thereby having an interest in perhaps 100 or more different corporations.

Mutual funds vary widely in their method of organization, management, and type of securities they buy. Each mutual fund follows certain policies. One mutual fund may invest its funds principally in securities that pay very high dividends. Another may invest its funds in securities that may have greater opportunity for growth in value. In all cases, however, the purpose of mutual funds is to provide a wide variety of investment, managed by experts. Thus, an individual who has only a small investment to make and who is not an expert may benefit by investing in a mutual fund.

Small Businesses

For some people, owning and operating a small business is one of the most important dreams and objectives in their lives. These people may be able to save their money until they have enough to go into business for themselves. Before deciding to invest one's life savings by buying an existing business or starting a new business, however, one should make a very careful study of all the problems involved. Owning and operating a small business is not easy; one should have some experience in the business before attempting to operate it alone.

Buying a franchised business (McDonald's, Taco Bell, Wendy's, Holiday Inn, or Avis Rent A Car, for example) is a popular way of going into business for oneself. A *franchise* is the right to operate a business in a given area. Before buying a franchise, you should consult an attorney to protect your rights and your investment. Some franchises have very specific requirements. For example, some stipulate from whom you must buy supplies, equipment, and merchandise; whether or not you can sell the business to someone else; and whether or not you can expand the business.

Investing in a partnership (a business owned by two or more people) involves complicated legal responsibilities in most states. Even though one of the partners may not be actively engaged in the business, in many states he or she is equally responsible for debts of the firm. For instance, suppose that you become a part owner of a business but allow your partner to operate it. The business fails to make a profit, and the creditors demand payment. If your partner cannot pay, the creditors can demand payment from you.

Illus. 12-2
Owning and operating a small business is not easy.

Real Estate

Anyone planning to invest in real estate should first consider the desirability of the location and the quality of the property. After that, the following seven points should be considered:

1. Can the property be rented?
2. At what price can the property be rented?
3. What will be the annual cost of repairs?
4. What will be the taxes and assessments?
5. What will be the yearly loss from depreciation?
6. During what percentage of time will the property be vacant?
7. What will be the approximate net earnings (earnings after taxes and other operating expenses have been paid)?

Real estate is subject to fluctuations in price. The current cost of a piece of property is therefore no indication of its future value. The community may change rapidly with a resulting decrease or increase in the value of the property. Because of a change in business conditions, the value of the property may be raised or lowered.

The purchase of unimproved real estate (with no buildings) is usually an investment made in the hope that it can be resold at a profit. A person well acquainted with managing property may find real estate more suitable than any other type of investment. If, however, one is not in a position to manage real estate with buildings on it, it may not prove to be a suitable investment.

Buying a Home. Buying a home (rather than renting one) is considered an investment because it often adds to one's wealth. When buying a home, many of the same points should be considered as when buying real estate for profit.

Buying Real Estate by Mail. Do not buy real estate through mail advertising. There have been thousands of unhappy investors who have lost a lot of money this way. Never buy real estate unless you see it first. Also, you want truthful answers regarding location of shopping areas, availability of utilities, amount of taxes, cost of improvements, and availability of a clear title (see Chapter 18). Always check with the Better Business Bureau in the state where the real estate is available. Check also with an official in your state (usually the secretary of state) to see if the seller got permission to advertise and sell in your state.

Collectibles or Tangibles

As a protection against inflation, some people use their savings to buy objects such as paintings, jewelry, coin and stamp collections, antiques, or gold bullion. They hope that the increase in value of these collectibles or tangibles over the years will be greater than the rate of inflation. A profit is made only when the objects are sold, provided, of course, that they have increased in value.

To invest successfully in collectibles or tangibles, one must not only have excess savings but must also be very knowledgeable about the object to be purchased. However, a number of publications are available to help the investor in collectibles. Also, tangible asset advisers in private firms specializing in financial planning are available to assist the novice investor. In the past few years investing in collectibles has gained status and popularity.

INVESTMENT PROCEDURES

There are many things to consider when investing one's money. There are decisions to be made as to the type of investment—stocks, bonds, or real estate, for example. Decisions have to be made as to the purpose of the investment—growth in value of original investment or a steady income from the investment. Safety of the investment, sources of information about investment opportunities, and the marketability of one's investment are also things to consider.

Investing and Speculating

A form of investing is buying assets, such as stocks and bonds, with the hope of receiving a certain income over a long period of time. Usually the investor selects those assets that are safe and have a proven record. The risk is usually low; therefore, the return will be modest but dependable. Some examples of dependable securities are many corporation stocks and bonds and most government bonds.

Speculating is buying securities or other assets with the hope of earning substantial gains over a short period of time. Usually the speculator selects those assets which have not yet developed a reputation for reliability, but which appear to have promise of rapid growth. Since the risk is great, either large gains or losses can result. Two examples of speculation are commodity futures (buying an agricultural product today to be delivered at a future date) and stocks in newly formed businesses.

Sources of Investment Information

Today there are private firms that specialize in providing complete financial planning services. These firms hire professional attorneys, accountants, certified financial planners, insurance advisers, securities advisers, tangible asset advisers, real estate brokers, and economists. Thus, they are in a position to provide total financial planning for the individual investor. Several stock brokerage firms are adding financial planning departments to provide similar services.

For the average investor, there are excellent monthly financial services available to which one can subscribe to obtain current investment information. Helpful and current financial information is also available in some newspapers and magazines (*The Wall Street Journal, Forbes, Barron's, Business Week, Money, Fortune*, for example). Most city libraries have financial information about the earnings, dividends, assets, and credit ratings of corporations.

Growth in Value

Certain industries are characterized as growth industries. The demand for the industry's product is growing at a rate significantly faster than GNP or competing industries. Profits from sales are not paid as dividends but are usually reinvested in the corporation for future expansion. If an investor were to buy the stock of a growth company, the investor could probably expect a rise in the value of the stock in the future. But the higher the projected growth rate, the greater the risk that such projections will not be realized and that the stock will not increase in value as expected. If one is interested in investments that will probably increase in value (with some risk), good common stocks of certain industries or even good real estate might be the answer.

Safety of Principal

The safety of the principal invested in a corporation bond is really only as good as the corporation itself. The same can be said for common and preferred stocks. We have already learned that common stocks may increase or decrease in dollar value. Preferred stocks have preferred claims on earnings or assets or both, but they may decrease in value if the corporation has financial trouble. The face value of bonds will not increase in dollar value. However, a discounted bond (one sold below face value) appears to have an increase in face value since the bond must be redeemed at maturity for full face value even though the buyer paid less than face value.

One's investment in a government bond is only as safe as the government itself. Cities, counties, and states have credit and financial ratings just the same as businesses.

Three main factors should be considered as to the safety of the principal when one invests in real estate:

1. whether the investor receives a good legal title to the property,
2. the location of the property, and
3. economic conditions

Checking on the title involves legal assistance. In checking on the location, one should make sure that the property is in a location that will not decrease in value. Some residential neighborhoods are gradually depreciating in value while others are increasing in value mainly because of the location. Economic conditions affect the value of real estate just as they affect the value of all other investments.

Satisfactory Income from the Investment

The safety of the principal is very important. If the principal is lost, there will be no income. However, the amount of income from the investment is also an important consideration.

Rate of Return. A sound investment should have a yield that is higher than the rate of inflation. A conservative rate of interest on a good bond will be determined by the conditions that exist at the time the bond is offered for sale. A high-grade bond sometimes pays no more than 8 percent interest on the face value, but these rates change.

Regularity of Income. Most investors are interested in having a steady and reliable income over a period of time. The continuous payment of interest or dividends is therefore one of the first considerations in evaluating a security.

The history of a corporation's earnings and dividends can be determined from the records of any stock listed on an exchange. However, expert advice is needed to determine possible future earnings.

Margin of Safety. For investment purposes, a good corporation should earn considerably more money than it pays out as bond interest and stock dividends. Unless the corporation is regularly earning more than is needed for these purposes, there is not an adequate margin of safety.

Liquidity

When an investment can be turned into money quickly and without loss of value, it is said to be a *liquid investment*. Some of your investments should be liquid in the event you encounter emergencies. If, for example, you need $2,000 to replace a furnace that broke down in the middle of winter, you wouldn't want to wait several months for a piece of real estate you owned to sell. Real estate is not considered a liquid investment. On the other hand, if you have money in a bank savings account, you can withdraw it whenever the bank is open. Savings accounts are the most liquid of all investments.

Marketability of Securities

Although a true investor is not interested in buying a security with the thought of selling it immediately, he or she must consider this possibility. For most investors, the most desirable securities are those that are listed for public sale on stock exchanges or at least those securities that are sold directly through brokers. A *broker* is a person who specializes in the study of securities or other assets, advises investors, and arranges for the purchase or sale of securities or other assets. The least desirable security for a small investor to buy would be stock in a new corporation with an unproven record.

Buying and Selling Securities

Securities are usually bought and sold through brokerage firms. These firms buy and sell listed securities through stock exchanges. They also deal in *over-the-counter securities,* which are not listed on any stock exchange. You pay the broker or dealer a commission for buying or selling a security for you.

Stock Exchanges. There are two main types of markets through which stocks and bonds are easily bought and sold. These are the local stock exchanges in various cities and the national exchanges located in New York City. The two national exchanges are the New York Stock Exchange and the American Stock Exchange. Regional stock exchanges in various cities have connections with the national exchanges.

Illus. 12-3

There are two main types of markets through which stocks and bonds are easily bought and sold. These are local exchanges in various cities and national exchanges in New York City.

Buying and selling stocks on a security exchange is carried on by means of the auction method. A stock may be offered for sale at a certain price, or someone may bid for the same stock at a different price. A sale is made when someone buys the stock at the price offered. These offers and bids are going on regularly so that anyone owning a stock has a pretty good idea of the price at which the stock can be sold.

Listed and Unlisted Securities. A security that is said to be *listed* on a stock exchange is one on which there are regular quoted prices on either regional or national exchanges. It may be listed and traded on both regional and national exchanges.

Unlisted securities are not listed on stock exchanges but may be bought and sold through individual brokers. Transactions in unlisted securities are called *over-the-counter transactions.* An unlisted stock (such as most bank stocks) may be as good as a listed stock; however, it may not be as well known as a listed stock and thus harder to sell. A financial planner or broker can give you sound advice regarding unlisted stock.

The prices at which stocks, bonds, and mutual funds are bought and sold daily are printed in most newspapers. Quotations for a few of the stocks listed on the New York Stock Exchange are shown in Figure 12-1.

Figure 12-1

Quotations for a Few of the Stocks Listed on the New York Stock Exchange

The current dividend in dollars per year
The hundreds of shares sold during the day
The highest price in dollars at which a sale was made during the day
The lowest price at which a sale was made during the day
The last price at which a sale was made during the day
The net change between the closing price and the closing price of the preceding day

52 Weeks High	52 Weeks Low	Stock	Div.	Yld %	P-E Ratio	Sales 100s	High	Low	Close	Net Chg.
33 1/8	15 1/8	Newell	.70	2.2	15	266	32 1/2	32 1/8	32 1/2	- 1/8
40 7/8	21 1/2	Nwhall s	.40	1.0	18	36	40	39 5/8	40	1/4
20 1/4	14	Newhll	6.20e	34.0	3	30	18 3/4	18	18 1/4	- 5/8
10	6 3/8	NwhlRs	.78e	9.9	6	15	7 7/8	7 3/4	7 7/8	+ 1/8
53 7/8	40 1/8	Newmt	1.00	2.2	...	114	45 1/4	44 5/8	44 3/4	- 1/4
2 1/8	9/16	Nwpark		...	...	204	11/16	5/8	11/16	...
25 1/2	17 1/2	NiaMP	2.08	9.2	8	9347	23 1/4	21 1/2	22 5/8	- 3/8
36	27 1/4	NiaMpf	3.40	9.8	...	z50	34 3/4	34 3/4	34 3/4	+ 5/8
37	28	NiaMpf	3.60	10.0	...	z1050	36 3/8	36	36	1/2
41	30	NiaMpf	3.90	9.8	...	z1330	41	40	40	...
56 1/8	37	NiaMpf	4.85	9.0	...	z260	54	54	54	1
61	41	NiaMpf	5.25	9.1	...	z1950	59	58	58	- 2
72	47 1/2	NiaMpf	6.10	8.7	...	z420	71	70	70	+ 1 1/2
88 1/4	59	NiaMpf	7.72	8.7	...	z6730u	89	87 3/4	89	+ 3/4
17	14 1/2	NiagSh	1.71e	10.5	...	65	16 1/4	16	16 1/4	+ 1/8
15 5/8	11 3/4	Nicolet	.12	.8	18	311	15	14 3/4	14 7/8	...
33 7/8	19	NICOR	1.80	6.5	917	899	27 5/8	27 1/8	27 1/2	...
33	21 3/4	NICO pf	1.90	6.8	...	2	28 1/8	28 1/8	28 1/8	- 1/8
16 1/4	9 5/8	NoblAf	.12b	1.2	...	x248	10 1/4	10	10 1/4	+ 1/8
19 1/4	10 1/2	NordRs		...	11	295	19 1/8	18 5/8	18 3/4	+ 1/8
99 1/4	62	NorfkSo	3.40	3.8	11	893	91 1/4	89	89 1/2	- 1 1/8
33	20 1/2	Norstr s	1.28	4.1	12	111	31 1/4	31 1/8	31 3/8	- 1/8
53 1/4	46 1/2	Norstr pf	3.73e	7.1	...	500	52 7/8	52 3/4	52 7/8	+ 3/8
25 5/8	13 3/4	Nortek	.08	.3	12	415	23 7/8	23 1/4	23 3/4	...
85	51 1/4	NACoal	1.10	1.4	8	34	81 1/2	80 1/2	80 5/8	- 5/8
48	31 5/8	NAPhil	1.00	2.2	20	181	46 5/8	45 3/4	45 7/8	- 5/8
19 3/4	15	NEurO	2.02e	11.4	8	62	17 7/8	17 1/2	17 3/4	+ 1/8
22 7/8	14 1/2	NoestUt	1.68	8.4	8	2270	20 1/2	19 7/8	20	5/8
12 7/8	8 3/8	NIndPS	1.56i	...	...	5152	11 1/8	10 1/2	10 3/4	- 3/8
47 1/4	33 1/4	NIPS pf	4.00e	9.1	...	19	44	43 1/8	44	+ 1
65 1/2	44 5/8	NoStPw	3.52	5.7	10	812	63 3/4	62 1/8	62 1/8	- 1 5/8
42	31 1/2	NSPw pf	3.60	9.0	...	z610	41	40	40	...
52	36 3/4	NSPw pf	4.08	8.0	...	z400	51 1/4	51 1/4	51 1/4	+ 1/4
51 1/4	36	NSPw pf	4.11	7.7	...	z1800u	53 1/4	53 1/4	53 1/4	+ 1 5/8
58	41 1/2	NSPw pf	4.56	7.8		z130u	58 1/8	58 1/8	58 1/8	+ 1/8
88 1/8	59 3/8	NSPw pf	6.80	7.6		z13000u	89 1/4	89 1/4	89 1/4	+ 7/8
39 1/2	25 1/4	NorTel	.40	1.3		2359	31 1/8	30 1/2	30 5/8	1/8

52 Weeks High	52 Weeks Low	Stock	Div.	Yld %	P-E Ratio	Sales 100s	High	Low	Close	Net Chg.
34 3/8	25 3/8	Questar	1.72	5.8	9	110	30 1/2	29 7/8	29 7/8	...
40 3/4	19 5/8	QkReil	.28a	.9	17	184	33 1/8	31 3/8	31 5/8	- 1 3/8
		– R – R – R –								
9 3/8	5 1/4	RBInd	.04i	.5	...	15	8 1/8	8	8	- 1/8
65 1/4	39 3/4	RCA	1.04	1.6	24	4669u	65 3/8	65 1/8	65 3/8	+ 1/8
53	36	RCA pf	3.50	6.6	...	z200	53	53	53	+ 1
148 1/2	92 3/4	RCA pf	4.00	2.7	...	3u	149	149	149	+ 1/2
45	35	RCA pf	3.65	8.1	...	210	44 7/8	44 3/4	44 7/8	+ 3/8
20	8 3/4	RJ Fin	.14	.8	14	126	18 5/8	17 5/8	17 3/4	- 3/4
48	24 3/4	RJR Nb s	1.48	3.3	12	7479	44 7/8	43 1/2	44 3/8	- 1/2
124	108	RJR pf	11.50	9.3	...	3u	124 1/4	124 1/4	124 1/4	+ 1/4
139 3/4	123 3/4	RJR pf	12.96	9.4	...	209	137 5/8	137 1/2	137 5/8	+ 1/4
11 7/8	6 1/4	RLC	.20	1.8	30	530	11 3/8	11	11 1/4	+ 1/4
4 1/2	2 7/8	RPC		...	...	29	3	3	3	...
28	16 5/8	RTE	.60	2.5	12	82	24 1/2	23 5/8	23 5/8	- 1/2
18 1/4	9 3/4	Radice		...	11	381	17	16 3/4	16 3/4	+ 1/8
69 1/2	39 3/4	RalsPur	1.10	1.7	14	923	66 1/8	64	64 3/8	- 1 1/8
11	6 1/4	Ramad		...	20	1894	9 5/8	9 1/4	9 1/4	- 1/4
24 1/4	16 1/8	Ranco	.84	3.6	11	40	23 1/4	23 1/8	23 1/8	- 1/8
4 3/4	2 1/2	RangrO		...	...	17579	3 3/4	3 3/8	3 1/2	- 1/4
140	59	Raycm	.44	.4	29	8516	107	98	106	- 20
13 7/8	9 3/8	Raymk		...	...	21	10 3/8	10 1/8	10 3/8	+ 1/4
27 1/4	19 5/8	Raynr n		...	...	41	26 1/2	26 1/8	26 1/4	1/8
67 3/8	44 3/8	Raythn	1.60	2.4	14	2992	66 1/4	65 3/8	66	- 1/2
10 1/2	1 3/4	ReadBt	.04	1.5	...	4831	2 7/8	2 5/8	2 5/8	...
19 3/8	6 1/2	RdBat pf	2.12	19.3	...	45	11	10	11	+ 1/2
22 1/2	7	RdBat pf	2.88e	28.8	...	5	10	10	10	+ 1/8
16 7/8	12 3/8	RltRef	1.64	10.0	11	22	16 5/8	16 3/8	16 3/8	+ 1/4
16	8 5/8	RecnEq		...	39	397	14 3/8	14	14	- 3/8
12 5/8	7	Redmn	.32	3.2	18	549	10 1/8	9 5/8	10	- 1/4
15 1/2	8 5/8	Reece		...	69	4	12 3/8	12 3/8	12 3/8	...
15/16	1/4	Regal		...	...	105	7/8	13/16	7/8	...
43 1/8	29 3/4	ReichC	.80	2.3	...	233	35	34 5/8	34 7/8	...
16	6 1/4	RepAir		...	10	3004	15 1/2	15 3/8	15 1/2	+ 1/8
6 1/4	1 1/4	RepA wt		...	...	345	5 3/8	5 3/8	5 3/8	...
14 1/4	7 1/4	RepGyp	.30	2.4	14	104	12 3/4	12 1/2	12 3/4	+ 1/8
49 1/2	29 1/8	RpNY s	1.12	2.4	11	166	45 7/8	45 1/4	45 3/4	...

Buying on Margin. Most investors pay cash for securities. However, some regular dealers on the stock market buy on margin. When *buying on margin,* the buyer authorizes the broker to purchase stock and pays only part of the price in cash. The broker lends the buyer the remaining amount of the purchase price, charges interest on this amount, and holds the stock as security for the loan. The buyer hopes to make a profit if the stock increases in value. If the stock decreases in value, however, the buyer may be forced to put up additional cash or have the stock sold by the broker at a loss. In order to control speculation, federal laws govern how much of any security sale may be made on margin.

Investment Clubs. Many investment clubs exist so that the members can study and make investments on a regular basis as a group. The usual procedure for investment clubs is to meet weekly or monthly and to study various investments regularly. They often have an expert as an adviser. At each meeting decisions are made about new possibilities for investment and whether any of the old investments should be sold and the money reinvested in another security. Membership in an investment club is a good means of learning about investments.

INFORMATION EVERYONE SHOULD KNOW ABOUT INVESTMENTS

1. Most people should invest, but not speculate or gamble.
2. The important factors to consider in selecting investments are:

   a. growth possibilities,
   b. safety of the principal,
   c. satisfactory and certain income,
   d. liquidity, and
   e. marketability of securities.

3. Do not listen to tipsters; consult only reliable sources of investment information.
4. Beware of the typical methods of deception practiced by unscrupulous promoters offering quick or unusually large money-making propositions.

VOCABULARY BUILDER

buying on margin   municipal bonds
franchise   mutual fund
IRA   over-the-counter securities
liquid investment   preferred stock

REVIEW QUESTIONS

1. What is the difference between saving and investing?
2. On what type of government bonds is the interest subject to federal income taxation?
3. What is the advantage of buying shares in a mutual fund?
4. What words of caution would you give a person considering investing his or her life savings in a business which that person will own and operate?
5. Before investing in real estate, what are some of the factors that should be investigated to determine its desirability?
6. What is the difference between investing and speculating?
7. What are the main sources of investment information available to an investor?
8. What are some of the factors that determine the safety of the principal of an investment?
9. If you were investing in stocks for dividend income, what factors should be considered?
10. How are securities usually bought and sold?

DISCUSSION QUESTIONS

1. "All municipal bonds provide very safe investments." Do you agree with this statement? Why?
2. If a definite income with maximum safety is desired, what investment would you recommend?
3. How is buying a home an investment?
4. Why are shares in mutual funds recommended for many investors who do not know much about stocks and bonds?

5.   Assume that you have $3,000 to invest and wish to continue working at your present job. What do you think of the idea of investing this money in a partnership with two other people in a neighboring town?

6.   "A bond is an investment; a stock is a speculation." Discuss this statement. Is it true or false?

7.   A person who is earning 5.5 percent interest on a savings account considers buying bonds that pay interest at a rate of 9 percent. What are the advantages and the disadvantages of this plan?

PART 3

Special Activities

CLASS PROJECTS

1. Itemize a list of expenditures you make during one school year. Which of these expenditures would you classify as fixed expenses and which as variable expenses?

2. Using the cash spending plan and the daily cash record in Chapter 9 as models, prepare a spending plan of your own based on your past experience and a daily cash record with columns that will meet your own needs. Keep a record of your income and expenditures for at least two months.

3. Make a record of the number of impulse items you buy for one week. Keep an account of the nature of each impulse item as well as the cost of each.

4. You decide to take advantage of the automatic bill payment service offered by your bank to pay your electric, water, and telephone bills each month. Assume that you would have to pay 10 cents for each check you write and 22 cents for every letter you mail. What would you save in postage and checks over one year using this modern bank service?

5. Consult your school or city library for articles on buying a franchised business. How much money is usually needed to buy the franchise, to build a building to franchise specifications, and to cover the start-up costs of operating the business in the early weeks or months until the business starts to realize a profit? What restrictions are placed on the owner of some franchised operations by the parent organization? Prepare a report for the class.

COMMUNITY PROJECTS

1. Check your newspaper or the latest edition of the *Statistical Abstract of the United States* in your library to see what the annual inflation rate is. Then assume you had $100 in a savings account that paid interest at 6 percent compounded quarterly. How was the purchasing power of your savings and interest affected by inflation?

2. Check a local supermarket that stocks non-brand (generic) grocery items. Select 10 or 12 items (canned goods, detergents and cleansers, and paper products) and make a three-way price comparison (generic label, supermarket's own brand, and a national brand) on these products. Be sure that your price comparisons are based on the same quantity of the product (you may have to resort to unit pricing). Set up your findings for bulletin board display similar to the example below.

Product	Non-brand Price	Supermarket's Brand Price	National Brand Price
Green Beans (16 oz.—454 g)	33¢	38¢	40¢

Summary

Total savings—No-brand over Supermarket's Brand ____%

Total savings—No-brand over National Brand ____%

Total savings—Supermarket's Brand over National Brand ____%

3. Select a committee to go to a bank that advertises itself as a full-service bank to obtain information about the various types of services offered by the bank, including those mentioned in Chapter 11. Describe each service and indicate whether there is a charge for it. Then prepare a bulletin board display indicating in one column the nature of the services provided and in the second column the fees, if any, charged for each of the services.

4. Contact a local broker, financial planner, or bank official who provides investment counseling. Ask what kinds of financial information he or she would want to know about a prospective client before advising that person about investments.

5. Assume that, with the help of your teacher, you have $1,000 to invest in stocks. Obtain as much information as you can about the stocks of various corporations and then select the stocks in which you would want to invest your money. Assume that you buy the stocks and set up a record of your imaginary purchases. In this record show the cost of each stock and the fees charged by the broker. Keep a record of dividends and after a period of time (determined by your teacher) compute the value of the stock that is owned and the amount of dividends received. Write a report on your income or loss and evaluate the worth of the stock and compare it to the worth at the time it was purchased.

PART 4
Consumer Credit

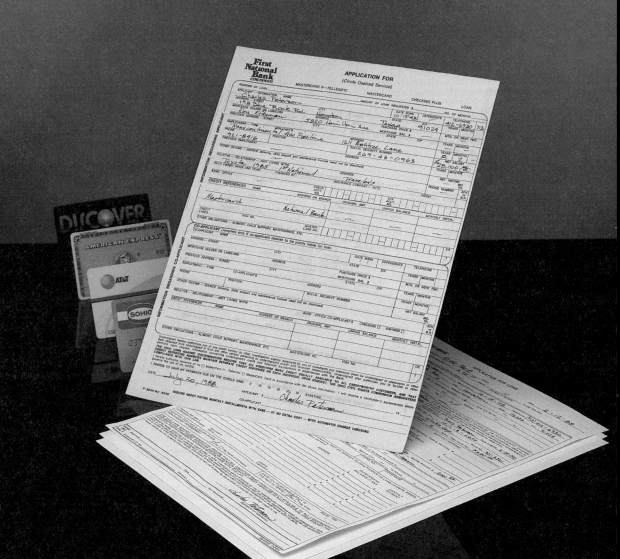

13

Understanding Credit

Credit is used by business and industry in the production and distribution of goods and services. Credit is used by consumers in buying the goods and services provided by business firms. The American family uses many forms of credit to improve its level of living. The development of a variety of good sources of credit, combined with the improved judgment of consumers, has led to the current widespread use of consumer credit. The purpose of this chapter is to help you understand credit, its importance to you, and how to use it most wisely.

After studying this chapter, you will be able to:

1. explain the four functions of credit,
2. explain how credit may help shape an individual's or a family's financial growth and security,
3. identify the common kinds of consumer credit,
4. explain what qualifies one to obtain credit, and
5. state the economic problems caused by using credit.

CREDIT

Credit demands careful management. Unwise use of credit can cause people, businesses, and even governments to go bankrupt.

Nature of Credit

Credit is a form of debt that occurs whenever cash, goods, or services are provided in exchange for a promise to pay at a future date. Most people and business organizations use credit in one form or another. Based on the faith of one individual in another, credit, like money, represents immediate buying power. A person or a firm has ability to buy now when a promise to pay at some time in the future is acceptable to the seller.

Credit Increases Buying Power. *Buying power* (or value of money) is measured by the quantity of goods that a given amount of money will buy. Like money, credit is valuable because it provides buying power. If everyone, including business firms and the federal government, had to pay cash for everything bought, business would slow down almost to a standstill. Like money, the value of credit is determined by its acceptability. When credit is used wisely, it is just as useful as money.

Wise Use of Credit. Proper use of credit has a steadying effect on the economy by helping to eliminate the usual increases and decreases in business. However, unwise use of credit can cause violent changes in business conditions.

If credit is too easy to get and is used too much, debts may not be paid when due. When this situation occurs on a national scale, many lenders suffer losses. Buying then decreases, causing a weakening of business conditions and a drop in production and jobs. Too much credit can also cause inflation. This occurs if there is more money available than goods and services to buy. Prices go up on these limited goods and services, causing inflation.

Credit may sometimes let persons start businesses that really should not be started. Industrial expansion that takes place largely on the basis of consumer credit depends on consumers' future earning power. Should consumers' earning power fail to grow, these industries are likely to have great losses in their businesses. Because businesses can be expanded rapidly through the use of credit, they are sometimes overconfident. Businesses must often use credit and offer credit. In order to offer credit, businesses must have faith in others and faith in the future.

Effect of Credit. The ease with which credit may be used increases the flow of goods to consumers. If the head of a household has a job and can expect to continue to earn money, the family can buy now on credit.

If a family uses credit wisely, it can plan carefully to meet all payments and enjoy many goods without having cash at the time of purchase. Goods bought on credit should last beyond the time the last payment is made.

FOUR MAJOR FUNCTIONS OF CREDIT

1. *Stabilizes the economy.* Credit steadies economic activity as it lets individuals and businesses buy goods and services even when income is temporarily limited. Through borrowing, the government may help the economy by spending money for roads, schools, unemployment benefits, and so forth.
2. *Promotes business growth.* Many people start new businesses and thousands of others continue in business through the use of credit. For example, many individuals are able to start small businesses (such as barber shops, auto repair shops, and boutiques) by getting loans from financial institutions.
3. *Expands production.* Business firms may increase the production of goods and services by means of long-term loans from banks, insurance companies, and other financial institutions. By borrowing, you, too, may increase your productive (earning) power by getting more education or by investing borrowed money at a rate of return higher than the cost of the borrowed money.
4. *Raises standard of living.* The general standard of living is raised when such things as homes, automobiles, furniture, appliances, insurance, and health service are bought on credit. Through credit, demand is created, production is increased, and jobs are created. A young family does not need to wait for savings to build up before buying things that make life comfortable.

If people fail to meet the legal and moral obligations of credit and cannot pay their debts, they may get into serious legal trouble. They will lose their good credit rating, and their buying power and standard of living will decrease.

Goods bought on credit should last beyond the time the last payment is made.

Kinds of Credit

Credit comes in many forms and may be grouped in many ways. Three groups quickly come to mind: government credit, business credit, and consumer credit. The instruments of credit most often used include drafts, promissory notes, conditional sales contracts, and real estate mortgages. These are defined and discussed in Chapters 14, 15, and 18.

Government Credit. Governments build highways, schools, hospitals, and many other projects for public use. Often a government will pay only part of the cost of a project from tax funds already collected. Governments, like individuals, borrow when they spend more than their current income. The usual practice is to sell bonds, with the interest and the amount borrowed to be paid back out of future taxes. A *bond* is a written promise to pay a specified amount plus interest at a certain time.

A local government will usually levy enough taxes to pay its police, fire fighters, and teachers and to cover the cost of other operating expenses. It will, through the sale of bonds, use credit when it must build a new school, a courthouse, or a city park. Table 13–1 shows amounts of federal, state, and local government debt in the United States.

Table 13–1

Government Credit Outstanding
1976–1984 (in Billions of Dollars)

	1976	1978	1980	1982	1984
Federal Government	$597	$780.4	$914.3	$1,147	$1,667
State and Local Governments	236	280.5	335.6	404.6	464
Total Government Debt	$833	$1,060.9	$1,249.9	$1,551.6	$2,131

Source: U.S. Bureau of the Census, *Statistical Abstract of the United States: 1986* (Washington, D.C.: U.S. Government Printing Office, 1985).

Business Credit. Businesses use *commercial credit* to cover the cost of producing and marketing goods. A manufacturer buys raw materials and promises to pay for them in 30, 60, or 90 days. A *retailer* (a business that sells directly to consumers) buys goods from a *wholesaler* (a business that buys large quantities of goods and sells smaller quantities to retailers) on similar terms. A farmer may buy seed or fertilizer and pay for it when the crop is harvested.

Businesses also use commercial credit when buying productive resources such as land, buildings, and machinery. Through borrowing, a restaurant can obtain land for a parking lot; an automobile manufacturer can acquire a new building; and an oil company can set up a new refinery. Bonds, maturing over periods of ten or more years, are often sold for such purposes. Table 13–2 shows total corporate and farm production debt in the United States.

Consumer Credit. *Consumer credit* is debt incurred by a consumer for goods and services needed for personal and family

Table 13–2

Manufacturing Corporations and Farm Production
Credit Outstanding
1976–1984 (in Billions of Dollars)

	1976	1978	1980	1982	1984
Manufacturing Corporations Debt	$188	$222	$292	$371	$405
Farm Production Debt	104.1	141.1	182.3	217.2	212
Total Corporate Manufacturing and Farm Production Debt	$212.1	$363.1	$474.3	$588.2	$617

Source: U.S. Bureau of the Census, *Statistical Abstract of the United States: 1986* (Washington, D.C.: U.S. Government Printing Office, 1985).

use. Consumer credit helps many people to buy the goods and services needed to satisfy their immediate wants. You may borrow money from a financial institution so that you can pay for a car or for modernizing your home. You may use install-ment buying in which you make a down payment on a washer and dryer and pay the rest in 12 or 18 months. Also, you may frequently use your credit card for buying at service stations or your favorite department store. Many people prefer credit buying to paying cash simply because it is handier. Some find it easier to pay for things by means of regular monthly pay-ments than to save up the same amount of money. Also, the danger of losing money or having it stolen makes the use of credit attractive to many people.

Debts on which payments are to be made at periodic inter-vals are known as *installment debts* or *installment credit.* Such consumer debts may arise from purchases of goods and ser-vices for personal and family use or from obtaining loans to pay for such purchases.

Debts for which the full payment is to be made in a single payment at a stated maturity date are known as *noninstall-ment debts* or *noninstallment credit.* Less than 25 percent of all consumer credit is in the form of noninstallment debt. Over 75 percent is in the form of installment debt. Table 13–3 shows the total of consumer installment and noninstallment credit outstanding in the United States.

Table 13–3
Consumer Credit Outstanding
1976–1984 (in Billions of Dollars)

	1976	**1978**	**1980**	**1982**	**1984**
Installment Debt	(193.5)	(273.6)	(301.4)	(335.0)	(460.5)
Automobile credit	67.7	101.6	112.2	126.3	172.6
Revolving credit	17.2	48.3	58.5	69.6	101.6
Mobile home credit	14.6	15.2	18.8	22.4	24.6
All other loans	94.1	108.5	111.8	116.7	161.8
Noninstallment Debt	(55.4)	(64.3)	(74.8)	(85.9)	(116.6)
Single payment	28.8	35.8	42.4	47.1	61.9
Charge accounts	13.2	12.0	13.1	14.4	19.2
Service credit	13.4	16.4	19.3	24.3	35.5
Total Installment and Noninstallment Credit Outstanding	248.9	337.9	376.2	420.9	577.1

Source: U.S. Bureau of the Census, *Statistical Abstract of the United States: 1986* (Washington, D.C.: U.S. Government Printing Office, 1985).

ESSENTIALS OF CREDIT

The economy of the United States has been called a credit economy because the use of credit is so widespread. If we are to have a sound economy, we must understand credit and use it wisely.

Importance of Credit

Credit is a vital force in our economy. It is of economic and social importance to every family and business organization. Credit was first used in business transactions to make *barter* (the exchange of goods for goods) more flexible. Credit was used before the existence of money. The custom of charging interest began early, and the cost of credit is something that has been reckoned with in all of recorded history.

The use of credit by consumers is similar to its use by government and by private businesses. Whenever an immediate need for cash, goods, or services is met through the proper use of credit, the economy of the nation is strengthened and the level of living is raised. The immediate need is actually met because of the faith one person has in the honesty and responsibility of another—faith that the debt will be repaid at maturity or that each payment will be made on time.

Charge Accounts

Many stores and business firms sell merchandise through *charge accounts*. This transaction is an arrangement between a customer and a store or business firm whereby the customer receives merchandise at the time of the sale in return for a promise to pay later. The two types of charge accounts are regular and revolving.

Regular Charge Account. Under the *regular charge account* plan, customers are expected to pay their accounts in full on receipt of their bills or within a stated number of days from the billing date. Sometimes there is a limit on the total amount that may be charged during a given period. Some examples of businesses that offer regular charge account services are American Express, Diners' Club, Carte Blanche, and many large department stores, clothing stores, and mail-order stores.

Revolving Charge Account. The *revolving charge account* is a plan which allows the payment for purchases to be extended over a period of time. The customer and the store representative determine at the time the account is opened the maximum amount that may be owed at any one time. New purchases may be charged to the account at any time, so long as the total amount owed by the customer does not go over the maximum. A service charge of from 1.04 to 1.8 percent of the amount due is charged each month (from 12.5 to 21.6 percent a year) for this type of account. Each state determines what percentage business can charge. Some examples of businesses that offer revolving charge account privileges are oil companies (for example, the Standard Oil Company and Shell Oil Company), large mail-order stores (for example, Sears, Roebuck and Company), large department stores, and all-purpose credit cards.

The privilege of charging purchases may be withdrawn by a business firm if the customer fails to pay the amount owed. A charge account may be a disadvantage for people who have a tendency to spend beyond their income or their ability to pay. A brief summary of the advantages of charge accounts to customers follows.

ADVANTAGES OF CHARGE ACCOUNTS

1. Charge accounts are a very convenient and simple way to buy.
2. Payment for purchases can be delayed until a predetermined date.
3. A record of purchases is made automatically.
4. Since money is not needed at the time of purchase, the danger of losing money while shopping is minimized.
5. Charge accounts make it easy to order merchandise by mail or telephone.
6. Salespeople and owners may learn to know a charge customer, which may result in better service.
7. Payment for several purchases may be made at one time.
8. Charge accounts enable customers to take advantage of sales.

Credit Cards

Credit cards are issued by many firms such as banks, oil companies, restaurants, hotels, airlines, and telephone companies to identify customers who have valid accounts. A *credit card* is an identification card that allows a customer to charge purchases of goods and services. There are two basic types of cards: pay-as-you-go cards and buy now, pay later cards.

Pay-As-You-Go Cards. These credit cards are generally used for travel, entertainment, and leisure activities. They include American Express, Diners' Club, and Carte Blanche. There is an annual charge or membership fee for these cards. For this membership fee, a variety of services is provided which other credit cards do not provide, such as guaranteed check cashing at hotels and airline counters, free travel insurance, and emergency card replacement. Usually no credit limit is imposed on the cardholder. (A *credit limit* is the maximum amount of money that can be owed at any one time.) The cardholder is expected to pay the entire charge upon being billed.

Buy Now, Pay Later Cards. MasterCard® and VISA® are two of the best-known, all-purpose credit cards. Banks, savings and loan associations, and credit unions issue these cards to customers, who can use them at millions of participating businesses. The business firms send all bills to the bank, savings and loan, or credit union, which in turn sends the customer one bill for total monthly purchases. Most users make only a minimum monthly payment, and the financial institution charges interest (usually 1.04 to 1.8 percent a month) on the unpaid balance each month.

Financial institutions offering MasterCard® and VISA® often charge annual membership fees. These cards can also be used to get instant loans up to a limited amount at the bank, savings and loan, or credit union, or at one of their 24-hour teller facilities. A credit limit is imposed on the cardholder.

Credit Terms

No down payment is required for purchases made through a charge or open account. The time allowed between the date of purchase and the date the payment is due is the length of the *credit term*. A common credit term for charge accounts is 30 days; however, some credit terms may be for a shorter time

Illus. 13–2
Business firms send all credit card bills to the bank or savings and loan, which in turn sends the customer one bill for total monthly purchases.

period. A service charge is made on the past-due balance and added on at the next billing. States allow charges of from 1.04 to 1.8 percent for each 30 days that the debt is past due. Thus, when a consumer postpones paying a debt, the cost of that credit is 12.5 to 21.6 percent a year.

Under a plan known as *cycle billing*, the balance owed by a customer becomes due regularly on a certain day of the month regardless of the date of the last purchase. This means that a bill for a purchase made late in a customer's credit month becomes due in less than 30 days. Large stores use cycle billing because it spreads the work of preparing monthly statements over an entire month.

Cost of Charge Accounts

Retailers selling on credit and issuing their own cards incur extra costs on every sale. The principal extra costs result from:

1. the office work necessary for recording sales and collecting accounts,

2. losses because of customers who fail to make payments, and
3. the tendency of charge customers to return goods for exchange.

Retailers that fail to investigate a customer's ability to pay before charging sales to the account are apt to have high losses from failure to collect debts. One may well expect to find high prices in stores that recklessly advertise generous credit terms to everyone. Stores that have sound credit policies have practically no losses from customers who fail to make payments. Also, some stores that regularly sell on credit often provide delivery service and other conveniences. These services, combined with possible higher costs due to charge accounts, may cause the store to sell at higher prices than a cash-and-carry store. We must not assume, however, that a merchant who sells on credit must necessarily sell at higher prices than a merchant who sells only for cash.

Firms issuing all-purpose credit cards like American Express or VISA® collect from participating retailers a percentage of every charge sale made on their credit card. This charge covers the card-issuing companies who stand to lose money if the cardholders fail to pay for purchases charged to these accounts.

USING CREDIT

At one time or another almost everyone needs to use credit. It is important that we can get credit when it is needed.

Establishing a Credit Rating

Our *credit rating* or *credit worthiness* is an indication of our ability to secure goods, services, and money in return for a promise to pay. It represents our ability to incur debts because some lender trusts us. A favorable credit rating does not come automatically. It comes as the result of slow growth. It must be nurtured, fostered, strengthened, and improved. It is an asset of tremendous value to those who develop it over a long period of years. It can be destroyed easily; it is sensitive to abuse; and it usually continues only as long as it is justified. A favorable credit rating over a period of time is enjoyed only by persons who deserve it and who protect it.

A common formula for determining the credit worthiness of a person or a business consists of the "three Cs"—character, capacity, and capital.

Lack of capacity, capital, or character can affect one's credit rating adversely, making it difficult to borrow money or buy goods and services on credit.

Character. *Character* is revealed in one's conduct, attitudes, and achievements. It does not necessarily have any relation to one's wealth. It represents the principles for which one stands. One's reputation is a reflection of how other people evaluate one's character traits. We are not able to borrow money or buy goods and services with the promise to pay later if others judge our character to be questionable.

Capacity. *Capacity* is merely another term for earning power. It represents one's ability to earn money and to pay debts when they become due. An individual may have an honorable character and perfectly good intentions of paying a debt; but without the ability or capacity to pay, the person cannot pay satisfactorily. It is often more difficult to judge character than it is to judge capacity. Capacity, or earning power, can be measured with some accuracy, but character is an intangible quality.

Capital. The third measuring standard, *capital*, applies only to people who have property (land, home, cars, or anything else of value). Naturally our capital affects our ability to pay debts when they become due and, consequently, affects our credit standing. People with a temporary lack of earning power but with substantial capital may still have favorable credit ratings; that is, others will be willing to make loans to them based on their promises to pay.

Establishing a Line of Credit

One's credit rating or credit worthiness refers to the chances or the probability that one will pay a debt when it becomes due. We have just learned that it depends on the trust or confidence others have in our intention to pay. *Line of credit* means the maximum amount a lender or creditor will permit a customer to charge at any one time.

To establish your credit rating and your line of credit, the usual procedure is to go to your favorite store and discuss the matter frankly with the credit manager or the owner. The credit manager will request information about your character, capacity, and capital. Such information should be provided accurately and completely. The credit manager must have such information as a basis for determining how much credit to extend to you.

Figure 13–1 shows a typical application for credit for department store customers. In some cases the forms are more complicated, but in general they require the same information.

Credit Agencies

In general there are two types of credit agencies: agencies that provide credit ratings on individuals and agencies that provide credit rating information on businesses.

Banks sometimes give confidential credit information on individuals and businesses. It is therefore important to maintain satisfactory relations with a bank if a good credit rating is desired.

Figure 13–1
An Application for Credit

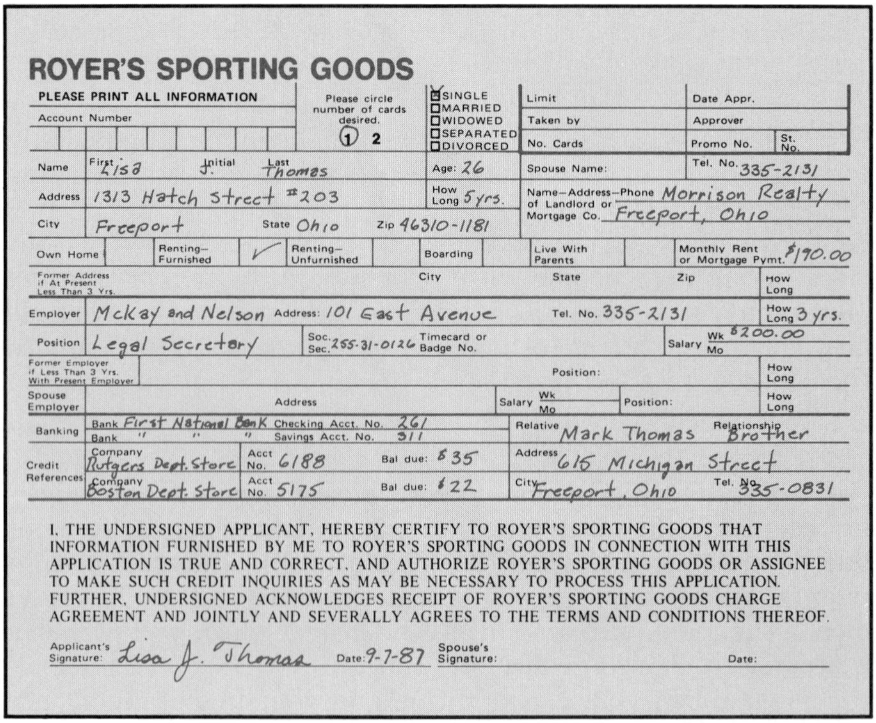

ROYER'S SPORTING GOODS

PLEASE PRINT ALL INFORMATION | Account Number | Please circle number of cards desired. (1) 2 | ☑ SINGLE ☐ MARRIED ☐ WIDOWED ☐ SEPARATED ☐ DIVORCED | Limit | Taken by | No. Cards | Date Appr. | Approver | Promo No. | St. No.

Name: First Lisa, Initial J., Last Thomas | Age: 26 | Spouse Name: | Tel. No. 335-2131

Address: 1313 Hatch Street #203 | How Long 5 yrs. | Name—Address—Phone of Landlord or Mortgage Co.: Morrison Realty, Freeport, Ohio

City: Freeport | State Ohio | Zip 46310-1181

Own Home | Renting—Furnished ✓ | Renting—Unfurnished | Boarding | Live With Parents | Monthly Rent or Mortgage Pymt. $190.00

Former Address if At Present Less Than 3 Yrs. | City | State | Zip | How Long

Employer: McKay and Nelson | Address: 101 East Avenue | Tel. No. 335-2131 | How Long 3 yrs.

Position: Legal Secretary | Soc. Sec. 255-31-0126 | Timecard or Badge No. | Salary Wk $200.00 Mo

Former Employer if Less Than 3 Yrs. With Present Employer | Position: | How Long

Spouse Employer | Address | Salary Wk Mo | Position: | How Long

Banking: Bank First National Bank Checking Acct. No. 261 | Bank " " Savings Acct. No. 311 | Relative Mark Thomas | Relationship Brother

Credit References: Company Rutgers Dept. Store Acct No. 6188 Bal due: $35 | Address 615 Michigan Street

Company Boston Dept. Store Acct No. 5175 Bal due: $22 | City Freeport, Ohio | Tel. No. 335-0831

I, THE UNDERSIGNED APPLICANT, HEREBY CERTIFY TO ROYER'S SPORTING GOODS THAT INFORMATION FURNISHED BY ME TO ROYER'S SPORTING GOODS IN CONNECTION WITH THIS APPLICATION IS TRUE AND CORRECT, AND AUTHORIZE ROYER'S SPORTING GOODS OR ASSIGNEE TO MAKE SUCH CREDIT INQUIRIES AS MAY BE NECESSARY TO PROCESS THIS APPLICATION. FURTHER, UNDERSIGNED ACKNOWLEDGES RECEIPT OF ROYER'S SPORTING GOODS CHARGE AGREEMENT AND JOINTLY AND SEVERALLY AGREES TO THE TERMS AND CONDITIONS THEREOF.

Applicant's Signature: Lisa J. Thomas Date: 9-7-87 Spouse's Signature: Date:

Private credit agencies collect information and issue confidential reports for the benefit of their subscribers, who are retailers. Each subscriber contributes information about customers to the agency. Additional information is gathered from local newspapers, notices of change in address, death notices, and court records. Such information is valuable to retailers in protecting them from loss on accounts. If a customer moves, retailers will want to know of the change in address. If a customer dies, retailers will want to be sure that claims are presented. If someone is taking court action against a customer, other retailers will want to know in order to protect their own claims.

The Associated Credit Bureaus of America has more than 3,000 credit bureau members serving over 600,000 business firms. Any of these local credit bureaus can develop a report on any individual in North America and in many foreign countries within a short period of time. Through the interchange of information, the credit records of over 100 million consumers are already compiled and are readily available to members of the Associated Credit Bureaus of America. The services of this nationwide credit reporting system are an advantage to you if you have safeguarded your credit. You can move from one community to another, and your credit record will follow you or it can be checked on very easily. However, a bad credit reputation also will follow you wherever you go.

In 1971, the Fair Credit Reporting Act prevented credit agencies from giving out wrong credit information about consumers. An individual who has been denied credit, employment, or insurance because of an inaccurate credit-agency report may ask to know the source of that report. The individual then has a right to be told the nature, substance, and sources of the information on file at the credit agency. The individual may have wrong information and information that cannot be proven removed from the file. The Act also allows consumers the right to examine information in their credit files, and they can add a short statement to the files giving their side of the story.

Responsibility for Debts

Responsibility for paying one's debts is one of our oldest moral and ethical principles. In addition to this principle, laws have been enacted specifying a person's legal responsibility for debts. Furthermore, one's relationship to lenders in case of failure to pay has also been fixed by law.

Parents generally are legally responsible for debts incurred by their children when permission has been given to the children to make purchases and charge them to the parents' account. For instance, if it has been customary for a child to use a charge account of the parents, the parents are responsible for the debts.

Creditor's Remedies. If a person does not or cannot pay a debt, the *creditor* (the one to whom money is owed) has several legal courses available. The account can be turned over to a lawyer or a collection agency for collection. The merchandise may be repossessed. Or suit may be brought in court against the *debtor* (the one who owes money) to enforce payment of the debt. In some instances, a person's salary may be garnisheed or attached.

Garnishment. If a debtor refuses to pay a debt, the creditor may have a court order issued against the debtor. This court order would require the employer of the debtor to pay part of the debtor's wages to the creditor until the debt has been paid. This procedure is called *garnishment* or *garnisheeing* of wages. Some states do not permit garnishment. Those states that do must abide by the federal Consumer Credit Protection Act of 1968. This act states that the most that can be taken from a debtor's weekly take-home pay is the lesser of:

1. 25 percent of take-home pay, or
2. the difference between a debtor's take-home pay and $100.50 (30 times the current federal minimum wage of $3.35 per hour).

States may exceed the federal maximum and use 40 or 50 times minimum wage. The larger the multiplier, the smaller the amount that can be garnisheed. An illustration of the amount that can be garnisheed is given in Table 13–4.

Attachment. If you owe a debt and refuse to pay or cannot pay as agreed, you may be sued in court and forced to pay it. A common procedure in such a case is for the creditor to ask the court for an attachment on some of your property until the case is settled. An *attachment* is simply a legal process whereby the property attached comes under the control

Table 13-4
Garnishment of Wages

Weekly Take-Home Pay	Alternatives to Determine Amount to be Garnisheed	
	Wages × 25%	**Wages − $100.50**
$200	$200 × 25% = $50.00*	$200 − $100.50 = $99.50
$125	$125 × 25% = $31.25	$125 − $100.50 = $24.50*
	*The amounts that can legally be garnisheed	

of the court until the case is settled. Property on which an attachment order has been placed may not be sold and may not be moved except by court approval. The court can order the property sold to pay the debt.

Debtor's Remedies. When a person is unable to pay a debt, that person has a number of courses available. It may be possible to borrow money to pay the current debt. It may be possible to make an arrangement with the creditor to pay off the debt in small installments over a period of time. Or, the debt may be discharged by a statute of limitations or bankruptcy proceedings.

Arrangement. This is usually the most desirable plan for both the debtor and the creditor. In most cases debtors want to pay their debts and creditors want to be paid without having to take legal action against the debtors. Therefore, creditors are usually quite willing to make an arrangement for the debtor to make small regular payments over a long period of time until the debt has been paid. Usually, as a part of this arrangement, the debtor cannot make additional credit purchases from the creditor until the original debt has been paid.

Statutes of Limitations. The *statutes of limitations* in most states set a time limit after which a creditor cannot enforce a legal claim. For instance, in one state if an account is not collected within five years, the creditor cannot sue for the amount. If the debtor, however, makes a payment or a promise to pay at any time during the five years or at any time thereafter, the account is revived or reinstated.

Bankruptcy. If one is unable to pay debts when they become due, one is *insolvent*. If the debts are greater than the total value of one's *assets* (things of value that are owned), a federal court may declare the person to be *bankrupt*. Recognizing the impossibility of paying one's debts, a person may ask the court to declare him or her bankrupt. This process is known as *voluntary bankruptcy*.

Any one of a person's creditors who holds a past-due debt against the person may also petition or ask the court to declare that person bankrupt. This process is known as *involuntary bankruptcy*.

Bankruptcy cancels all of a debtor's former debts after the debtor's property is divided among his or her creditors and enables that person to start to acquire property again. Property acquired after bankruptcy proceedings have been completed is not subject to claims for prior debts. The great advantage of bankruptcy to creditors is that they all receive, in proportion to their claims, a part of the net proceeds resulting from the sale of the bankrupt's property. No one creditor gets an unfair preference over others.

Bankruptcy should not be looked upon as an easy way out of paying one's debts. When bankruptcy has been filed against a person, that person may have to operate strictly on a cash basis for a number of years. This means, in most instances, one might be denied the use of charge accounts, credit cards, and loans for automobiles and other consumer goods. One may even be denied admission to a hospital unless one can prove that one has the cash (or insurance) to pay the hospital bill. After declaring bankruptcy, a person cannot declare bankruptcy again for six years.

Consumer Credit Laws

Since 1975, some laws regarding credit have been passed that are important for consumers. Some of these laws will be discussed briefly.

Nondiscrimination. The Equal Credit Opportunity Act was directed toward credit discrimination on the basis of sex, marital status, race, color, religion, age, or national origin. In the past women were often denied credit by stores, lending institutions, and credit card companies. This practice is now illegal. Women applying for credit must be judged by the same standards as men. If women have steady incomes and can qualify in other respects as good credit risks, they are equally entitled to credit.

Illus. 13–3

In the past, women were often denied credit by stores, lending institutions, and credit card companies. This practice is now illegal.

Billing Errors. Under the Fair Credit Billing Act, consumers can preserve their credit ratings while settling disputes with stores and credit card companies. If you think there is an error on your bill or some charge you don't understand, you must notify the creditor in writing within 60 days after the bill was mailed to you. The creditor must respond to your inquiry within 30 days and must resolve the problem within 90 days. During this time the creditor cannot report you as delinquent to any credit agency for your failure to pay the portion of your bill that is under dispute.

Cash Discounts. Since stores pay credit card companies 4 to 7 percent for the privilege of accepting their card, many cash customers feel they are entitled to discounts on their purchases. In the past most credit card companies would not permit stores who honored their cards to offer cash discounts to cash customers. Now stores have the right to offer cash discounts as long as the offer is made to all potential customers. The law does prohibit retailers from adding extra charges to credit card purchases.

Credit Collections. The Fair Debt Collections Practices Act makes it illegal for a creditor to threaten or harass a debtor by posing as an officer of the law or courts. Late night telephone calls demanding payment are also illegal under this act.

The Truth in Lending Act. Under the Truth in Lending Act (also known as the Consumer Credit Protection Act), the creditor must inform the consumer exactly how much is being charged for the use of credit. In the past it was not always easy for consumers to determine how much they were paying for credit. This act requires the creditor to state the annual percentage rate and the amount in dollars and cents being charged for the credit.

FACTS EVERYONE SHOULD KNOW ABOUT CREDIT

1. Consumer credit is debt incurred for goods and services for personal and family use.
2. In its many forms, credit is a useful tool if it is not used unnecessarily and does not cost too much.
3. Because it is convenient and often is a means of adjusting high and low points in spending, credit is used by people at all income levels.
4. Each credit transaction remains incomplete until all legal responsibilities and repayment obligations of the debt are met.
5. A good credit rating must be earned and maintained if one wants to get credit when it is needed at a reasonable cost.
6. If it becomes impossible to pay one's debts, prompt action should be taken to notify creditors and to establish an adjusted payment schedule that can be met.
7. When credit is used as a substitute for careful money management, there is usually a tendency to overuse it.
8. When overuse of credit forces a person to declare bankruptcy, there is a weakening of the economic and social structure.

Economic Problems of Credit

The use of credit tends to increase purchases and stimulate business. Government officials, bankers, business people, and many others constantly watch the figures that are collected to show the amount and the nature of debt that is owed by individuals. If consumer debt increases too fast and is not being paid off, it indicates that consumers buying on credit are not able to pay their debts. Such a condition is an indication that we might be entering a period of bad business conditions.

When great numbers of people buy more on credit than they can repay, we experience an overexpansion of consumer credit. The result may be that many businesses lose money because they cannot collect for goods sold on credit. We are all affected by bad business conditions that arise when great numbers of people cannot pay their debts.

VOCABULARY BUILDER

buying power	credit rating
capacity	garnishment
capital	retailer
character	revolving charge account
consumer credit	wholesaler
credit	

REVIEW QUESTIONS

1. What makes credit truly valuable?
2. How widespread is the use of credit today?
3. What are the main functions of credit?
4. What could be a major disadvantage of using charge accounts?
5. How does a revolving charge account work in a retail store?
6. What extra costs are incurred by business in making charge sales?
7. What are some of the agencies through which credit information can be obtained?
8. What is the purpose of statutes of limitation?
9. What relief may an individual debtor obtain under the bankruptcy laws?

10. Explain the purpose of the following consumer credit laws:
    a. the Equal Credit Opportunity Act,
    b. the Fair Credit Billing Act,
    c. the Fair Debt Collection Practices Act, and
    d. The Truth in Lending Act.
11. Why are government officials, bankers, and business people sometimes concerned about the amount of debt owed by individuals?

DISCUSSION QUESTIONS

1. What are some examples (other than buying a car or modernizing a home) of the high and low points that develop in a family's spending pattern where credit can be useful?
2. What are some of the kinds of goods and services that consumers most frequently buy on credit? What are the advantages and the disadvantages of buying them on credit?
3. Most people appreciate the advantages of using credit cards but are unaware of the disadvantages and dangers. What are some disadvantages and dangers of using credit cards?
4. a. Do you think you can open a charge account in your parents' name and use the charge account?
    b. Can you use your parents' charge account if it has been established by them?
5. How may the use of credit affect the individual consumer, the community, and jobs in industry?
6. How can a good credit reputation at your present place of residence help you if you move to another city?
7. Nancy Wong has been away from her job without pay for six weeks because of illness. She is now behind in paying her bills. She owes $75 to a department store, $30 to an oil company, and $150 to her doctor. How should Nancy handle this situation?

14

Using Installment Credit

Using installment credit means buying and then making regular payments over a period of months. Installment credit can also mean borrowing money to make a purchase and making payments on the loan. In this chapter you will learn how consumers can use installment credit wisely and how it can cause serious trouble if used unwisely.

After studying this chapter, you will be able to:

1. tell the difference between charge account buying and installment buying,
2. identify the three types of installment contracts,
3. describe under what conditions one should buy on the installment plan,
4. explain how the Truth in Lending Act affects installment contracts, and
5. state what wise users of installment credit have to consider.

NATURE OF INSTALLMENT CREDIT

Buying on an installment plan differs from buying on a regular charge account or a revolving charge account in four ways:

1. a down payment is usually required;
2. a finance or carrying charge is added to the price;

3. payments, usually of equal amounts, are spread over a specified period of time; and
4. if payments are not made as scheduled, protection is provided to the seller in the form of a security agreement.

Installment Buying

Estimates indicate that nearly 45 percent of our yearly retail sales are credit transactions. About 75 percent of these credit sales are made on the installment plan. More than half of the automobiles, furniture, and household appliances sold are purchased on the installment plan. Many families cannot pay cash for these major purchases. Under the installment plan, however, these families are able to buy with little or no cash. The opportunity to buy now and pay later has increased mass consumption of goods and services. If purchases could be made on a cash basis only, sales would decrease rapidly and business activity throughout the nation would slow down.

Characteristics of Installment Contracts. Installment contracts are usually written in triplicate. One copy is kept by the purchaser; another copy is filed in some local recording office; and the third copy is kept by the seller. The purpose of recording an installment contract is to make the record public so that anyone can tell whether a claim has been made against the property listed as security.

Installment contracts may differ in their wording and content but all types are similar. In each case the buyer must agree to do certain things. For example, the buyer must agree to make the payments as specified. The balance of the contract may be collected immediately if one payment is missed. In some states, the salary or wages of the buyer may be garnisheed if payments are not made. The buyer may also be held responsible for paying taxes, insuring the property for damage or loss, and keeping it free from other claims.

Types of Installment Contracts. A *security agreement* is a written statement signed by the buyer indicating that the seller has a right to repossess the item purchased and to sue for the purchase price if payments are not made as scheduled. This signed agreement also includes a general description of

Illus. 14–1

Estimates indicate that nearly 45 percent of our yearly retail sales are credit transactions.

the article sold. Figure 14–1 is an example of a security agreement for installment sales. Such agreements may be in one of the following forms:

1.   chattel mortgage contract,
2.   conditional sales contract, or
3.   bailment lease contract.

Figure 14–1

Retail Installment Contract and Security Agreement

Seller's Name: *HOWARD'S HOUSEHOLD APPLIANCES*
INDIANAPOLIS, INDIANA

Contract # *1402*

RETAIL INSTALLMENT CONTRACT AND SECURITY AGREEMENT

The undersigned (herein called Purchaser, whether one or more) purchases from *Howard's Appliances* (seller) and grants to *HIM* a security interest in, subject to the terms and conditions hereof, the following described property.

PURCHASER'S NAME *MR. ROBERT M. WEAVER*

PURCHASER'S ADDRESS *7234 N. COLLEGE AVE.*

CITY *INDIANAPOLIS*   STATE *IN*   ZIP *46224-2935*

QUANTITY	DESCRIPTION	AMOUNT
1	*WASHING MACHINE*	*295.00*

Description of Trade-in:

	Sales Tax	*15.00*
	Total	*310.00*

1.	CASH PRICE	*$295.00*
2.	LESS: CASH DOWN PAYMENT	$*60.00*
3.	TRADE-IN	
4.	TOTAL DOWN PAYMENT *60.00*	$*60.00*
5.	UNPAID BALANCE OF CASH PRICE	$*235.00*
6.	OTHER CHARGES:	

SALES TAX		*$15.00*
CREDIT LIFE INSURANCE		*2.00*
7.	AMOUNT FINANCED	$*252.00*
8.	FINANCE CHARGE	$*25.00*
9.	TOTAL OF PAYMENTS	$*277.00*
10.	DEFERRED PAYMENT PRICE (1+6+8)	$*335.00*
11.	ANNUAL PERCENTAGE RATE	*18.5*%

Insurance Agreement

The purchase of insurance coverage is voluntary and not required for credit.   (Type of Ins.)

insurance coverage is available at a cost of $ *2.00* for the term of credit.

   I desire insurance coverage

Signed *Robert M. Weaver* Date *1/8/87*

   I do not desire insurance coverage

Signed_____ Date_____

Purchaser hereby agrees to pay to *HOWARD'S HOUSEHOLD APPLIANCES* at their offices shown above the "TOTAL OF PAYMENTS" shown above in *12* monthly installments of $ *22.90* _____(final payment to be $ *23.10*), the first installment being payable *FEBRUARY 8* 19*87*, and all subsequent installments on the same day of each consecutive month until paid in full. The finance charge applies from   *1/8/87*

Signed *Robert M. Weaver*

NOTICE TO BUYER: YOU ARE ENTITLED TO A COPY OF THE CONTRACT YOU SIGN. YOU HAVE THE RIGHT TO PAY IN ADVANCE THE UNPAID BALANCE OF THIS CONTRACT AND OBTAIN A PARTIAL REFUND OF THE FINANCE CHARGE BASED ON THE "ACTUARIAL METHOD." [Any other method of computation may be so identified, for example, "Rule of 78's," "Sum of the Digits," etc.]

Most installment sales are called *secured credit sales* because of this written, signed security agreement. In a secured credit sale the possession and risk of loss pass to the buyer. The seller has a security interest in the article until it has been paid in full.

Chattel Mortgage Contract. A *chattel mortgage contract* applies to goods that are movable, such as automobiles. It is a claim against the goods mentioned in the contract. The seller gives title of the goods to the buyer, and the buyer becomes the owner. The chattel mortgage permits the seller to retain a claim against the goods until the debt is paid.

Conditional Sales Contract. A *conditional sales contract* is the most common type of agreement used to provide security for the seller. Under this plan the title to the goods remains with the seller until all payments have been made in full. The title to the property is then transferred to the buyer.

Bailment Lease Contract. In a *bailment lease contract* the buyer rents an article and, after payment of sufficient rentals to equal the purchase price, has the option to take title of the article. Sometimes a small additional sum, such as $1, may be required before the title of the article is given to the renter-buyer.

QUESTIONS TO ASK YOURSELF BEFORE SIGNING AN INSTALLMENT CONTRACT

1. What is the cash price of the article?
2. How much money is actually advanced?
3. What are the total finance or carrying charges?
4. What are the insurance, investigation, legal, recording, and other charges in addition to the purchase price and carrying charges?
5. How do the installment costs compare with costs of other ways of borrowing, such as a personal loan at a bank or credit union?
6. Are all the facts about the contract known and fully understood?
7. Are all figures in the contract correct? Are all blanks filled in?
8. Specifically, what security has been given? Does it include merchandise previously bought or to be bought in the future?
9. May wages be garnisheed in case of delinquent payments?
10. May the buyer pay off the contract before the due date and thus save having to pay all the interest?
11. Will fair notice be given before repossession?
12. What rights does the buyer have in case of repossession?

Finance Companies

Most stores and business firms do not have enough money to finance their sales if they sell on an installment plan. They need the money from sales immediately to invest in replacement merchandise so they can maintain a high level of sales. Therefore, they use the services of a finance company.

Sales Finance Company. A finance company that deals only in installment contracts arising from sales by business firms is sometimes known as a *sales finance company*. In effect, the sales finance company purchases the installment contracts from the business firm at the time of the sale, thus immediately replenishing the merchant's cash. In some instances the customer's payments are made to the merchant, but more often they are made directly to the finance company.

The following example illustrates how a sales finance company operates. Mr. Baker buys a refrigerator from Ace Appliance Company for $500. Under the terms of the installment

Illus. 14–2

Most stores do not have enough money to finance their sales if they sell on an installment plan. Therefore, they use the services of a finance company.

contract, the debt is to be paid monthly over a period of two years. Ace Appliance Company sells (discounts) the installment contract to Top Finance Company for $450. Top Finance Company collects the $500 from Mr. Baker. *Discounting* is the act of financial institutions buying installment contracts from merchants at prices lower than the prices appearing on the contracts.

There are several thousand finance companies in the United States that deal in installment credit.

Some finance companies confine their transactions to the purchase of one kind of installment contract, such as contracts arising from the sale of automobiles. The large automobile manufacturers own a finance company or have an agreement with one to handle the installment contracts on cars sold by their dealers.

Consumer Finance Company. As pointed out in Chapter 11, consumer finance companies make small loans to consumers. Instead of buying installment contracts from business firms, consumer finance companies make installment loans directly to consumers to purchase durable goods, pay debts, pay emergency expenses, or make home repairs.

Rights of Buyers and Sellers in Secured Credit Sales

In secured credit sales, both the buyer and the seller have legal rights. It is important for an installment buyer to know these rights.

Rights of Credit Buyers. Even though the buyer may not have paid the seller the full purchase price, the buyer may sell his or her rights in the article to a third party. The third party, or new buyer, however, is still subject to the original security agreement. This means that if the first buyer did not pay the seller in full, the seller has the right to repossess the article from the second buyer. This is true even though the second buyer does not owe anyone for the article.

The credit buyer also has the right at any time to demand from the credit seller a written statement saying exactly how much is still owed.

In case of repossession, the buyer has the right to be notified by the seller reasonably in advance of when the article is to be resold. This gives the buyer the opportunity to buy back the article before the time of resale. However, the buyer must pay the balance owed plus any expenses and legal fees incurred by the seller in the course of the repossession. The credit buyer also has the right to any surplus resulting from the resale of a repossessed article. *Surplus* is defined as any amount over the balance due, including interest; costs of repossession, storage, and resale; and attorneys' fees.

Right Against Holder in Due Course. The *holder in due course* is the purchaser of an installment loan contract. The buyer is allowed to sue the holder in due course if the merchandise proves to be faulty. For example, if a store sells merchandise on an installment contract and later sells (discounts) the contract to a bank or sales finance company (holder in due course), the bank or finance company becomes liable if the merchandise proves to be faulty. In the past the buyer had no recourse. The seller, who no longer held the installment contract, would refuse to make good on the faulty merchandise. The holder in due course (the bank or sales finance company) would refuse to make good on the merchandise because it didn't sell the merchandise to the buyer.

Right of Prepayment. Most stores will allow a buyer to prepay the balance of an installment contract. This *right of prepayment* (paying off the contract before it comes due) saves the buyer some interest charges. However, many of these stores apply the *Rule of 78s* (note last line in Figure 14–1) to buyers who prepay a loan. The theory behind this practice is that lenders are entitled to more interest in the early months of the contract when their risks are greater and less interest near the maturity date when their risks are less.

The Rule of 78s works this way: Write the numbers 1 to 12 in a column. Add the numbers; the total is 78. The first month's interest charge (on a 12-month contract) is 12/78 of the total finance charge; the last month's interest is 1/78 of the total finance charge. Assume you bought a portable electric typewriter for $188, paying $20 down. The balance is to be paid in 12 equal installments with interest at 18 percent a year ($30.24 total interest or $2.52 interest each month). At the time of your seventh installment, you decide to prepay the contract. Applying the Rule of 78s, the store would charge you a total of only $24.42 interest (63/78 of $30.24), representing a savings of $5.82 ($30.24 - $24.42). The 63 in the formula is arrived at by adding upward from 12 in the column through 6

(12 + 11 + 10 + ... 6). The last five numbers in the column, which are not counted, represent the five months still remaining in the contract.

Rights of Credit Sellers. The seller has the right to sue for the amount due plus interest if the buyer does not honor the contract. The seller also has the right of repossession even without a court order. If after repossession and resale of the article the seller does not recover the original purchase price, the seller has the right to demand the difference from the buyer. This is true even though the buyer no longer has possession of the article. The seller may waive this right; however, the buyer should get this waiver in writing.

USING THE INSTALLMENT PLAN

If used wisely, installment buying can be of benefit to consumers, to business, and to the economy in general. It can, however, be a harmful practice if abused.

Illus. 14–3
Installment buying is a poor practice if it is abused.

Buying on the Installment Plan

Installment buying may be harmful to consumers if they buy luxuries or other goods they don't really need. On the other hand, buying on an installment plan may be both economical and wise if it is used carefully and with common sense. For example, the purchase of furniture on the installment plan would be justifiable if the payments could fit into the spending plan. Using the installment plan to buy good furniture is better than spending all available funds to buy cheap furniture that will soon wear out and have to be replaced. An auto mechanic would be justified in buying a good set of tools on the installment plan. Another example of using installment buying wisely is taking advantage of sales on needed merchandise. For example, a washer and dryer normally selling for $500 are on sale for $400 (20 percent off). If the finance charge on the installment contract is $72 (18 percent), $28 can be saved even when buying on credit ($100 − $72 = $28).

Often a family's income is committed to such an extent that additional payments on installment purchases are neither possible nor wise. For example, let us assume that the monthly income of a family is $1,500 and that the family's monthly expenses are $675, not including housing. Further, assume the payments on a mortgage, taxes, and insurance on the house in which the family lives are $575 a month; on an automobile, $180 a month; and on a refrigerator, $50 a month. This is a total of $1,480 of each month's income that is committed. Under these conditions, to purchase a television set on an installment plan would be very unwise. Both the seller and the buyer of merchandise should consider the advisability of the buyer contracting an installment debt.

Before Buying on the Installment Plan. Before buying an article on the installment plan, it is wise to consider the following alternatives:

1. buying from another seller who offers better terms,
2. paying cash from savings or waiting until one has saved enough money,
3. borrowing from a bank or another lending agency and paying cash, and/or
4. borrowing on a life insurance policy and paying cash.

Finance Charges for Installment Credit. When goods are sold on an installment plan, the seller or the one financing the

GUIDES TO FOLLOW WHEN MAKING AN INSTALLMENT PURCHASE

1. Make as large a down payment as possible.
2. Pay the balance as quickly as possible.
3. Buy only durable goods that will be of value long after the final payment.
4. Plan your income and your expenditures to be sure that you can pay all debts.
5. Don't use the full extent of your installment credit. Leave a safety margin for unforeseen expenses and possible reductions in income.
6. Consider before you buy whether it is more profitable or desirable to save your money and wait until you can pay cash.
7. Check other ways to get what you want which may be cheaper.
8. When possible, wait for sales to buy goods on installment, thus saving principal and interest.

sale incurs costs that would not arise with cash or charge sales. The expenses of checking the credit rating of the buyer, making the loan, collecting, bookkeeping, insurance, repossessing, reselling, and general office expenses must be covered. This is done either by increasing the selling price or by adding separate charges.

In an installment sale, the total due is paid in regular installments over a period of time. The finance charge or carrying charge is generally included as a part of the amount due. In some instances the charges are listed separately, such as charge for credit investigation, credit life insurance, service charge, and interest. The total *finance charge* is often confused with interest, but it is legally very different. Although the finance charge includes interest on the money loaned to the consumer, it also includes other costs such as those already mentioned. In some states maximum finance charges are regulated, but in many states they are not. The charges vary for different kinds of goods and among the firms that sell on the installment plan.

The Truth in Lending Act requires creditors to state the finance charges in terms of both a monthly and an annual percentage rate on all installment and noninstallment (single-payment contracts) credit. For example, the creditor must show that 1.5 percent a month is charged, which is equal to an annual percentage rate of 18 percent. The creditor is not required by law, however, to indicate what portion of the finance charge is interest and what portion of it is bookkeeping expense or credit investigation expense. Table 14–1 shows typical finance charges for purchasing new automobiles on the installment plan.

Table 14–1

Finance Charges on New Car Loans

Amount Financed	Length of Contract	Total Finance Charges (14%)	Total Amount of Loan	Monthly Payment
$1,000	12 months	$ 140	$1,140	$ 95.00
1,500	12 months	210	1,710	142.50
2,000	18 months	420	2,420	134.44
2,500	24 months	700	3,200	133.33
3,500	36 months	1,470	4,970	138.05
4,500	48 months	2,520	7,020	146.25

In some cases the finance or carrying charges may seem to be unduly high, yet in most instances they are reasonable when the extra costs of making and collecting installment loans are considered. When dealing with a reputable business firm, finance company, or bank, there is not so much a question of whether the cost of buying on an installment plan is fair or unfair. Rather, there is sometimes a question of whether the merchandise is needed enough to justify paying the finance or carrying charges.

Credit Life Insurance. *Credit life insurance* is also called *consumer-credit insurance*. This kind of insurance is short-term insurance on the life of the buyer. Under the terms of the purchase contract and the life insurance policy, the money from the insurance will pay off any remaining debt in case of the buyer's death.

Usually credit life insurance is rather expensive. Any reliable insurance agent can tell you what you should pay for this kind of insurance. Sometimes the cost of the insurance is included in the total cost of the installment purchase. If it is not shown as a separate item, the buyer has a right (under the Truth in Lending Act) to know how much of the finance charge is for credit life insurance. Some dealers make credit life insurance optional; many do not.

WARNINGS ON INSTALLMENT BUYING

1. Do not allow yourself to be rushed into signing a contract until you know all the facts.
2. Refuse to sign any contract if you are not given an exact duplicate copy.
3. Do not sign any contract before all the blanks are filled in.
4. Do not pledge any security other than the article being purchased.
5. Pay only what is shown on the contract.

Using Installment Credit Wisely

When making wise use of installment credit, there is more to consider than simply comparing quoted percentage rates. The length of time the installment contract is to run and the *deferred payment price* (total of the cash price or principal plus the finance charge) of the merchandise must also be considered. For example, assume you were going to buy a black and white television set for $125 on the installment plan. Store A offers to finance the set for 6 months at an 18 percent annual rate. Store B offers to finance the set for 12 months at an annual rate of only 15 percent. In comparing annual percentage rates alone, it would appear that you would pay less in finance charges at Store B. In reality, you pay less at Store A even though the annual percentage rate is 3 points higher.

	Store A	Store B
Amount financed	$125	$125
Length of time financed	6 mos.	12 mos.
Annual percentage rate	18%	15%
Dollar finance charge	$ 11.25	$ 18.75
Deferred payment price	$136.25	$143.75

Assume that Store C offers to sell you a television set for $125 financed for 1 year at an annual rate of 18 percent. Store D offers to sell you the same model television set for $135 financed for 1 year at an annual rate of only 15 percent. Even though the finance charge is less and the annual percentage rate is lower at Store D, the deferred payment price (total of the cash price plus the finance charge) is $7.75 higher ($155.25 − $147.50) than at Store C.

	Store C	Store D
Amount financed	$125	$135
Length of time financed	12 mos.	12 mos.
Annual percentage rate	18%	15%
Dollar finance charge	$ 22.50	$ 20.25
Deferred payment price	$147.50	$155.25

When shopping for credit, the wise consumer considers the length of time the installment contract is to run and the deferred payment price as well as the annual percentage rate.

PRINCIPLES OF INSTALLMENT BUYING EVERYONE SHOULD KNOW

1. Installment buying really means borrowing money.
2. A chattel mortgage, conditional sales contract, or bailment lease contract provides security for the seller.
3. Installment selling involves extra costs that must be paid by the buyer.
4. The finance or carrying charge is the difference between the cash price and the total cost paid under an installment contract.
5. Deferred payment price is the best single standard for comparing finance charges among creditors and retailers.
6. Buying on an installment plan costs more than buying on a regular charge account or paying cash.
7. An installment buyer should fully understand the provisions of a contract before buying.

VOCABULARY BUILDER

bailment lease
chattel mortgage
conditional sales contract
credit life insurance

holder in due course
Rule of 78s
sales finance company
discounting

REVIEW QUESTIONS

1. How does buying on the installment plan differ from buying through a charge account?
2. How is the seller protected under each type of installment contract?
3. What are the common elements in all installment contracts?
4. What are some things you should check before entering into an installment contract?
5. Under a secured credit sale, what rights do the buyer and the seller have?
6. In what type of situation might buying furniture on the installment plan result in a savings?
7. Before you buy on the installment plan, what are some alternatives to consider?
8. What costs other than interest costs are often included in finance charges?
9. Under the Truth in Lending Act, what information about finance charges must a creditor give a debtor?
10. What two important things, other than the annual percentage rate of finance charges, does the wise consumer consider when shopping for credit?

DISCUSSION QUESTIONS

1. How important is installment buying to our economy?
2. a. What do you think would happen to automobile sales if automobiles could no longer be purchased on the installment plan?
   b. What do you think would happen to automobile sales if dealers did not require any down payment?

3. How should purchases on the installment plan be worked into one's spending plan?

4. Why should you know if credit life insurance is a part of your installment contract?

5. Assume that you have made a purchase on the installment plan at a time when the store is very busy. The manager suggests that you merely sign the installment contract, and it will be filled out and a copy mailed to you later. Is this a good practice if you know the store manager well?

6. Why is the deferred payment price considered the best single standard for comparing finance charges among creditors?

15

Obtaining Personal Loans

At times, both individuals and families need to borrow money. Loans to meet personal and family needs are usually small. In many instances small loans or personal loans enable individuals and families to:

1. meet financial emergencies such as unexpected medical and hospital bills,
2. buy necessary household equipment,
3. make permanent additions and improvements to the home, and
4. do other things that cannot wait until the money could be saved.

Borrowing money to go to school falls in the personal loan category.

After studying this chapter, you will be able to:

1. explain when obtaining a personal loan is justified,
2. list the most desirable sources for personal loans, and
3. list a number of guides to follow when borrowing.

WHEN TO OBTAIN PERSONAL LOANS

In order for you to be able to borrow money, you must establish a good credit rating in ordinary buying. If you have a good credit rating, you can usually borrow the money you need when you need it.

Before borrowing, you should always consider how great your need for the goods or services you intend to buy really is. Under some circumstances, you may be exercising very good judgment when deciding to borrow money; under other conditions, it may be very unwise to borrow. The advantages and disadvantages of borrowing for a specific purpose should be carefully determined and analyzed as a basis for making your decisions.

Take the Miller family as an example. Their washer and dryer are ten years old and have been breaking down regularly. They saw an ad in the newspaper for a washer and dryer which normally cost $600 on sale for $500. This sale price represents a 16.66 percent ($100 ÷ $600) savings over the original cost of $600. Mrs. Miller can borrow $500 from her company's credit union for one year at 14 percent interest. Her monthly payments would be $47.50, which would make the total deferred payment price for the washer and dryer $570. Provided the Millers can afford the additional monthly payments of $47.50, borrowing in this instance makes good sense for the following reasons:

1. Costly repair bills are avoided.
2. Even with borrowing, the deferred payment price of the washer and dryer ($570) is less than the price before the sale ($600).
3. A washer and dryer are important household needs.

On the other hand, the Newtons decided to trade in their 1985 model car (valued at $6,000 and getting 25 miles per gallon) for a new 1988 model (listed at $8,000 and getting 30 miles per gallon). Their reason for trading was that the new model would give them better mileage and save them money. They drive their car an average of 14,000 miles a year. At $.95 a gallon for gas, their old car costs them $532 a year (14,000/25 × $.95) in gas; the new car would cost them only $443.33 in gasoline (14,000/30 × $.95), a savings of $88.67 ($532 − $443.33) a year. To buy the car, however, they would need to borrow $2,000 for one year at 14 percent, costing them $280 in interest or $191.33 ($280 − $88.67) more than they would save in gas. Their monthly payments would be $190 ($2,280 ÷ 12). In this instance borrowing does not make good sense for the following reasons:

1. The interest is more than three times as great as the savings in gas.

2. Their budget may not be able to handle an additional $190 in monthly fixed payments.
3. Their two-year-old car is still quite serviceable.
4. Depreciation is at its highest the first two years of the life of a car.

How to Shop for a Loan

You should shop for a loan with the same care that you would use in shopping for furniture or appliances for the home. The primary factors to be considered in shopping for a loan are:

1. reliability of the lender,
2. real cost of the loan to the borrower, and
3. special terms or conditions of the loan that affect the borrower.

The Truth in Lending Act requires lenders to give borrowers a written statement showing:

1. annual percentage rate (APR);
2. total finance charges;
3. starting date for payments;
4. the number of payments, their amounts, and their due dates;
5. the total of all payments;
6. penalties for default or late payment, or for paying off the loan early, and
7. the nature of any security held by the lender.

Types of Loans

Two types of loans are based on the methods of repayment. One type permits you to repay in a lump sum (single-payment loan). The other and more common type permits you to repay in regular installments (installment loan).

Two other types of loans are based on security. One type is an *unsecured loan*. In other words, you merely sign a contract, binding yourself to its terms. This is also known as a *signature loan*. Your character and honor are sufficient to enable you to obtain a loan. If you fail to abide by the contract, you can be sued for the amount due. The other type is a secured loan. A *secured loan* means that you have to pledge or turn over to the lender some kind of property called *collateral* (bonds, stocks, rights to proceeds from an insurance policy, or personal property such as an automobile, furniture, or livestock). Such

Illus. 15-1
A secured loan means that you have to pledge or turn over to the lender
some kind of property called collateral.

items serve as security for the loan. The lender has a claim
against this property until you repay the loan. If you fail to
repay the loan, the lender can keep the property or sell it to
satisfy the claim against you.

Another type of protection that a lender sometimes
requires is the signature of an additional person. That person
becomes jointly responsible with you and promises to pay if
you fail to do so. This person is called a *cosigner* or a
comaker. Studies have shown that a large percentage of
cosigners end up having to pay the balance of the loans. Thus,
one should be most cautious in cosigning a loan for another
person. Figure 15–1 shows a loan agreement signed by comak-
ers.

When you borrow money, you are usually required to give
the lender a written promise to repay the money at a specified
time. The written promise is sometimes in the form of a promissory note, although it may be a letter containing the details
or a special contract form.

Figure 15–1
A Personal Loan Agreement (Secured Installment-Loan Agreement)

Installment-Loan Contract

PURPOSE *Personal use*

THE FIFTH THIRD BANK   No. *1531*

$ *600.00*   CINCINNATI, OHIO *January 5*   19 *—*

12 months after date, for value received, the undersigned promise(s) to pay to the order of The Fifth Third Bank (hereinafter called the "Bank"), the sum of *Six Hundred* ___ Dollars, in *11* consecutive monthly installments of $ *56.00* each, commencing *Feb. 5*, 19 *—*, and on even date of each succeeding month, and a final installment of $ *56.00* on *Jan. 5*, 19 *—*, with interest from maturity at maximum legal rate in State of execution, until paid.

Upon failure to pay any installment as herein agreed, or in the event of the death, insolvency, bankruptcy, or failure in business of any of the undersigned, all unpaid installments under this Note shall, at the option of Bank, become immediately due and payable, without demand or notice (after calculation of the Pre-payment Rebate as per item 7, below). Further, if any monthly installment stipulated herein is not paid on or before ten days after the due date thereof, in addition to all other rights and remedies of Bank given by law or the terms of this Note, the undersigned promise(s) to pay to Bank a sum calculated at the rate of 5¢ for each dollar of such defaulted installment; but in no event shall the delinquent charge of any such defaulted installment exceed $3.00. Acceptance of such delinquent charge by Bank shall not constitute a waiver of any default or any rights of Bank hereunder.

(ADDITIONAL TRUTH IN LENDING ACT DISCLOSURES)

1. **Proceeds of Loan** $ *600.00*
2. **Other Charges:**
    †a. Credit Life Insurance $ *—*
    ††b. Credit Accident & Health Ins. $ *—*
    c. Official Fees $ *—*
    d. Other ___ $ *—*
    Total Other Charges $ *—*
3. **Amount Financed** (1 + 2) $ *600.00*
4. **FINANCE CHARGE*** $ *72.00*
5. **Total of Payments** (3 + 4) $ *672.00*
6. **ANNUAL PERCENTAGE RATE**   *22.15* %

*FINANCE CHARGE includes interest and group credit life insurance premiums paid by Bank for its benefit if purpose of loan is for Home Improvement or unsecured personal use.

7. **PREPAYMENT REBATE:** Borrower may prepay the obligation under this Note in full at any time prior to maturity and receive a refund credit computed in accordance with the Rule of 78's. Such rebate will be computed after first deducting from the Finance Charge an acquisition charge in the amount of $10.00.

OPTIONAL INSURANCE
Borrower authorizes Bank to obtain for Borrower only the following insurance coverages to remain in effect during the entire term of this loan.

†2a. **Credit Life Insurance** on the life of Borrower provided by ___

in accordance with the separate Application, Notice, Certificate and Policy being issued herewith.

††2b. **Credit Accident and Health Insurance for Borrower** provided by ___

in accordance with the separate Application, Notice, Certificate and Policy being issued herewith.

NOTICE TO BORROWER: You are not required to obtain Credit Life and/or Credit Accident and Health Insurance, and such is not a factor in Bank's extension of this credit. ACKNOWLEDGING the foregoing, Borrower requests and authorizes Bank to obtain each insurance coverage set forth above.

Borrower's Signature ▶ ___

Date ___

8. **AGREEMENT NOT TO ENCUMBER OR TRANSFER PROPERTY:** As an inducement to the making of this loan, Borrower will execute an agreement whereunder Borrower agrees to pay all taxes and assessments levied against the real property located at ___ and agrees not to transfer or assign any interest of Borrower therein, and agrees to not permit any lien or other encumbrance to be placed against said real estate, without the consent in writing of Bank. Said agreement further provides that, upon breach of any of these covenants, the payments due under this Note may be accelerated, whereby the entire remaining unpaid balance of the principal, and interest earned to the time of acceleration (after calculation of Prepayment Rebate), would be immediately due and payable.

9. **SECURITY INTEREST:** As collateral security for the payment of this and any and every liability and liabilities of the undersigned to Bank, however created, direct or contingent, due or to become due, now existing, and whether the same may have been or shall be participated in, in whole or part by others by trust agreement or otherwise, or in any manner acquired by or accruing to Bank, whether by agreement with the undersigned or by endorsement to Bank by anyone whomsoever, the undersigned do hereby assign to and pledge with said Bank the following property, to wit ___

in which property Bank has been granted a security interest by ☐ Security Agreement ☐ Pledge Agreement (check one if applicable), executed by the under-signed on even date herewith, default under the terms of which could result in default under this Note.
The others of the undersigned jointly and severally agree to make each of the said installments promptly if the said Borrower should default in making the same. The undersigned hereby severally waive presentment, demand for payment, protest, notice of protest and notice of nonpayment of this Note.

BORROWER ACKNOWLEDGES RECEIPT OF A COMPLETED COPY OF THIS NOTE AND THE ABOVE INFORMATION AT THE TIME OF SIGNING

ADDRESSES (GIVE COMPLETE ADDRESS)
1516 Baker Street, Cincinnati, O.
2819 Fenway Drive, Norwood, Ohio
5027 Monroe Avenue, Cincinnati, O.

SIGNATURES (WRITE IN FULL AND IN INK)
James C. Higgins   BORROWER
Emma Washburn   CO-MAKER
C. F. Angelo   CO-MAKER

A *promissory note* is an unconditional written promise to pay a certain sum of money at a certain time. The note is usually made payable to a person or to a business. The one who signs a promissory note is the *maker* or *borrower*. The person to whom the note is payable is the *payee*. Figure 15–2 is an example of a promissory note.

Figure 15–2

A Promissory Note (Unsecured, Single-Payment Agreement)

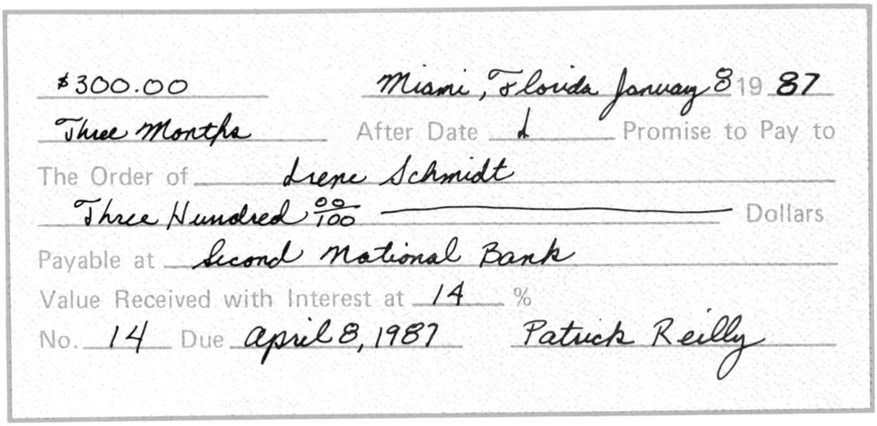

Charges for Loans

Many borrowers wonder why higher interest is charged on small personal loans than on large loans. Let us take the case of a loan of $300 to a person who applies to a lending agency for the first time. Let us also assume that the interest on a loan of this size, to be paid in 12 monthly installments, would be $54 (18 percent). The lending agency must investigate the applicant, close the loan, keep records, collect the money, allow for a percentage of loss on loans never repaid, and earn something on the investment. When one takes these expenses into consideration, it can be seen why rates are higher on small loans than on large loans. With the same amount of effort, the bank might handle a $5,000 auto loan or even a $50,000 mortgage.

WHERE TO OBTAIN PERSONAL LOANS

Personal loans may be obtained from a variety of sources. When in need of a personal loan, you should explore and compare these sources to get a loan that meets your needs at a competitive price. Table 15–1 lists holders of consumer installment credit and the amounts outstanding with each.

Borrowing from Banks

Many of the small loans obtained by consumers come from commercial and savings banks (discussed in Chapter 11).

Table 15–1

Consumer Installment Credit Outstanding
(in Billions of Dollars)

Holder	Credit Outstanding	Percent of Total
Commercial banks	236.4	46.1
Finance companies	110.4	21.5
Credit unions	76.3	14.9
Savings and loans	38.5	7.5
Retailers	37.4	7.3
Mutual savings banks	9.5	1.9
Gasoline companies	4.4	.9
Total	512.9	100.0

Source: Adapted from *Federal Reserve Bulletin* 71, no. 12 (December 1985).

Banks are one of the chief sources of personal loans. Commercial banks are especially active in this field. Banks make personal loans in four ways:

1. Single payment loans for which the borrower signs a promissory note
2. Installment loans for which the borrower signs a personal loan agreement
3. Credit card loans based on credit cards issued to customers by the bank
4. Revolving loans based on a special checking account

With a single payment loan, the lender will ask the borrower to sign a promissory note. At the close of the loan period (often 60 or 90 days), the borrower repays the full amount borrowed plus the interest.

When a borrower gets an installment loan, the loan is repaid in a series of installments, usually monthly. The amount of each installment includes both principal (amount borrowed) and interest.

Various types of credit card loans are available from commercial banks. The bank issues a credit card, which the consumer can use at participating businesses. The businesses send all bills to the bank, which in turn sends the customer one bill for total monthly purchases. Examples of such bank credit cards are VISA® and MasterCard®. Some bank credit cards

Illus. 15–2

Commercial banks are especially active in the field of making small personal loans.

can be used to obtain instant loans up to a limited amount at the bank.

Many commercial banks have established a somewhat permanent borrowing plan called a *revolving loan*. The plan works like this: You apply to the bank for a revolving loan. If you have a steady income and a good credit rating, you will be granted a revolving loan of a certain amount. A checking account will be opened for you. You will not be charged any interest on the loan until you write checks on the account. Interest is usually charged at 1.5 percent a month on the outstanding average account balance plus a charge for each check. Under this revolving loan plan you will be required to repay the loan, including the interest and the check service charge, in monthly installments. However, you may continue to borrow (by writing checks) so long as you don't borrow over the agreed upon line of credit.

Borrowing from Savings and Loan Associations

Savings and loan associations, sometimes called building and loan associations, cooperative banks, building associations, homestead associations, or savings associations, make both home and business loans. They also make small personal loans up to 100 percent of a depositor's savings account. Interest rates on large personal loans (up to $10,000), home mortgage loans (up to $100,000), and home improvement loans (up to $35,000) are comparable to commercial bank rates.

Borrowing from Life Insurance Companies

Many life insurance policies build up a cash value. A policyholder may borrow from the insurance company up to the cash or loan value of the policy. A table of loan values at the end of each year is shown in most policies. In some states, insurance companies may require 90 to 180 days' advance notice before making a loan on a policy.

Relatively low interest rates are often charged borrowers because they are actually borrowing their own money. No credit investigation is required; therefore, no fee. The insurance company has no control over how the money is used by the borrower. The loan may be for a short or long period, and one does not need to repay the loan at all if one does not choose to do so. If interest is not paid, it will be added to the amount of the loan. If death occurs before the loan is repaid, the amount of the loan plus accumulated interest will be deducted from the face value of the policy.

When one borrows on life insurance, the insurance protection is reduced by the amount of the loan because the loan is deducted before the amount of the insurance is paid. It is rather easy to borrow on life insurance, and the insurance companies usually do not try to seek repayment of the loan. Because of these facts one may be slow to make repayments and, therefore, not have adequate insurance when it is needed.

Borrowing from Consumer Finance Companies

Consumer finance companies are small-loan companies that lend primarily to persons of moderate means who may not have established a credit rating. They also lend to those who may not have security as collateral for loans from other sources. These companies are legitimate institutions and fill an important place in our economic system. The licensed consumer finance company should not be confused with loan sharks (unlicensed lenders), discussed later in the chapter.

About 70 percent of the loans made by consumer finance companies are covered by a security agreement or by a comaker. The rest are made on the borrower's signature only. Loans are usually made for a period of one to three years.

Consumer finance companies frequently make a smaller loan than a bank, and they frequently accept applications that banks might refuse.

Most states have laws governing the operation of consumer finance companies. Some states permit maximum loans of only $300. However, other states allow consumer finance companies to lend up to $10,000 for unsecured loans and up to $50,000 for secured loans. Consumer finance companies must have a license if they operate in states where there are laws governing this kind of institution. In most of the states the laws are modeled after the Uniform Small-Loan Law and the Model Consumer Finance Act.

Interest rates are often two to three times higher than bank rates. You should consult the small-loan law in your state before you borrow to learn what the maximum rate of interest and the amount of the loan may be.

Borrowing from Credit Unions

A credit union is a cooperative organization of people who agree to pool their savings and to make loans available to members at relatively low interest rates. The members of a credit union are people who work for the same employer, are members of the same church, labor union, or fraternal order, or live in the same community. As of 1985 there were 19,500 credit unions and over 52 million members in the United States. They are chartered under either federal or state laws.

Interest rates on loans are low because many small credit unions have little or no expense for rent, salaries, credit investigations, or collections. Credit unions organized under federal law are exempt from federal income taxes. A credit committee makes all credit investigations, and losses from bad debts (loans which debtors fail to repay) are usually low.

Members pay a small entrance fee and buy one or more shares, which usually sell for $5 to $25 each. The members set policy and hire managers to operate the credit unions. Each member has one vote, regardless of the number of shares he or she owns. *Dividends* (the part of the profit that each shareholder receives) are paid to savers. In many credit unions, partial interest rebates (a return of a part of the interest paid on the loan) are paid to borrowers. For example, assume that Ted Jones had borrowed $1,000 for one year at an annual percentage rate of 15 percent. Mr. Jones paid a total of $150 in interest. At the end of the year the board of directors decided to return to borrowers 5 percent of the interest paid during the year. In this case Ted Jones would have received a rebate of $7.50 ($150 × 5 percent = $7.50).

Loans are made to members only. The maximum amount for loans may be determined by the board of directors provided it does not exceed $2,500 for unsecured loans from credit unions organized under federal law. Although more than half of the loans are not secured, comakers sometimes sign the notes with the borrower; and occasionally a chattel mortgage is signed by the borrower to get the loan.

Borrowing from Pawnbrokers

The rate of interest charged on loans obtained from pawnbrokers is often extremely high. To get a loan from a pawnbroker, one must turn over personal property, such as jewelry or tools, as a pledge or *pawn*. The maximum amount of the loan is usually extremely low in proportion to the value of the property; it is seldom more than 50 percent of the appraised value. Loans from pawnbrokers must be paid in full before pledged property will be returned.

Illus. 15–3

To get a loan from a pawnbroker, one must turn over personal property, such as jewelry or tools, as a pledge or pawn.

States allow pawnbrokers to charge high interest rates. Since banks and small loan companies do not accept personal property as collateral, some people with poor credit ratings have no other source for borrowing small amounts of money. Since these people are such poor credit risks and the pawned property could not be sold by a pawnbroker for anything near its true value, pawnbrokers are allowed to charge high rates. In most states the highest legal rate pawnbrokers may charge is 100 percent.

In some states, if the loan is not paid by a stated time or within the length of time provided by state law, the property pawned may be sold. If there is a surplus from the sale, it is supposed to be given to the borrower. In other states, if the property pawned is not redeemed by a stated time, title passes to the pawnbroker.

GUIDES FOR BORROWING

1. Borrow from a licensed company that is under state supervision.
2. Borrow no more than is necessary.
3. Borrow no more than you can repay according to your agreement.
4. Understand your obligations and the obligations of the lender.
5. Understand the amount of the loan, the cost of the loan, and the specific details about repayment.
6. Read the contract carefully before you sign it.
7. Get credit for every payment and receive a canceled contract when you have completed the payments.

Borrowing from Unlicensed Lenders

There are still some states that do not have any small-loan laws. In these states unlicensed lenders, commonly known as *loan sharks*, are sometimes sources of loans for many persons with low incomes who are unable to get loans elsewhere. Unlicensed lenders also operate in states that do have regulatory laws. Studies have shown that the lowest rate commonly charged by these illegal lenders is 120 percent a year. It is common for the rate to be 500 percent a year, and examples have been found of rates as high as 2,600 percent a year.

The rates alone are not the only evils. Some of these unscrupulous lenders never allow their clients to get out of debt. The borrower is sometimes required to pay the whole loan at one time or no payment will be accepted. The borrower is constantly in debt because he or she can never get enough money together to pay the whole loan.

FACTS EVERYONE SHOULD KNOW ABOUT LOANS

1. One's real need should be determined before borrowing money to purchase goods or services.
2. One should shop for a loan as carefully as one would for the purchase of an expensive good.
3. Most loans require security of some kind.
4. The range of costs for small loans is very great.

VOCABULARY BUILDER

bank discount	payee
collateral	promissory note
cosigner or comaker	secured loan
maker	unsecured loan

REVIEW QUESTIONS

1. When you need to obtain a loan, what should you take into consideration?
2. When it is necessary to get a small loan, what are the factors that one should consider in selecting a place to borrow money?
3. Why is the interest rate on a small bank loan of $300 made to an individual higher than the rate on a bank loan of $10,000?

4. In what four ways do banks make loans?
5. What is the major disadvantage of borrowing on a life insurance policy?
6. Who usually borrows from consumer finance companies?
7. Why are interest rates on loans from credit unions often lower than rates from other lending institutions?

DISCUSSION QUESTIONS

1. Cite two or three examples of when you would be justified in applying for a loan.
2. Your friend asks you to cosign a note for him so that he can obtain a loan at a bank. You do so. What is your obligation?
3. Why is it recommended that you shop for a loan as carefully as you shop for expensive goods?
4. When might it be advisable to borrow from the cash value of one's life insurance policy?
5. Dr. Franklin, a highly respected citizen, felt insulted when she applied for a loan at a bank and was asked for considerable information on her assets, debts, and income. She believed that the bank had no right to this confidential information. What is your opinion?

PART 4

Special Activities

CLASS PROJECTS

1. Assume that your billing date for a charge account is the 25th of each month and that you have 25 days from the billing date to pay the entire bill without incurring a finance charge. Also assume that on April 28 you made a charge purchase of $500.
   a. By what date must you pay the $500 charge without incurring a finance charge?
   b. How many days of free credit did you receive with this $500 charge purchase?
   c. Assume you had borrowed $500 from a bank at 18 percent for the same number of days as the free days of credit you received. What would you have paid in interest charges?
2. Luis Camargo buys clothes for $100 on a revolving credit plan. The store requires him to make payments of $20 a month. It charges 1.5 percent interest on the unpaid balance at the beginning of each month, and it calculates this credit charge before deducting each payment. To determine the cost of this revolving credit, prepare a table

using the following headings. The first month's calculation is given as an example. The fifth and final payment will be the amount of the beginning balance plus the finance charge.

Payment No.	Balance at Beginning of Month	Finance Charge 1.5%	Balance Plus Finance Charge	Amount of Monthly Payment	New Balance
1	$100.00	$1.50	$101.50	$20.00	$81.50
2					

3. Bobbi Lehman is considering the purchase of a sewing machine on the installment plan. From a local store, she obtains the following information about the model she wants:

Cash price	$180.00
Sales tax	10.80
Down payment required	20.00
Credit life insurance	2.00
Finance charge (18% annual rate)	31.10
Monthly payments:	
11 at	17.00
12th	16.90

a. What is the total amount financed?
b. What is the total amount paid in installments?
c. What is the deferred payment price?
d. How much more would it cost to buy on the installment plan than to pay cash in full when purchased?

4. Al Hochgesang purchased a stereo sound system for his automobile. The system cost $280. After a down payment of $30, Al agreed to pay the balance in 12 equal installments with interest at 12 percent a year. Apply the Rule of 78s and answer the following questions:
a. What does the interest for 12 months amount to?
b. How much interest is Al charged if he prepays his installment contract at the eighth month?
c. How much interest did Al save by prepaying his contract?

5. The Kim Wong family has a monthly take home pay of
    $1,500. Their variable living expenses (food, clothing, utili-
    ties, personal items, entertainment) are budgeted at $525.
    Their monthly fixed expenses are $450 for a mortgage
    including taxes and insurance, $225 automobile payment,
    $50 for a U.S. savings bond, $50 for payment on a washer
    and dryer, and insurance premiums of $40. They would
    like to remodel their kitchen which has been estimated to
    cost $4,000. The Wongs would need to secure a second
    mortgage for 5 years at 12.5 percent interest. Can the
    Wong family's budget handle this added fixed cost
    monthly? Support your answer with calculations.

COMMUNITY PROJECTS

1. Assume that you lost your or your parents' MasterCard®
    or VISA® credit card. Inquire of an employee of a local
    bank that issues either of these cards to find out to what
    extent you are responsible for charges made to the card by
    the finder.
2. Make a survey in your community of stores honoring
    credit cards to see how many of them will give a cash dis-
    count to cash customers. Report your findings to the class.
3. Obtain an installment contract form from two or three
    retail stores in your community. Compare these forms
    with the sample form on page 243 to see what differences
    exist. Check to see if the forms include such items as
    security agreement, option for credit life insurance,
    method of payment, amount of each installment, deferred
    payment price, annual percentage rate, right of prepay-
    ment, and conditions of prepayment.
4. Investigate a number of retailers (car dealers, mobile home
    dealers, furniture and appliance dealers) in your commu-
    nity to see what their policies are regarding the percentage
    of the total price in the form of a down payment required
    on installment purchases of their goods and the typical
    length of time to finance the purchases. Report your find-
    ings to the class.

5. Investigate the cost of borrowing $1,000 for one year from the following sources (if available in your community):
   a. Local bank
   b. Savings and loan association
   c. Consumer finance company
   d. Credit union
   Present your findings and conclusions to your class.

PART 5
Transportation and Shelter

16

Owning a Car

The purchase of a car is usually one of the earliest large financial expenditures made by a young person. For this reason you should make sure you know how to get your money's worth when buying either a used or new car.

After studying this chapter, you will be able to:

1. name the expenses involved in owning a car,
2. define depreciation and explain how depreciation can be used to determine the optimum time to purchase a used car,
3. name sources of information which will aid consumers shopping for a new or used car,
4. explain the performance tests and inspection tests which should be used when shopping for a used car,
5. use the Used Car Buyers Guide when shopping for a used car,
6. explain alternative sources of new cars available to new car shoppers, and
7. use the appropriate resolution procedures if repair or warranty protection is unsatisfactory.

COSTS OF OWNING A CAR

For the young person with a new driver's license and money saved from summer jobs, the desire for a car can seem as important as eating. Many first-time car buyers think of automotive costs in terms of the initial price of the car and the price of gasoline and oil. A careful examination of the costs associated with car ownership shows that some costs occur whether or not the vehicle is driven, and other costs are directly related to the amount of travel. The first group of costs is generally referred to as ownership costs and the latter group as operating costs.

Ownership Costs

Ownership costs include depreciation, insurance, finance charges, registration and title fees, scheduled maintenance, accessory costs, and garage expenses. Ownership costs are likely to vary from one geographic location to another, but everyone faces the same type of expenses when owning a car.

Depreciation. *Depreciation* is the loss in value of a vehicle during the time it is owned due to:

1. passage of time,
2. a decline in the mechanical and physical condition of the vehicle, and
3. the number of miles the vehicle is driven.

Depreciation is the greatest single cost of owning a car. In the majority of cases, the age of a vehicle is more important than its mileage in determining the resale or trade-in value of a car. Such factors as brand popularity, body style, size, and color are also considered in determining value, but age and mileage are the major factors that influence resale value. For most cars, the greatest depreciation by far occurs in the first few years. As the vehicle gets older, the depreciation rate decreases. Generally cars depreciate 25 to 30 percent during the first year, 18 to 20 percent the second, 14 to 15 percent the third, 10 to 11 percent the fourth, 9 to 10 percent the fifth, 6 to 8 percent the sixth, and 2 to 6 percent the seventh.

Insurance Costs. Insurance costs are determined by the amount of coverage, the purpose for which the car is used, and the location in which it is operated. Automobiles are continuously exposed to the possibility of damage and theft. For more detailed information on automobile insurance, see Chapter 19.

Finance Charges. Car buyers either pay interest on money they borrow to buy their vehicles or they forego interest they would have earned if they have used savings to pay for the car. Lending institutions and car dealerships have numerous financing plans available to car buyers. These financing plans differ depending on the portion of the car cost being financed, the interest charged, and the length of the loan term. The cost of financing a car should be considered in calculating the cost of owning a car. Alternative methods of financing a new car can result in considerable savings, so different plans and lenders should be carefully compared before a particular financing plan is selected.

License, Title, and Sales Taxes. These items are payments to the state in which the car is registered. The license fee customarily is due each year, whereas the registration of title and sales tax is due only once when the car is purchased.

Other Costs. Other charges associated with owning a car are sometimes overlooked. These may include garage fees and dealer preparation and transportation charges for a new car. In some areas garage costs are high, whereas in other areas the costs are low or there is no cost.

Operating Costs

Operating costs include nonscheduled repairs and maintenance, gasoline, oil, tires, parking, and tolls. The more a car is used, the higher the operating costs.

Repairs and Maintenance. Numerous repairs and replacement of parts must be made during the life of a car. They include such items as wheel alignments and the replacement of tires, batteries, light bulbs, fan belts, brake linings, mufflers, spark plugs, etc. Although there are some people who service and repair their own cars, the public generally does not assume these tasks, so car owners must pay for the labor costs at dealer garages, independent garages, or service stations.

Gasoline and Oil. Gasoline is a major cost for vehicles of all sizes. The single largest factor in determining gasoline costs is the vehicle size. The difference in gasoline costs between a standard size car and a subcompact over a few years can be significant. Oil costs for a new or relatively new car are mainly

Illus. 16-1

Gasoline is a major cost for vehicles of all sizes. The single largest factor in determining gasoline costs is the vehicle size.

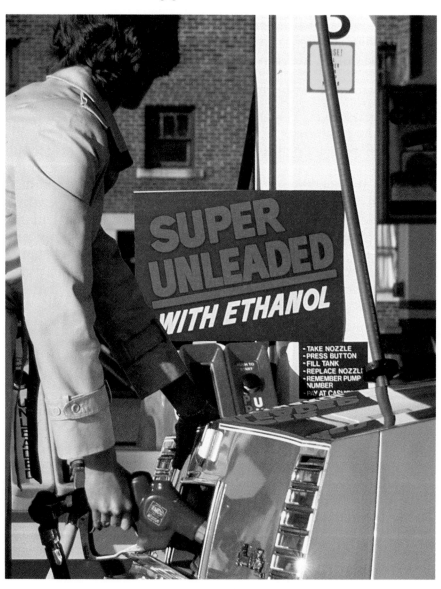

dependent on the manufacturer's instructions for oil changes. In the early years of a car, little, if any, oil is burned. Currently, many manufacturers recommend oil changes every 7,500 miles.

Tires. The average life of a tire ranges from 20,000 to 40,000 miles depending on the type of tire and the driving conditions. If the car is driven with reasonable care and the wheels are properly aligned, the wear can be kept to a minimum.

Parking and Tolls. Parking and tolls include metered curb parking, fees charged in parking lots, and toll charges for using private or public highways and bridges.

Holding Down Costs

According to U.S. Department of Transportation estimates, gasoline and oil costs, including taxes, account for approximately 26 percent of the total cost of owning an automobile throughout the life of the car. Substantial savings can be achieved by conserving fuel. Preventive maintenance procedures are recognized as essential in holding down operating costs. Keeping records on automobile expenses, particularly fuel consumption, is highly recommended. Any significant decrease in these figures could signify a need for an engine tune-up. Driving habits also are an important factor in costs, not only for fuel consumption but also for repairs, maintenance costs, and replacement of tires.

CHOOSING A CAR

The type of car you buy should be governed by your needs. The choice of an automobile depends on several considerations. For example, how much space do you need? Do you plan to use the car to transport goods, etc.? These and other requirements will determine whether you need a large or small car, a powerful motor or a smaller one.

Think carefully about the type of car you need before you start looking, and when you decide on your requirements, don't be side-tracked from your needs and price range. Remember that cars with greater horsepower, extra size and flashy styling cost more to purchase, operate, and insure.

Before Going to Car Lots

Every April, *Consumer Reports* publishes a comprehensive survey of its readers' experience with a wide variety of U.S. and foreign cars. This comprehensive guide concentrates on frequency of repairs and other problem areas. On such points as durability, reliability, and longevity, it pays to take into consideration the advice of the *Consumer Reports* testers.

Set a Price

Before you start looking for a car, decide on the amount of money you can spend and don't go over this figure. It is advisable to include such costs as taxes, registration, license, and insurance. If you are buying a used car, be prepared to spend a couple hundred dollars over the purchase price for repairs.

Optimum Time to Buy a Used Car

Generally, the best buy in a used car is one that is only two or three years old. The smart buyer can take advantage of a new car's rapid depreciation during the first two or three years of the life of a car. According to the "N.A.D.A. Official Used Car Price Guide," a new car loses approximately 50 percent of its value in the first two years. Assuming that the normal life of a car is seven years, after two years a buyer can get five-sevenths (70 percent) of the useful life of the car for approximately one-half (50 percent) of its original cost. Therefore, the best time to purchase a used car is when it is two or three years old.

BUYING A USED CAR

When young, first-time car buyers go shopping for a used car, their prime considerations are price, gas mileage, style, appearance, power, and the equipment they want on the car—though not necessarily in that order. Knowing where to buy, what to avoid, and how to inspect a used car can help a buyer get a good deal. Without knowing the right way to shop, used car buyers may find themselves saddled with cars that may be unsafe and require costly repairs to correct defects that could have been detected before they signed any papers.

Where to Shop

Should you buy from a private party? a new-car dealer who also sells used cars? a dealer of used cars only? a car rental agency? These are questions commonly asked by first-time car buyers.

New-Car Dealers. New-car dealers who sell used cars tend to charge more for used cars, but often they keep the best used-car trade-ins that come their way for their own used-car lot. New car dealers usually try to get rid of trade-ins in poor condition by selling them to wholesalers who, in turn, often sell these to used-car dealers. The new-car dealer who sells used cars has his reputation, and that of the manufacturer, on the line. In most cases, the dealer wants you back for repeat business.

Used-Car Dealers. Dealers who sell only used cars generally have less extensive service facilities or no service facilities at all, and their cars are often the less desirable trade-ins received by new-car dealers. When buying from a used-car dealer, find out how long the dealer has been in business at the same location. The longer the used-car dealer has been in business at the same location, the better your chances that a bad reputation has not forced the dealer to move.

Private Party Sales. If you know of a car that's had proper care from a friend or relative, and the price is right, it can be a good way to get a used car. You can also buy a good used car at a low price by watching the classified ads in the local newspaper and by buying from a private party. Private parties sell perfectly good used cars, but you should consider the possibility that if the car was running well the owner would be less likely to dispose of it. When buying from a private party, everything is up to you. Inspect it carefully; take it to your mechanic or a diagnostic station to have it inspected. Get a clear title to avoid getting stuck with a car that has been stolen or one that is about to be repossessed by a bank or finance company because the owner has not made the loan payments. When buying from a private party, there are no warranties and you have to do all the paperwork yourself, including payment of taxes, and the handling of title transfer and registration.

Car Rentals. Many car-rental agencies buy new cars every year and sell their older cars after using them for only a year.

You can often pick up a good used car from these car rental agencies. Although cars bought from rental agencies have accumulated a lot of mileage in a short time, most cars from such agencies have received better-than-average maintenance.

Inspecting the Car

According to car experts, you can tell the real condition and value of a used car by carefully examining important components of the car.

Outside the Car. Look carefully at the car's exterior. Check for new or refinished chrome or repainted parts. Any paint on the chrome or underside of the hood or trunk lid indicates repainting. This may indicate that the car has been in an accident. Inspect the car carefully for signs of rust damage. Vulnerable areas are around the bottom of doors, below rocker panels, and at the bottom of rear fenders. A small amount of rusting is normal, but press a rusted spot with your finger to determine the extent of the rust damage.

Illus. 16-2

According to car experts, you can tell the real condition and value of a used car by carefully examining important components of the car.

Press down hard on each corner of the car to determine the condition of the shock absorbers. A car should bounce upward once and then return to a level position. More bouncing means worn shock absorbers. Run your finger around the tailpipe. Black, gummy deposits could mean carburetor trouble or worn piston rings. Also, closely inspect all tires, including the spare in the trunk. Take a close look at tire tread. You can expect to see a certain amount of wear, but excessive wear in the center of the tire or on the edges can be a sign of wheels that are out of alignment.

Inside the Car. The car's interior can tell much about the care of the car. Look for signs of dampness or water stains on the carpet, floor, walls, and glove compartment. Such stains could indicate that the car has leaks or has been in a flood. Press the accelerator and brake pedals. Both should feel firm and spring right back. Turn the steering wheel to the right and left to determine the play (movement) in the steering wheel. More than two inches of play in either direction may indicate that the front end is misaligned and that steering components are loose. Power steering should be tested while driving the car.

Test every accessory including the radio, heater, windshield wipers, windshield washer, dome and dashboard lights. All accessories and lights should be checked for proper function. For this reason it is advisable to shop with a parent or friend to assist in checking for brake lights, turn signals, etc.

Examine the accelerator, brake pedal, and floor mats for signs of heavy use. If wear seems excessive, consider this a sign of long and/or hard use. New floor mats in an older car may be an indication that the seller is trying to hide something.

Check the Odometer. Federal law prohibits tampering with mileage figures, but there are still dealers who alter *odometers* (the device on a car that records the number of miles driven). In fact, odometer tampering is more prevalent than people think. The National Highway Traffic Safety Administration estimates that about three million of the eighteen million used cars sold each year have had their odometers rolled back an average of 30,000 miles. The 1972 Odometer Protection Law prohibits:

1. disconnecting or resetting the odometer with intent to change the mileage reading;

2. operating a vehicle with a nonfunctional odometer with intent to defraud;
3. advertising, selling, using, or installing a device which causes an odometer to register incorrectly;
4. knowingly falsifying the written odometer statement; and
5. removing the notice attached to the door frame at the time of odometer service. This provision is applicable only when an odometer is serviced, repaired, or replaced, and cannot be adjusted to reflect the true mileage.

Federal law requires that anyone selling a vehicle or transferring ownership in some other way must provide the buyer with a signed statement indicating the mileage registered on the odometer at the time of the transfer. The disclosure statement must contain the following information, and must be signed by the person transferring ownership to you:

1. odometer reading at time of transfer;
2. date of transfer;
3. seller's (transferer's) name, address, and signature;
4. make, body type, year, model, vehicle identification number (and last plate number of the vehicle if it had previously been titled and registered); and
5. if the seller has reason to believe that the mileage reading is incorrect, the disclosure statement must indicate that the actual mileage traveled is unknown.

Before purchasing a used car be sure to inspect the odometer disclosure statement and compare it with the mileage registered on the odometer.

Under the Hood. Under the hood you should check for frayed drive belts or cracks in hoses and other engine components. The rubber hoses should be firm, not brittle or leaking. Check the battery for cracks or posts and clamps that are heavily corroded. Check to make sure the oil is clean, and look for oil and lubrication stickers.

Road Test. Drive the car on an expressway, urban roads, and varying terrains. The steering should not have more than two inches of play. Loud noises from power steering might mean problems. Test brakes by making several sharp stops. The tires should not screech. The car should not pull to one side or the other. Check acceleration response. Look at the exhaust; blue or black exhaust indicates a worn engine.

Mechanical Inspection. The final step before purchasing a used car should be a mechanical inspection. Naturally, this inspection should be performed only on the used car which you are certain has met all the other inspection tests. For a nominal cost ($35 to $50), have a mechanic check the car's engine cylinder compression, brake and wheel bearings, rear axle and differential, the transmission, and exhaust system. Ask the mechanic to approximate the cost of repairing defects that turn up. You can use this estimate of repair costs as leverage to lower the price of the car.

Using the Buyers Guide

The Federal Trade Commission's Used-Car Rule requires auto dealers to complete and affix a Buyers Guide to the side window of all used vehicles, demonstrators, and company vehicles offered for sale. The Buyers Guide will state:

1. whether the vehicle comes with a warranty and, if so, what specific warranty protection the dealer will provide;
2. whether the vehicle comes with no warranty (as is) or with implied warranties only;
3. that you should ask to have the car inspected by your own mechanic before you buy;
4. that you should get all promises in writing; and
5. what some of the major problems that may occur in any car are.

The Buyers Guide gives the used-car buyer important warranty information. In the past, lack of information and misunderstanding about warranties frequently were a major source of consumer problems. Figure 16-1 on pages 270-271 is an example of a Buyers Guide.

As Is. About half of all used cars sold by dealers come without a warranty, or *as is*. In other words, if you have problems with the car after you buy it, you must pay for any needed repairs yourself. The dealer has no further responsibility for the car once the sale is completed and you drive off the lot.

Implied Warranty Only. Under most state laws, almost every purchase you make from a merchant is covered by an implied warranty, unless the seller tells you in writing that implied warranties do not apply. If a vehicle does not come with a written warranty, it is still covered by implied warranties unless the Buyers Guide is marked as is. Some states do not permit as is sales. In these states, dealers must sell their cars with implied warranties. Implied warranty coverage varies from state to state. If a state does not permit as is sales, or if the dealer offers a vehicle with only implied warranties, a disclosure entitled "Implied Warranties Only" will be printed on the Buyers Guide in place of the as is disclosure.

Full or Limited Warranty. If dealers offer a warranty on a used car, they must fill in the warranty portion of the Buyers Guide. A full warranty provides the following terms and conditions:

1. Warranty service will be provided to anyone who owns the vehicle during the warranty period.
2. Warranty service will be provided free of charge, including such costs as returning the vehicle or removing and reinstalling a system covered by the warranty, when necessary.
3. At your choice, the dealer will provide either a replacement or a full refund if the dealer is unable, after a reasonable number of tries, to repair the vehicle or a system covered by the warranty.
4. No limit is placed on the duration of the implied warranty.

If any of the above statements is not true, then the warranty is limited. A full or limited warranty need not cover the entire vehicle. The dealer may specify only certain systems for coverage under a warranty.

By giving a limited warranty, the dealer is telling you that there are some costs or responsibilities that the dealer will not assume as covered by the warranty. The warranty that the dealer offers may give you some idea of what the dealer thinks about the condition of the vehicle. Also check the percentage of the repair cost that the dealer will pay. The Buyers Guide provides the used-car buyer with valuable information and should be carefully considered when buying a used car.

Figure 16-1
Buyers Guide

BUYERS GUIDE

IMPORTANT: Spoken promises are difficult to enforce. Ask the dealer to put all promises in writing. Keep this form.

_____   _____   _____   _____
VEHICLE MAKE   MODEL   YEAR   VEH NUMBER

_____
DEALER STOCK NUMBER (Optional)

WARRANTIES FOR THIS VEHICLE: _____

☐ AS IS - NO WARRANTY

YOU WILL PAY ALL COSTS FOR ANY REPAIRS. The dealer assumes no responsibility for any repairs regardless of any oral statements about the vehicle.

☐ WARRANTY

☐ FULL ☐ LIMITED WARRANTY. The dealer will pay_____% of the labor and _____% of the parts for the covered systems that fail during the warranty period. Ask the dealer for a copy of the warranty document for a full explanation of warranty coverage, exclusions, and the dealer's repair obligations. Under state law, "implied warranties" may give you even more rights.

SYSTEMS COVERED: DURATION:

_____   _____
_____   _____
_____   _____
_____   _____
_____   _____
_____   _____
_____   _____
_____   _____

☐ SERVICE CONTRACT. A service contract is available at an extra charge on this vehicle. Ask for details as to coverage, deductible, price, and exclusions. If you buy a service contract within 90 days of the time of sale, state law "implied warranties" may give you additional rights.

PRE PURCHASE INSPECTION: ASK THE DEALER IF YOU MAY HAVE THIS VEHICLE INSPECTED BY YOUR MECHANIC EITHER ON OR OFF THE LOT.

SEE THE BACK OF THIS FORM for important additional information, including a list of some major defects that may occur in used motor vehicles.

☐ IMPLIED WARRANTIES ONLY

This means that the dealer does not make any specific promises to fix things that need repair when you buy the vehicle or after the time of sale. But, state law "implied warranties" may give you some rights to have the dealer take care of serious problems that were not apparent when you bought the vehicle.

Below is a list of some major defects that may occur in used motor vehicles.

Frame & Body
Frame-cracks, corrective welds, or rusted through
Dogtracks — bent or twisted frame

Engine
Oil leakage, excluding normal seepage
Cracked block or head
Belts missing or inoperable
Knocks or misses related to camshaft lifters and push rods
Abnormal exhaust discharge

Transmission & Drive Shaft
Improper fluid level of leakage, excluding normal seepage
Cracked or damaged case which is visible
Abnormal noise or vibration caused by faulty transmission or drive shaft
Improper shifting or functioning in any gear
Manual clutch slips or chatters

Differential
Improper fluid level or leakage excluding normal seepage
Cracked or damaged housing which is visible
Abnormal noise or vibration caused by faulty differential

Cooling System
Leakage including radiator
Improperly functioning water pump

Electrical System
Battery leakage
Improperly functioning alternator, generator, battery, or starter

Fuel System
Visible leakage

Inoperable Accessories
Gauges or warning devices
Air conditioner
Heater & Defroster

Brake System
Failure warning light broken
Pedal not firm under pressure (DOT spec)
Not enough pedal reserve (DOT spec)
Does not stop vehicle in straight line (DOT spec)
Hoses damaged
Drum or rotor too thin (Mfgr Specs)
Lining or pad thickness less than 1/32 inch
Power unit not operating or leaking
Structural or mechanical parts damaged

Steering System
Too much free play at steering wheel (DOT Specs)
Free play in linkage more than 1/4 inch
Steering gear binds or jams
Front wheels aligned improperly (DOT specs)
Power unit belts cracked or slipping
Power unit fluid level improper

Suspension System
Ball joint seals damaged
Structural parts bent or damaged
Stabilizer bar disconnected
Spring broken
Shock absorber mounting loose
Rubber bushings damaged or missing
Radius rod damaged or missing
Shock absorber leaking or functioning improperly

Tires
Tread depth less than 2/32 inch
Sizes mismatched
Visible damage

Wheels
Visible cracks, damage or repairs
Mounting bolts loose or missing

Exhaust System
Leakage

DEALER

ADDRESS

SEE FOR COMPLAINTS

IMPORTANT: The information on this form is part of any contract to buy this vehicle. Removal of this label before consumer purchase (except for purpose of test-driving) is a violation of federal law (16 C.F.R. 455).

Source: Federal Trade Commission, Bureau of Consumer Protection, *Facts for Consumers* (May 1985).

BUYING A NEW CAR

Millions of new cars are purchased in this country each year. Many people who buy new cars are happy with them and many are unhappy. Much of the difference between those who are satisfied and those who are not depends on the type of preparation and buying procedure followed by the new-car buyer.

Just Looking

Before going to a car dealership to see new cars, look at consumer magazines and automobile magazines. Both types of magazines are available in your public library. Consumer magazines, such as *Consumer Reports*, generally pay close attention to practical things like roominess, gas mileage, and road tests. Automobile magazines also report on performance, style, and road tests, but the consumer has to keep in mind that such magazines depend on auto industry advertising to keep them in business and some (not all) will find something nice to say about all cars. It pays to read both types of magazine to get the objective view of automotive experts and engineers.

Comparison shopping at various dealerships is a valuable practice when shopping for a new car. Some car-buying authorities suggest that the best deals can be made at highly competitive, high-volume dealerships. Other experts suggest that the small-volume dealers are in a position to make a better deal because of lower operating expenses, less advertising, and fewer salespeople. After you have determined the make and model car which you think you want, make a list of the dealerships that sell it. It often pays to compare price, reputation, service facilities, and convenience.

Auto Buying Services and Auto Brokers

Many individuals and families are eligible to buy new cars for prices that are only $100 to $250 above dealer's cost. *Auto-buying services* and *auto brokers* are alternative sources of new cars that can save the new-car buyer considerable amounts of money. Auto-buying services specialize in fleet or volume sales and sell cars to large companies. Some of these services allow car buyers to obtain from their employer a purchase certificate entitling the employee to order any car from

Illus. 16-3
Comparison shopping at various dealerships is a valuable practice when shopping for a new car.

the auto-buying service. Other companies limit the choice of cars to certain models and makes. In either case the buyer does not have to go through a salesperson at a dealership.

For persons who are not eligible for company auto-buying services, auto brokers like United Auto Brokers can order most domestic cars for $75 to $125 above cost. An auto broker can sell new cars directly to consumers at a low cost because dealership showrooms or salespeople are not involved. These brokers will ship the car to a cooperating dealer who works with them. An additional $75 courtesy delivery charge may be added to the cost if there is no cooperating dealer in your area.

Be Prepared to Bargain

The Federal Automobile Disclosure Act requires a price sticker to appear on every new car. The sticker price is not the amount you are expected to pay. You must be prepared to negotiate the price of the new car. Don't be afraid to drive a hard bargain. It's a competitive market and car dealers are eager to sell their cars. All dealers are different. Some are willing to make deals that others are not. In order to bargain, you must do your homework in advance. Most consumer magazines, such as *Consumer Reports* and *Edmund's New Car Prices*, provide dealer's cost information which makes it possible to know how much bargaining room there is. The *manufacturer's suggested retail list price* is the maximum price which manufacturers believe should be paid for the car. Most car dealers are independent business people who are prepared to negotiate the price.

Don't be confused by trade-in offers. Dealer A may have offered $2,500 for your trade-in on a $8,500 car. Dealer B may have offered you only $2,300 for your trade-in. But Dealer B has agreed to sell you the new car for $8,100. It may be obvious to you that Dealer B is offering a better deal. But many people jump at the highest trade-in offer they get. Remember, it is the price difference between the trade-in and the new car that really matters.

Shop for Credit

If it is necessary to finance a new car, it pays to shop around for credit as carefully as for the car. Many dealers offer their own financing, which is convenient but may also be more expensive. You will want to consider the following sources for financing a new car.

Dealers. New-car dealers generally offer credit arrangements to prospective buyers. The dealer may use the services of lending subsidiaries of the manufacturer, such as General Motors Acceptance Corporation, or may arrange financing through a local financial institution. The customer then makes payments to the financing agency.

Banks. Banks offer both installment and single-payment automobile loans. Most specialize in new-car loans with the car as security. If you have a dependable income, most banks will provide automobile loans at moderate rates of interest.

Credit Unions. Credit unions make installment loans to members for both new and used cars. Usually the car is pledged as security but the interest rates often are the lowest available to borrowers.

Consumer Finance Companies. Consumer finance companies make installment car loans, but at higher rates than are available from other sources. When financing a car, new or used, it pays to shop for the best price for the car and the lowest cost of financing.

After the Purchase

One of the common frustrations of new-car buyers occurs when new cars develop repeated repair and maintenance problems. For this reason it is important for the consumer to understand the appropriate procedures to follow when seeking redress.

Warranty Protection. A new-car warranty places certain obligations on you. If you do not do what is required of you, your dealer or manufacturer may refuse to honor the warranty. For this reason, read the warranty until you understand it. Most warranties cover only factory-authorized repairs, parts, and labor. Most dealers can quickly recognize a problem which requires new parts and labor. When the car is under warranty, a dealer may complete the repair and mark the bill "No Charge" without itemizing the repair or telling you what has been done. Always insist on itemized receipts for everything done to your car, whether under warranty or not. Keep the itemized receipt for as long as you own the car.

One of the common complaints of new-car owners is that the same repairs are needed again and again. After the warranty runs out, the owner may have to have repairs done at his expense. By keeping itemized receipts, you can avoid this problem by showing that you have evidence that you tried to have it fixed under warranty.

Manufacturer's Customer Relations. When new-car owners are not satisfied with repairs or have received inadequate warranty coverage, they should complain to the manufacturer. You should send your first letter to the manufacturer's zone or district representative. The address can usually be found in the owner's manual. The letter should provide all the details necessary to identify your car, when purchased, where bought, current mileage, whether or not under warranty, etc. Describe the problems involved, what has been done to correct the problem, and what course of action is required to resolve the problem. If there is not a satisfactory resolution to the problem, it may be necessary to write a similar letter to the manufacturer's customer relations office at the headquarters address. Most manufacturers have established procedures for complaint resolution.

Lemon Laws. In recent years a growing number of state laws, called *lemon laws*, have been passed to help new-car owners who cannot get a car fixed in a reasonable length of time. Lemon laws vary from state to state, but basically they establish the type of vehicle covered, define what a lemon is, set a period during which a vehicle is eligible for protection, and establish a procedure to resolve disputes.

Most states say a car is a *lemon* if within its first year, or 12,000 miles, the vehicle is hampered by a serious defect that an authorized facility has not been able to repair in four attempts, or if the vehicle has been out of service for 30 days. Lemon laws are not meant to provide a way of unloading a car you decide you do not like. Defects must be covered by the manufacturer's warranty and must substantially reduce the use, safety, and value of the vehicle. Also, the owner must continue to maintain the car as required in the warranty and owner's manual.

Illus. 16-4

In recent years a growing number of state laws, called lemon laws, have been passed to help new-car owners who cannot get a car fixed in a reasonable length of time.

Arbitration. If appeals to the manufacturer do not work and your car problem does not fall under lemon law protection, you can seek one of two types of arbitration available to most new-car buyers. *Auto Line* is a third party mediation service operated by Better Business Bureaus throughout the United States. This arbitration program succeeds in mediating disputes in about 90 percent of consumer complaints. Members of the arbitration panels are community volunteers, with the manufacturers picking up administrative expenses. Decisions reached by arbitration panels are usually binding on manufacturers but not on car owners, who are free to sue in court if they are dissatisfied with the results of arbitration.

The National Automobile Dealers Association sponsors *Autocap,* another dispute-settling program. Similar to *Auto Line*, this industry-sponsored complaint-handling program has been organized by state and local automobile dealers associations. Some of them settle disputes by using panels which have both consumer members and industry members; others use a single mediator or an industry committee.

FACTS EVERYONE SHOULD KNOW ABOUT OWNING A CAR

1. The costs associated with owning a car include both ownership and operating costs.
2. The optimum time to buy a used car is when the car is between two and three years old.
3. New-car dealers who sell used cars are often the most reliable source of used cars.
4. The final step in the selection of a used car should be a mechanical inspection by an impartial mechanic.
5. The FTC's Used Car Buyers Guide provides important warranty information.
6. New-car buyers can save money by comparison shopping and by using alternative sources of new cars such as auto-buying services and auto brokers.
7. Consumers who have problems with new cars can use several means of redress such as warranty protection, lemon laws, and arbitration.

VOCABULARY BUILDER

as is

depreciation

lemon laws

manufacturer's suggested
  retail list price

odometer

operating costs

ownership costs

REVIEW QUESTIONS

1. What are the two categories of costs associated with owning a car?
2. What is depreciation, and what factors cause a car to depreciate?
3. The cost of gasoline and oil account for approximately what percentage of the total lifetime cost of owning and operating a car?
4. Name the four primary sources of used cars.
5. How prevalent is the problem of odometer rollback for the used-car buyer?
6. State the major items of information provided by the Federal Trade Commission's Buyers Guide.
7. When buying a new car, what are some alternative sources of new cars available for consumers?
8. Which source of car financing usually offers the lowest interest rates?
9. When do lemon laws apply to new-car buyers?

DISCUSSION QUESTIONS

1. When buying a used car, what are some of the components of the car which should be inspected? Cite at least one item for inspection from inside the car, outside the car, under the hood, and on the road.
2. How can depreciation help the used-car buyer obtain a used car at the optimum time?
3. How can a used-car buyer benefit from using the FTC's Used Car Buyers Guide?
4. Does the state in which you live have lemon laws that apply to new car purchases? Describe the provisions of the lemon law in your state.

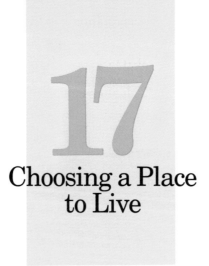

Choosing a Place to Live

Everyone must have housing. Many choices are available: one can buy a house, an apartment, or a mobile home; one can rent a house or an apartment; or one can build a house. Two big problems face the buyer, renter, or builder. First, he or she must decide what type of housing to buy, rent, or build. Second, a way must be found to pay for the housing. In this chapter we will look at problems relating to buying, renting, and building.

After studying this chapter, you should be able to:

1. list the advantages and disadvantages of owning a home,
2. state the direct and hidden costs of housing,
3. state the advantages and disadvantages of renting, and
4. list the rights and duties of both the owner and tenant when housing is rented or leased.

OWNING A HOME

Choosing adequate housing is one of the most important economic decisions an individual or a family must make. For many people, owning a home is the biggest expense of a lifetime. Simply deciding to buy a home is often one of the most significant choices a person or family can make.

Choosing adequate housing is one of the most important economic decisions an individual or family must make.

An individual or family should consider home ownership when:

1. payments can be made out of savings taken from current income,
2. the person or family expects to continue to live in the same area for three years or longer, and
3. more pleasure and satisfaction can be gained from owning than from renting.

When you own a home, you are responsible for its financing, repair, and maintenance. Usually these responsibilities provide individuals and family members with a sense of pride, enjoyment, and satisfaction.

Even though the thought of owning a home may appeal to you, it may not be economically desirable for you to buy or build. If a person expects to move to another location in a year or two, if property values are falling, if not enough money is available to make the down payment, or if there is any chance that the monthly payments cannot be made, buying would be unwise. All the costs of home ownership should be carefully figured and should then be included in a person's or family's spending plan. Table 17-1 presents advantages and disadvantages of owning a home.

Table 17-1
Advantages and Disadvantages of Owning a Home

Advantages of Owning a Home	Disadvantages of Owning a Home
Home ownership often gives a feeling of security and independence. Home ownership usually costs more than renting but provides a means of forced savings, that is, the money invested in the home. For many years, home ownership has proven to be a good investment because of the increase in value of property. The interest expense incurred in buying a home provides a tax benefit to the owner, whereas rental expenses do not.	The owner's investment in the home is not readily available for purchases. An owner must assume responsibility for financing, maintenance, and improvements; renters pay their rent and leave the other responsibilities to the owner. Home ownership makes moving from one community or city to another more difficult. Home ownership may require larger monthly payments (including expenses such as utilities and insurance) than renting.

HOME OWNERSHIP OPTIONS

Most young people do not have enough money to buy the home they would like. Home ownership requires careful planning. It is necessary to make certain choices to get the most satisfactory housing for the money that is available. A discussion of these choices follows.

Buying a New Home

Often a new home will cost more than an older home. In 1985, the average new home in the United States sold for approximately $85,000. The repairs for a new home usually cost less than those for an older home for many years. However, many people are unable to make large monthly payments in addition to the down payment required for a new home. For example, a monthly payment of $551.00 is necessary to *amortize* (pay off) a 12 percent loan of $50,000 over a 20-year period. Keep in mind that a substantial down payment (usually 10 to 20 percent of the purchase price) is generally required in order to get a loan.

When a new home is purchased, a buyer should also consider landscaping or any other general improvements that need to be made. These expenses are often larger than you would expect. Items such as landscaping, home modifications, furniture, draperies, and the like can greatly increase the cost of owning a home.

Buying an Older Home

An older home can frequently be bought at a lower price than a new home. In recent years, however, real estate prices have been increasing rapidly. In 1985, the average used home in the United States sold for nearly $75,000. But remember, location makes a big difference in the cost of a home. The median-priced older home in San Francisco cost $152,000, but in Pittsburgh, only $54,152.

Older homes frequently need repairs. The house may need a new roof, a new furnace, new plumbing, or electrical work. Sometimes an extra room must be added or existing rooms must be modified. These costs must be included in the buyer's spending plan.

Other costs that may seem unrelated to housing must also be considered. For example, most new homes are built some distance from a city; whereas older homes might be closer to places of employment. Therefore, transportation costs to and from work need to be considered.

The satisfaction that a person or family might receive from restoring an older home could be significant. A good deal of pleasure can be derived from fixing up an older house and fashioning it to your liking. Keep in mind, however, that many of your improvements are geared to your tastes and may not increase the cash value of the home if you decide to sell it.

Buying an Apartment

Some people want to combine the security of owning a home with the convenience of renting an apartment. The solution is to buy an apartment.

Cooperative Apartments. In many cities it is now possible to buy an apartment in a building that is shared by other individuals or families. Such an apartment is called a *cooperative apartment*. For example, a building may contain six apartments. Each apartment is owned by one person or family, but the whole apartment building is owned jointly or cooperatively by the six individuals or families. The six owners are jointly responsible for repairs, taxes, lawn care, security, and other expenses related to the entire building. When an individual or family buys an apartment, a contract is signed covering the buyer's portion of all the shared costs. The contract usually states that when one wishes to sell the apartment, approval of a majority of the other owners is needed.

Condominiums. An apartment that is owned separately instead of cooperatively is called a *condominium*. The owner pays a fee for central management and maintenance of the building and grounds. The owner of a condominium, unlike the owner of a cooperative apartment, owns only one unit and is responsible for taxes and repairs on that unit only. Also, the condominium owner can usually buy and sell the condominium without the consent of the other owners in the building or complex. The condominium owner is therefore more like a homeowner.

Buying a Mobile (Manufactured) Home

In recent years there has been a growing interest in manufactured homes among home buyers of all ages. Mobile homes provide moderately priced living quarters for people who need only a limited amount of space.

The mobile home owner must have land on which to park the mobile home or must rent space in a mobile home park and pay monthly rental fees. There are many attractive mobile home parks in convenient locations. Often these parks provide a foundation, water and electrical connections, central laundry facilities, and recreational facilities.

Many people rent mobile homes in established mobile home parks. This is especially true in recreational and retirement areas or in other places where temporary housing is required. The cost of renting a mobile home is frequently lower than the cost of renting an apartment or house. Table 17-2 presents advantages and disadvantages of mobile homes.

Table 17–2
Advantages and Disadvantages of Mobile Homes

Advantages of Mobile Homes	Disadvantages of Mobile Homes
Cost is usually much lower than that of other forms of housing Can be moved to other locations Upkeep costs are low Less housekeeping Less yard work	Zoning laws are strict on home location Living space is usually small Yard or lawn space is usually small Little storm protection is provided because of lightweight construction

Building Your Own Home

If you have the ability, you can save money by doing some of the construction of your home yourself; but generally it is better to hire a competent builder to do at least the main part of the work. If you intend to build a home and do not plan to do the work yourself, give some thought to the five ways to build a home recommended by the National Better Business Bureau.

FIVE WAYS TO BUILD A HOME

1. Engage the complete services of an architect.
2. Engage the limited services of an architect, using stock plans.
3. Engage a contractor or builder, using stock plans.
4. Buy stock plans and arrange with several contractors to complete different parts of construction.
5. Buy a modular (prefabricated) house and either hire a builder to erect it or do it yourself.

For a fee, an architect will draw up plans tailored to your needs. However, it is less costly to buy *stock plans* from a catalog and have the architect modify them to fit your needs. Also, as part of his or her service the architect can arrange for the best placement of the home on your lot, award all major

Illus. 17-2
If you have the ability, you can save money by doing some of the
construction yourself.

and sub-major contracts, and supervise the entire project. A
more common procedure is to engage a contractor or builder
to do the major construction. The contractor or builder will, in
turn, employ subcontractors for such items as plumbing, wiring, and brick work. If you are specially skilled, you might
want to serve as the general contractor yourself. In that case,
you work from either the architect's plans or stock plans and
arrange with several contractors to complete different parts of
the construction. This approach should only be used if you
have a great deal of experience in the construction business.
Generally, an experienced builder or contractor will save you
money in the long run.

When starting out, young people sometimes prefer to buy a
smaller, less expensive modular (prefabricated) home to avoid
the larger cost of owning a new home. When this approach is
used, the home is generally resold after some years, and the
money from the sale is used to purchase a more expensive
home. If you have the ability, you can sometimes do part of
the construction yourself or make improvements on the home

after you buy it. At the time the home is resold, the work you have put into the home—*sweat equity*—may make the house worth more on the market.

THE COST OF OWNING A HOME

The amount of money that people should spend for housing varies. Most authorities state that between 25 and 30 percent of a person's or a family's total monthly income can safely be spent for housing (including loan payments, insurance, taxes, utilities, and maintenance). Another rule of thumb suggests that the purchase price of a home should not exceed $2\frac{1}{2}$ to 3 times the buyer's annual take-home pay. This guide gives a prospective homebuyer a price range for shopping purposes until actual expenses can be estimated. Under current mortgage lending standards, buyers will usually qualify for a mortgage as long as the annual or monthly cost of the house does not exceed 28 percent of the homeowner's gross (total) income.

Down Payment

In most cases the buyer must pay part of the original price in cash. This is called a down payment. In some rare instances, housing can be purchased without a down payment. The most common down payment is 10 to 20 percent for an owner-occupied home and 20 to 30 percent for investment property. Some financial advisors recommend that a buyer make a down payment of at least 20 percent of the purchase price and still have sufficient funds available for improvements, furniture, and other moving-in costs. For most people the purchase of a home, especially the first home, involves careful financial planning and some sacrifice.

Monthly Payments

Most housing loans today are paid back through monthly payments. These payments usually go towards paying interest and a certain portion of the original purchase price, thereby reducing the balance of the loan. Sometimes the payments also include the cost of insurance and taxes. If insurance and taxes are not a part of the monthly payment, money must be set aside to meet these obligations. Also, some funds should be kept in reserve so a monthly payment can be met in case of a financial emergency.

Moving-In Costs

When you move into a house or an apartment, there are certain expenses that occur initially that do not recur until much later, if at all. Such expenses are for curtains, draperies, floor coverings, and landscaping. In addition to the down payment and the required monthly payment, resources must be available to meet all moving-in costs.

Economic Considerations of Buying Housing

There are two major economic considerations in buying housing for your personal residence. The first one is that interest paid on loans for housing is tax deductible. The way loan repayment plans are figured, most of the monthly payment is interest in the early years of the loan. (Tax savings can be substantial.) The second consideration is the increase in property value over time due to inflation. It should be noted, however, that inflation also increases the cost of buying another house should you decide to sell your present home.

RENTING OR LEASING HOUSING

Most authorities on housing agree that there are definite economic advantages to owning rather than renting or leasing. For most young people the advantages of owning a home cannot be realized since they are not able to afford a home. In such cases, they must rent while saving money for a down payment. Also, if a person plans to be in a community for only a year or two, it makes more sense to rent or lease than it does to buy. In some cases a person might value job mobility to such an extent that renting or leasing is preferable to buying. When a person rents or leases, that person can usually move on shorter notice than a home owner.

Some people may be uncertain about their future income. In such cases, it is usually better to rent until income stabilizes rather than purchase a home that may not suit the person's needs. There are other people who simply do not want the responsibility of owning a home. They feel more comfortable renting or leasing even if they could afford their own home.

Renting or leasing involves the legal rights, duties, and responsibilities of owner and tenant. It is necessary that both fully understand the relationship that exists between them.

Relations Between Owner and Tenant

The owner of a house or an apartment building who allows the property to be occupied and controlled by another is called a *landlord* or *landlady* or simply the owner. The one who occupies the property is called the *tenant* or renter. The tenant has the right of possession and use of the property, although the rights of the owner must be respected. When the agreement between the owner and renter expires, the owner has the right to regain possession of the property.

Leasing a Place to Live

The agreement between the owner and the tenant is known as the *lease*. The owner is the *lessor* and the tenant is the *lessee*. The lease may be oral or written, depending on the laws of each state. A written lease is desirable in most cases since it clearly defines the rights of both parties. In some states the lessor and the lessee must sign their names before a witness such as a notary public. Every state has laws regarding the basic rights of the lessor and the lessee. In any case, to avoid disagreements and possible lawsuits, leases should contain certain information.

USUAL CONTENT OF A WRITTEN LEASE

1. The date.
2. The names of the lessor and the lessee.
3. A description and an identification of the property.
4. The length of the tenancy (rental) period.
5. The amount and due date of the rental payment.
6. The amount of a security (damage) deposit, if any.
7. The manner of the payment (cash, certified check, mailed, delivered, etc.).
8. A statement of general and special agreements.
9. The signatures of the lessee and the lessor.

Distinction Between Leasing and Renting

Generally speaking, leasing and renting mean the same thing. However, some people think of renting as using property without a written agreement and of leasing as using property with a written agreement. The term *renting*, however, can be properly applied to the use of property both with and without a written agreement.

A tenant may use property under an agreement covering:

1. a definite period, or
2. an indefinite period with both parties having the right to end the agreement when they wish.

Any of these agreements may be written or oral, but the latter is more likely to be an oral agreement.

Renting or Leasing a House or an Apartment

One of the largest and most important items in a family spending plan is the cost of housing. It is also an important factor in determining the satisfaction of living. These factors of cost and satisfaction are as important in renting as in owning a home.

In deciding whether to rent or to lease a house or an apartment, it is important to consider the length of time for which you wish to occupy the property.

Renting a House or an Apartment. If you plan to live in a house or an apartment for only a short period of time, it is probably better for you to rent without a lease. Renting a home from month to month gives you greater freedom to move and to take advantage of decreases in rentals as living conditions change. You may find it necessary to move at an uncertain future date because of a change in your work. Thus, you should try to avoid signing a lease, particularly one covering a long time.

If you rent for an indefinite period, however, you may have to move if the owner wants the property for some other purpose. In most states, however, the custom or law requires the property owner to give the tenant at least 30 days notice.

Leasing a House or an Apartment. In some communities it is difficult to obtain a home without a written lease. Property owners do not want to run the risk of the property being vacant. They therefore prefer the protection of a written lease for a specified length of time. Most leases are written for one year.

Many families find that it pays them to select a home carefully with the intention of living in it for several years. By leasing for a long period, they can reduce moving costs and become better established in the community. By staying in one place a long time, a family has an opportunity to improve the property and perhaps plant a garden. Owners are usually willing to keep property in good repair if the tenants indicate a desire to stay a reasonable length of time.

Rights and Duties of the Tenant

The tenant is entitled to peaceful possession of the property. If deprived of that, the tenant may sue for damages. The tenant is also entitled to use the property for any purpose for which it is suitable, unless certain uses are forbidden by the agreement. The property may not be used for unlawful purposes.

The tenant must pay the rent when it is due. Leases usually require payment of rent in advance; but in the absence of an agreement to that effect, rent is not due until the end of each month. A security (damage) deposit is usually required. This deposit should be refunded at the end of the leasing period if the property is left as clean and sound as it was when it was first occupied, excluding ordinary wear and tear.

The tenant should carefully inspect the property to be rented or leased. In the absence of any agreement with the owner, the tenant accepts the property with the risk of defects being present except those that are hidden from the tenant. For example, if a tenant accepts a house with an obviously defective screen door, the owner may not be responsible for fixing it except by agreement. However, if the tenant accepts the property in the summer and finds in the fall that the furnace will not function, the owner is probably responsible since this is a hidden defect that could not have been noticed in the summer. In most states, the tenant is liable for injuries to guests resulting from defects that should have been reported to the owner and repaired. (See Chapter 19 for a discussion of insurance to cover these situations.)

If the lease is for a definite period of time, the tenant is not required to give notice when vacating the property. The lease may be ended, however, before the expiration of the period if an agreement is reached with the owner. If the lease is for an indefinite period of time, the tenant must notify the owner of any intention to give up the lease. The form and the time of notice are regulated by the laws of the community. Figure 17-1 is one form of notice of intention to terminate a lease.

Figure 17–1

A Tenant's Notice of Intention to Terminate a Lease

Bedford, Virginia, June 1, 19___

Mr. Robert Burdan

 I hereby give you notice that I will quit and deliver possession, July 1, 19___, of the premises at No. 417 Reading Road, in the city of Bedford, Virginia, which I now hold as tenant under you.

Shirley Korth

Illus. 17–3

The tenant should carefully inspect the property to be rented or leased.

If you, the tenant, do not believe the owner is living up to agreements of the lease, you can check on your rights at no cost. The state attorney general's office or a local tenants' group are good sources of information. Your city or county consumer protection agency or the legal aid society can tell you if a tenants' group exists.

Rights or Duties of the Owner

An owner does not have the right to enter the premises of a tenant without adequate notice (usually 24 hours) except to do what is necessary to protect the property. The owner must not interfere with the tenant's right of possession. If the tenant moves from the property, however, the owner may take possession.

At the expiration of the lease, the owner is entitled to take possession of the property. If the tenant refuses to give up possession, the owner may bring legal proceedings against the tenant.

The owner is entitled to receive the rent as specified in the lease. In some states, through legal proceedings, the owner may seize personal property of the tenant and have it sold to pay rent that is due. Unless the lease specifies otherwise, taxes and assessments (such as street repairs) must be paid by the owner.

The owner usually pays for all structural (basic building) repairs, such as foundation work, roofing, plumbing, and electrical work. The tenant usually is responsible for minor repairs that result from day-to-day use. The tenant should notify the owner when major repairs are necessary. In some states, the court will allow a tenant to use up a full month's rent to make necessary repairs if the owner does not make repairs after reasonable notice. Both the owner and the tenant are required to see that the house is kept in livable condition.

When the owner retains control over a portion of the property—as in the case of an owner who leases only part of a building to a tenant—the owner is liable for certain injuries caused by the defective condition of that part of the property over which control is maintained. For instance, Mr. Adams owns a two-story building. He lives on the first floor and retains control over the porch and the yard, but he rents the second floor to Mr. Brown. If Mr. Brown, a member of his family, or a guest is injured as a result of the defective condition of the porch or the sidewalk, Mr. Adams is liable for the injuries.

When a tenant occupies property for an indefinite period of time, the owner may obtain possession of it by giving notice to the tenant. The form of the notice and the time it must be presented are regulated by local customs or laws. Figure 17-2 is one example of a notice to vacate property.

Figure 17–2
An Owner's Notice Requesting a Tenant to Vacate Property

Cincinnati, Ohio, April 30, 19__

Miss Teresa Enlow
   I hereby notify you to surrender possession of the premises at 5942 Ridge Avenue, Cincinnati, Ohio, on or before June 1, 19__. Your lease of the said premises expires on June 1, and I shall take possession of the property on that date.

Mr. J. Michael Kuharic

FACTS EVERYONE SHOULD KNOW ABOUT THE LEGAL ASPECTS OF RENTING A HOME

1. Renting and leasing are legally the same, and agreements may be written or oral.
2. A tenant has a right to peaceful and uninterrupted possession of the property.
3. A tenant is generally obligated to make normal repairs, but not improvements.

Improvements and Fixtures

Unless there is an agreement to the contrary, improvements that are attached to the property become a part of the property and they belong to the owner. For instance, if the tenant builds a shed or a garage on the lot belonging to the owner, the tenant cannot tear it down or take it away without permission. If a tenant installs shelves or cupboards in a rented house, the tenant normally cannot take them away when moving. In some cases, however, courts have held that such fixtures attached with screws may be removed, whereas such fixtures attached with nails become a part of the property. Most courts hold that a tenant must have written approval from the owner to install or remove fixtures that are attached to the property. For example, a tenant may get written permission to fence in the backyard and to remove the fence when the property is vacated. The owner would probably require the tenant to fill in the holes caused by the removal of the fence posts and to resod these areas.

VOCABULARY BUILDER

condominium
cooperative apartment
landlord or landlady
lease
lessee

lessor
stock plans
sweat equity
tenant

REVIEW QUESTIONS

1. What are some of the advantages and disadvantages of owning a home?
2. What are some of the advantages and disadvantages of mobile homes?
3. What are the five ways recommended by the Better Business Bureau to build a home?
4. Why do some young people prefer to buy a prefabricated or kit home?
5. What is a general guideline that a person can follow in deciding the amount of monthly income that should go toward housing?
6. What are some of the costs of housing?
7. What economic considerations should be made when buying housing?
8. What are the economic advantages of renting or leasing housing rather than owning?
9. What elements are usually considered in a written lease?

10. What is the difference between leasing and renting?
11. When is the tenant entitled to a return of a security deposit?
12. Under what conditions is the owner liable for damages if an invited guest of the tenant is injured on the property?
13. Under what circumstances must the owner make repairs?
14. If a tenant makes improvements to property, when does an improvement become part of the property?

DISCUSSION QUESTIONS

1. Ms. Wells rents a home in a residential neighborhood. Ms. Wells decides to open a beauty shop in a spare room in the house and operate a lawful business. May she do so?
2. Compare the advantages and disadvantages of buying a new home versus buying a used home.
3. Why is location an important factor in selecting a house to rent or buy?
4. Why would some people prefer to buy a cooperative apartment or condominium rather than a house and lot?
5. Mr. Jones rented a house from Mrs. Scott. Mr. White was injured on a broken step while visiting Mr. Jones. Who is responsible for the injury?
6. Under what conditions may a TV antenna installed by a tenant be removed when the tenant moves?
7. When might it be better for a person or a family to rent or lease rather than to buy a home?
8. Why do lending institutions require a larger down payment for an investment property than they do for an owner-occupied property?
9. Could a tenant rent or lease his or her apartment or home to someone else (sublease) without approval of the owner?

18

Financing the Purchase of a Home

In recent years, interest rates have fluctuated substantially. During the 1980s interest rates on home loans ranged from as high as 16 percent to as low as 9 percent. Consequently, financing (finding money with which to buy) has in many instances become as important as the purchase price or the construction costs of a home.

After studying this chapter, you should be able to:

1. list and explain the three most common financing sources for real estate,
2. list the government agencies which provide assistance in buying and building housing,
3. explain the nature of a mortgage,
4. state the legal points that need to be investigated when buying real estate,
5. list the costs that must be paid by both the buyer and the seller at the time a real estate transaction is closed, and
6. explain the rights and duties of the mortgagor and the mortgagee, including the rights of each if a foreclosure takes place.

COMMON SOURCES OF LOANS

There are many sources from which money can be borrowed to purchase real estate. For average buyers, the most typical sources include commercial banks, savings and loan associations, mortgage bankers, insurance companies, and relatives. Only the most common sources of loans are discussed here.

Commercial Banks and Savings and Loan Associations

Banks and savings and loan associations are the most common sources of loans for residential real estate. In some states, savings and loan associations may be called homestead associations, savings banks, cooperative banks, or building and loan associations. In recent years, smaller savings and loans have been merging with other savings and loans, commercial banks, or other larger financial institutions.

Generally, banks and savings and loan associations collect the bulk of their deposits and make loans to customers within one hundred miles of their offices. These financial institutions extend loans for reasonably long periods, usually 15 to 30 years. The down payment required for owner-occupied residential property is usually 10 to 20 percent of the cost, assuming the cost does not exceed the appraisal (value as determined by a real estate specialist). The down payment required for rental or business property is usually 20 to 30 percent of the cost. Business conditions and the availability of money determine how easy it will be to get a loan from a bank or savings and loan association.

Private Lenders

Private lenders, who are not part of any organization, are free to operate as they please as long as they keep within the bounds of state laws on lending. They usually follow the methods of the lending institutions in their communities. They are frequently willing to lend a higher percentage of the property value than are financial institutions. Private lenders often include one's relatives or the seller of the property.

Interest rates for seller-financed loans tend to be lower than interest rates offered through commercial banks and savings and loans. One reason for this is that sellers often offer a lower interest rate to attract the buyer.

A common form of financing involving the seller of property is a *land contract*. Under a land contract, the seller permits the buyer to:

1. make a down payment which is generally smaller than that required by a commercial bank or savings and loan association and
2. pay off the balance owed in monthly payments with an interest rate which is generally lower than that available from other financial sources.

However, the title (ownership) of the property remains in the name of the seller.

GOVERNMENT INSURED REAL ESTATE LOANS

Government assistance designed to promote the construction or purchase of housing exists in many forms. The government does not make housing loans directly, but insures loans made by lending institutions in order to encourage them to offer long terms and low interest rates while requiring little or no down payment. The two most common forms of assistance for average home buyers are Federal Housing Administration (FHA) and Veterans Administration (VA) loans. These two sources of financing should be sought first if you desire government assistance.

Federal Housing Administration Loans

The Federal Housing Administration (FHA) of the Department of Housing and Urban Development provides federal insurance on loans that are obtained through an approved lending institution, such as a bank. The lending institution is protected because the FHA guarantees the payment of the loan. Money may be borrowed for:

1. repairing or improving a home,
2. building a new home, or
3. buying an existing home, apartment, mobile home, or multiple-family dwelling (an apartment building, for example).

A person who can make only a small down payment can sometimes obtain an FHA loan. FHA regulations, however, will not permit a loan to be made if it requires monthly payments exceeding a certain amount of the take-home pay of the principal wage earner of the family.

Loan lengths under the FHA vary but are generally thirty years for homes and multiple-family dwellings. The minimum down payment required on the purchase of a new home is less than that required for buying an older home. With FHA loans, the loan amount ranges between 95 and 100 percent of the appraised value or sales price, whichever is less, up to a maximum of $87,500 (1985). The interest rates permitted on FHA loans are regulated by law. These rates change from time to time as the law changes. However, FHA loan rates are usually slightly lower than other real estate loans because the FHA loans are insured by the federal government.

Veterans Administration Loans

For persons who served in the armed forces during World War II, the Korean War, the Vietnam War, and certain cold war periods, special loan privileges are granted by the Veterans Administration (VA). The privileges under *VA loans* (sometimes called GI loans) are similar to those obtainable under FHA loans. The loan must be obtained through a regular lending institution. The loan is then guaranteed by the federal government. This privilege helps veterans buy real estate and borrow money for business or agricultural purposes on favorable terms.

VA loans are insured by the Veterans Administration in about the same way FHA loans are insured. If a veteran fails to repay the loan, the Veterans Administration has the privilege of deducting this amount from any pension or other compensation the borrower may receive.

Interest rates on VA loans are fixed and are generally lower than those on other real estate loans. In addition to the interest rate, the borrower on a VA loan must also pay a small monthly charge for insurance. A down payment is recommended, but the VA loan law permits the Veterans Administration to guarantee loans up to $90,000 (1985) with no down payment if the lender is willing to make the loan for the full amount of the purchase price. As with FHA loans, VA loans are not permitted if monthly payments would exceed a certain amount of the take-home pay of the principal wage earner in the family.

Illus. 18-1
The Veterans Administration grants special loan privileges to persons
who served in the armed forces.

MORTGAGES

The key to home ownership is getting a mortgage loan. When
you borrow money for a home (a real estate loan) you will be
required to sign a *mortgage* which pledges the property to
secure the repayment of a debt. The terms of repayment of
the debt are set forth in a loan agreement that accompanies
the mortgage. Although there are numerous variations, essentially there are two types of home mortgages: fixed-rate mortgages and adjustable-rate mortgages.

Fixed-Rate Mortgages

Fixed-rate mortgages (FRMs) are amortized (paid off) at a
constant rate over a number of years, usually 15, 20, 25, or 30
years. Part of each monthly installment pays the interest,
while the remaining portion is applied to the principal
(amount borrowed). The interest rate charges and the
monthly mortgage payment remain the same (fixed), despite
changes in interest rates generally. Most conventional fixed-
rate mortgages are available for loan amounts of up to 80 percent of the appraised value or sales price of the home, whichever is less. See Table 18-1 to calculate the cost of a mortgage
based upon various interest rates.

Table 18-1
The Cost of a Mortgage
Monthly Payment to Cover Principal and Interest per $1,000 Borrowed

Mortgage Rate	15-year Loan	20-year Loan	25-year Loan	30-year Loan
9%	10.15	9.00	8.40	8.05
10%	10.75	9.66	9.28	8.78
11%	11.37	10.33	9.81	9.53
12%	12.01	11.02	10.54	10.29
13%	12.66	11.72	11.28	11.07
14%	13.32	12.44	12.04	11.85
15%	14.00	13.17	12.81	12.65
16%	14.69	13.92	13.59	13.45
17%	15.40	14.67	14.38	14.26

Note: Multiply the cost per $1,000 by the size of the mortgage in thousands. The result is the monthly payment including principal and interest. For example, for a $60,000 mortgage for 30 years at 10 percent multiply $8.78 × 60 = $526.80

Source: Comprehensive Mortgage Payment Tables (Boston: Financial Publishing Co., 1985).

Adjustable-Rate Mortgages

For many years home buyers had only one basic choice in financing a home, the fixed-rate mortgage. As interest rates began to fluctuate widely, mortgage lenders developed an alternative method of providing mortgages. This alternative is called a *variable* or an *adjustable-rate mortgage*. An *adjustable-rate mortgage (ARM)* is a loan with an interest rate that can be adjusted up or down an agreed upon number of times during the life of the loan. The interest rate is usually tied to changes in a monetary index, such as the interest rates on U.S. Treasury securities, or the rates financial institutions must pay their depositors.

In most cases, interest rates for adjustable-rate mortgages are lower than those for fixed-rate mortgages. Most adjustable-rate mortgages limit rate adjustments by using a *cap*. A *cap*, such as a two-percentage-point increase on the interest rate within a certain period of time, limits the total increase over the life of the loan. All the limits (caps) are imposed by federal law.

Another important factor to consider when borrowing for a real estate loan is the points which the lender may charge. A *point* is a one-time charge of one percent of the mortgage value, charged by a lender to raise the yield on a loan at a time when the availability of money is tight, interest rates are high, or other types of loans yield higher interest than home loans. In other words, points increase the yield lenders make on home loans to an amount competitive with other types of investments. For example, one point on a $50,000 mortgage would be $500 (1 percent of $50,000). Several points may be charged by a lender. One advantage to buying a home with a mortgage loan is that points and interest on the mortgage are tax deductible items.

LEGAL ASPECTS OF BUYING REAL ESTATE

Legal ownership of real estate is one of the important privileges and rights of free people in a market-oriented economy. The laws are concerned with:

1. public record and title of ownership,
2. transfer of title from one person to another, and
3. regulations about payment.

The services of a lawyer should be obtained when buying or selling real estate.

State laws require that most agreements relating to the purchase and sale of real estate be in writing in order to be legally binding on the parties involved. Thus, in buying or selling real estate, the safest practice is to have all agreements in writing and properly signed.

Title to Real Estate

The title to real estate is proof of ownership of the property. Each legal transfer of title to a piece of property is recorded in a register of deeds, which is usually kept in the county or parish courthouse. Generally, a loan on a piece of property cannot be obtained until the lender is certain that the title is clear. Therefore, it is advisable to have a competent lawyer examine the records and determine whether there is a clear title to the

Illus. 18-2
Legal ownership of real estate is one of the important rights of free
people in a market-oriented economy.

property. This examination, called a *title search*, traces the
history and legality of previous title transfers to determine
whether there are any back taxes due or any claims against
the property. The charge for the title search is either added to
the loan or paid as a special charge.

In some states, there are individuals and companies who
specialize in title searches. A report of the information taken
from the recorded history of the property is referred to as an
abstract of title. It is possible to obtain a *title-guarantee policy*, guaranteeing that the title is clear and that there are no
claims against it.

In order to get rid of doubts and to reduce the expense of
transferring the titles to property, some states have adopted a
special system of registering titles. This is known as the *Torrens System*. Under this system, a landowner applies for a registration of the title to the land. An officer examines the court
records, and, if the title is good, issues a *certificate of title*.
Each time the title is transferred thereafter a new certificate is
used. Under this system an abstract is usually not necessary.

A *deed* is written evidence of ownership of a piece of real
property and serves as a means of transferring a title from one

person to another. The one who transfers the title to the property to another is called the *grantor* of the deed, and the one to whom title is transferred is called the *grantee* of the deed. There are two general types of deeds: a warranty deed and a quitclaim deed. In a few states there is also a grant deed or limited warranty deed.

A *warranty deed* not only transfers the title from the grantor to the grantee, but also certifies that the title is free and clear from all claims and debts. The warranty deed is more commonly used than the quitclaim deed.

A *quitclaim deed* merely gives up the grantor's title to the property. The grantee assumes the risk that the title may not be good. In some communities a quitclaim deed is used instead of a warranty deed.

The important parts of a deed are the description of the property, signature, seal, witnesses's signature, acknowledgment, delivery, and acceptance. The laws in different states vary in some respects. To assure a clear title, the person granting the deed should become familiar with local laws. For instance, the laws in various states differ with regard to joint ownership of property by husband and wife. Some states require the signatures of both, whereas others require only one signature. In some states witnesses must sign in the presence of one another, whereas in others they must sign only in the presence of an authorized public officer. Because of the many technicalities involved, most people should obtain legal advice in granting a deed.

Closing Costs

At the time of sale, both the buyer and the seller incur certain costs. Generally, the buyer's costs are more than those of the seller. A buyer's closing costs include:

1. a title search (generally $100 to $150),
2. mortgage preparation (usually $25 to $50),
3. an appraisal fee (usually $25 to $150),
4. recording fees (usually $10 to $20), and
5. a credit report (usually $25 to $100).

The seller's closing costs consist primarily of paying the realtor's commission (if one exists), the preparation of the deed (usually $25 to $50), plus real estate taxes due.

Joint Tenancy

A *joint tenancy* exists when two or more persons own the same land or property. Under the laws of joint tenancy, when either party dies, the survivor becomes sole owner of the property. In some states, the method for passing the title to the survivor must be indicated in the deed.

Many states grant wives the legal right to share in a husband's property. This is called a *dower right* or *dower interest*. A similar right, called *curtesy*, is extended to husbands. In these states, a person cannot sell property without the signature of his or her spouse on the deed, even if the property was originally recorded in only one person's name on the deed. These rights, and the restrictions which arise from them, have been abolished in many states.

Rights and Duties of Mortgagor and Mortgagee

Any person who owns an interest in land, buildings, or even crops raised on land may mortgage that interest. The person who owns the land and borrows the money through a mortgage is called the *mortgagor*. The person who lends the money and holds the mortgage as evidence of the claim is called the *mortgagee*.

Illus. 18-3

Any person who owns an interest in land, buildings, or even crops raised on land may mortgage that interest.

In most states, the mortgagor is considered the legal owner of the property. The property is merely pledged as security for the payment of a debt, and the mortgage is the written contract acknowledging the debt. A mortgage on real estate includes equipment that has become so permanently attached to the real estate that it is considered a part of it. If a piece of land is mortgaged and a house is later built on the land, the house will be included in the mortgage.

The mortgagor is obliged not to destroy or damage the property. The mortgagee must not interfere with the occupancy of the property except through agreement with the mortgagor or through legal procedure. If a mortgagee sells a mortgage to a third person, the mortgagor must be given notice of the transfer.

When the debt is paid, the mortgage is automatically cancelled. It is wise, however, for the mortgagor to destroy the mortgage and obtain a written statement acknowledging the payment of the debt. The notice acknowledging the payment of the debt should be recorded in the proper place of registration—usually the county or parish courthouse.

Right to Cancel Second Mortgages

Some homeowners find it necessary to get a second mortgage on their home in order to have money to pay for major repairs or to build an addition to their homes. The Truth in Lending Act makes it possible for the homeowner to cancel this type of second mortgage after the contract has been signed. The holder of the second mortgage (lender) must give the homeowner a written notice of this right to cancel. From the date of this written notice, the homeowner has three business days in which to cancel the contract. This right to cancel can be very important to a homeowner who may have decided too hastily to sign a second mortgage on the home.

Mortgage Foreclosure

If the mortgagor fails to make payments on the mortgage, the mortgagee has the right of *foreclosure,* that is, of bringing a lawsuit to obtain possession of and title to the property. Foreclosure may consist of either a court order that transfers the title to the property from the mortgagor to the mortgagee or a court order that requires the property be sold to pay the mortgage.

A mortgage contract usually states that the mortgagor loses all rights to the mortgaged property if he or she fails to make payments at a specified time. However, the laws in most states permit the mortgagor to retain interest in the property by fulfilling the contract at any time before foreclosure of the mortgage.

If proceeds from the sale of the property exceed the total of debt and expenses relating to the sale, the mortgagor gets the difference. In most states if the proceeds are less than the amount of the debt, the mortgagee has a right to obtain a judgment against the mortgagor for the difference. This judgment is referred to as a *deficiency judgment.*

As a result of a deficiency judgment, the mortgagor is not released, under the laws of some states, from the mortgage debt just by giving up the property. For example, Mr. and Mrs. Yamota purchased a home. They paid $5,000 in cash and borrowed $45,000 on a mortgage to pay for the home. They failed to repay the money as agreed. The person who loaned the money and held the mortgage foreclosed through the proper legal proceedings. The property was sold to settle the claim, which at the time of the foreclosure amounted to $40,000. The property was sold for $38,000, which was paid to the mortgagee, leaving a deficiency of $2,000. The court granted a deficiency judgment of $2,000 against Mr. and Mrs. Yamota, which they are required to pay to the mortgagee.

One piece of property may have three or more mortgages against it at one time. If it is sold through foreclosure proceedings, the mortgagees are protected according to the preference given to their respective mortgages.

In many states a mortgagor who has lost property through foreclosure is given a certain time period (usually one year) in which to recover the property. The property may be recovered by paying the amount due plus interest at a stated rate.

Claims Against Real Estate

Any claim on real estate that arises from a debt is referred to as a *lien.* A mortgage is one type of lien; a judgment rendered by a court as the result of a lawsuit is another. Unpaid workers or material suppliers might also place a lien against property. This type of lien is referred to as a *mechanics lien.* For instance, a contractor who has constructed a building may hold a lien against the property for payment of the amount due. Whenever work is completed on property and payment is made, the owner should request a *waiver of lien* on materials and the cost of labor. This practice protects the homeowner from claims against the contractor in the event that the contractor fails to pay suppliers for materials used in construction. Figure 18-1 shows a waiver of lien.

Figure 18-1
Waiver of Lien

WAIVER OF LIEN - PARTIAL
MATERIALS OR LABOR (ILLINOIS)

STATE OF ILLINOIS,
} SS.
____DuPage____ COUNTY.   May 24 19 --

TO ALL WHOM IT MAY CONCERN:

Whereas, I the undersigned___Rymar Kitchens_____
_____have been employed by_____
_____Joseph A. Kreidl_____to furnish
_____cabinet material only_____

for the building_____known as Number_416 N. Batavia Ave._Street,

City of_Batavia_____

_____

in Section_____,Township_____Range,

County of _Kane_____   State of Illinois.

Now, Therefore, Know Ye, That I the undersigned, for and in consideration of $950.00
nine hundred and fifty dollars and other good and valuable considerations, the receipt whereof is hereby acknowledged, do_____hereby waive and release any and all lien, or claim, or right of lien on said above described building and premises under the Statutes of the State of Illinois relating to Mechanics' Liens, on account of labor or materials or both furnished up to this date by the undersigned to or on account of the said

___Joseph A. Kreidl_____
____for said cabinets._____.

Given Under _____¨ my____hand____and seal_____this_____24th day
of____May____19-.

David L. Bunnel ___ Seal
(Sole Owner) ___ Seal

Exact copy should be made and retained.

*State of Illinois
County of DuPage
24th day of May 19 --
Eleanor M. Vincent
Notary*

VOCABULARY BUILDER

abstract of title
adjustable-rate mortgage
deficiency judgment
fixed-rate mortgage
joint tenancy

mechanics lien
mortgage
title
Torrens System
waiver of lien

REVIEW QUESTIONS

1. What are the two most common forms of government assistance for the average home buyer? How do these agencies benefit the potential home buyer?
2. What are the three most typical sources of loans for the average home buyer?
3. What are the main advantages of a land contract?
4. How does a quitclaim deed differ from a warranty deed?
5. Which closing costs are paid by the buyer and which by the seller of real estate?
6. What are the rights and duties of the mortgagor and the mortgagee?
7. Under what circumstances does the homeowner have the right to cancel a second mortgage? How much time does the homeowner have to make this decision?
8. If the mortgagor fails to pay the claim against the mortgaged property, what right does the mortgagee have?

DISCUSSION QUESTIONS

1. Assuming that you have all sources of loans available to you, from what source do you think you could obtain the best mortgage loan? Give your reasons.
2. Although a house gradually gets older and deteriorates, why does a house sometimes increase in dollar value? Does it ever decrease in dollar value faster than it deteriorates? Why?
3. Which do you consider the better type of mortgage from the viewpoint of the borrower:
   a. a fixed-rate mortgage, or
   b. an adjustable-rate mortgage? Why?

PART 5
Special Activities

CLASS PROJECTS

1. Invite a local bank officer to your class to answer questions and give explanations about car financing. The class can prepare questions for the loan officer before the visit. Ask the banker to give tips and guidelines on when and how to finance a car.

2. Mark bought a six-year-old used car from his friend Donald for $1,200. Mark thought Donald had taken care of the car, and it sounded good when they drove it to school, so Mark decided it was a good buy. Besides, Donald needed the money for a tractor lawn mower for making money during the school year. Mark had the car only two weeks when the automatic transmission broke while driving to school. Towing and repairs cost $200. The mechanic told Mark that only a trained mechanic could have detected this repair problem. Evaluate Mark's purchase and consequences. What could he have done to avoid this used-car problem? As a class, compile a "Teenagers Guide to Buying a Used Car." Include in the guide the following:
   a. advantages and disadvantages of buying a used car,
   b. steps in finding a reliable used car,
   c. laws and regulations in your area which apply to buying a used car, and
   d. tips and precautions when buying a used car.

3. Form a committee to obtain from local and state government agencies or housing authorities information about laws and housing codes that apply to rental property in your community. As a class, analyze the provisions in the laws and codes and discuss how they might protect tenants and affect tenant-owner relationships. Have a

class committee interview an apartment owner about the behind-the-scenes work and responsibilities involved in managing and maintaining a building.

4. Six months ago, Mr. Krug bought from Mr. LeMoyne a lot valued at $12,000. Mr. LeMoyne delivered a quitclaim deed to the property. In reading tax-notice information in the local newspaper, Mr. Krug was surprised to learn a few days ago of an unpaid tax lien on the property for property taxes not paid over the past 3 years. Mr. Krug must pay $557 in taxes to retain undisputed ownership of the lot. Does he have any recourse to Mr. LeMoyne for this unexpected cost? Explain.

5. Donna Olson purchased an apartment in a condominium complex. She paid $14,000 in cash and borrowed $56,000 on a mortgage to pay for the apartment. She failed to repay the money as agreed. The financial institution which loaned the money and held the mortgage foreclosed. The apartment was sold to settle the claim of $56,000. The apartment was sold for $48,000. Does the mortgagee have a means of obtaining the remainder from the mortgagor? Explain.

COMMUNITY PROJECTS

1. Assume that you are buying a used car and you need a 2-year, $3,000 loan. Investigate the rates at various banks, savings and loan associations, credit unions, dealers, and finance companies in your community. You should find the following information:
   a. finance charge and APR;
   b. conditions for prepayment;
   c. penalty charges, if any; and
   d. number and amount of payments.

2. As a community project, draw up a cost control guide for car owners, outlining ways to reduce or control operating costs. Include driving habits that save on gas and maintenance costs, ways to cut auto insurance costs, simple do-it-yourself maintenance, and other useful information.

3. Interview older brothers, sisters, and students who bought their own cars within the last year or two. Try to find out what experiences they have had with operating costs and what advice they would give those who are considering a

car purchase. If possible, tape the interviews to share with the class.

4. Obtain from a local realtor or real estate board copies of standard rental leases used in the community. As a class, read and study the leases carefully. Identify and discuss any phrases or terms that are not clear and any troublesome clauses for tenants.

5. Call several banks or savings and loan associations in your area to obtain current mortgage interest rates. Using the different rates, figure what it would cost to finance a $75,000 condominium with 20 percent down. Investigate costs of home buying other than the mortgage. Explain each of the following:
    a. loan application fee,
    b. title search fee,
    c. lawyers' fees, and
    d. points.

6. Visit one or more mobile home sales lots. Note the construction and floor plans of various mobile homes. Obtain information about the prices of mobile homes, and ask the dealer how they are financed. Then discuss with other members of your class the advantages and disadvantages of mobile home living, the cost of such homes, financial arrangements for buying them, and other questions of interest to you.

7. Using your local newspaper or a newspaper from a nearby larger city, study the advertisements of real estate for sale. Make a list of the prices asked for houses, then compare prices for houses of different sizes, in different locations, and so forth. Note information in the advertisements about financing alternatives, if any is given. Make a report of your findings to the class.

PART 6
Insurance

Protection Through Property and Liability Insurance

Everyone in society is exposed to a variety of risks—accidents, sickness, death, disability, fire, theft, loss of property, and injury to others. Insurance provides protection from the financial consequences of these unfortunate events. The purpose of this chapter is to discuss ways in which the family may be protected against these risks through property and liability insurance. In the following chapters we will discuss life, health, and social insurance.

After studying this chapter you will be able to:

1. describe the nature of property and liability insurance;
2. state how insurance companies are organized, operated, and regulated to provide property and liability protection;
3. identify some of the hazards involved in home ownership and how the owner can be protected against these hazards; and
4. identify some of the hazards involved in automobile ownership and how an automobile owner can be protected against these hazards.

Illus. 19–1
Everyone in society is exposed to a variety of risks—accidents, sickness, death, disability, fire, theft, loss of property, and injury to others.

NATURE OF PROPERTY AND LIABILITY INSURANCE

Life has become complicated, particularly as it relates to home ownership and automobile ownership. Investment in a home accumulated over a period of years may be lost in a matter of minutes by a fire, tornado, or flood. Savings may be completely wiped out by a judgment resulting from a lawsuit involving an automobile accident.

Property insurance protects you against loss or damage to your property by such perils as fire, flood, wind, or vandalism. *Liability insurance* protects you against financial loss arising from your responsibility (*liability*) to pay for injuries to others or for damage to property.

Everyone in society faces risks; and there is no way to escape all of them. Yet there is a way to limit economic losses. This can be done by sharing economic losses with other people who face the same risks.

Sharing Losses

Insurance is based upon the idea of sharing economic losses. In theory, groups of families and individuals band together and agree that they will share equally in any loss sustained by one of the group. Members agree to pay a specified amount each month into a fund. The fund would be used to pay for a loss sustained by any one of the individuals or families in the group.

In practice, however, questions arise that must be resolved. For instance, how much would each individual or family pay? Who would hold the funds? How should the funds be invested? What would happen if losses were greater than the balance in the fund? How would the funds be used if no losses occurred in a given period? One critical question in any such arrangement is: Who will participate? Suppose that all of the individuals and families involved lived in one community and that a fire, tornado, or flood destroyed the entire community. Under such conditions, it is obvious that the fund would not be adequate to pay for all of the losses.

Insurance Companies Bear the Risk

Insurance companies are businesses that are organized to bring together people who face similar economic risks. Property and liability insurance companies are organized in such a way that they can handle all of the problems listed above. These insurance companies receive small payments from large numbers of people in many different communities. They invest part of these funds and use another part of them to pay for losses sustained by members. For example, assume that Elliot Insurance Company carries fire insurance on 100,000 homes, that each home has an average value of $60,000, and that each homeowner pays an average of $200 a year for fire insurance. The company would collect $20,000,000 a year from the owners of the property and use the money to pay its operating expenses and losses due to fires. Most property owners can afford to pay $200 a year, but they cannot afford to pay $60,000 for fire loss. In a sense, the 100,000 homeowners are pooling or sharing their risks, and the insurance company is the agent that handles the financial matters.

It may seem strange at first that a property insurance company can assume the risk of paying all losses and yet charge each policyholder only a small fee. The reason insurance companies can follow this practice is that they know from experience what losses can be expected. They can, therefore, keep in a reserve fund enough money to pay each loss as it occurs. It is true that unusual events, such as an exceptionally large fire, may cause unplanned losses; but over a long period of time, losses can be predicted fairly well. The reserve fund of an insurance company is used as a protection against unusual losses.

Insurance Contract

To understand an insurance contract, one must be familiar with certain definitions and the concept of insurable interest.

Definitions. An insurance agreement is a contract. An insurance contract is called a *policy*. The amount paid for insurance is called a *premium*. The person who buys an insurance policy is known as the *policyholder, insured,* or *assured*. The party from whom the insured buys the insurance and who agrees to pay the loss is called the *insurer* or *underwriter*. *Risk* is the possibility of loss. *Face value* (face amount) is the amount of insurance stated in the contract; *market value* is the actual cash value of the property destroyed. Market value may be greater or less than the face value of the contract; usually, however, no amount greater than the face value will be paid for any loss.

Insurable Interest. The purpose of property and liability insurance is the protection of the financial interest of the person who buys the insurance. The policyholder must have an insurable interest in the property. A person is said to have an *insurable interest* in property if the person will receive a financial benefit from the property. A person is also said to have an insurable interest in property if that person will suffer a loss from damage to or destruction of the property. For instance, both the owner of a home and the company that holds a mortgage on the home have an insurable interest. If the property is not insured and is later destroyed, the owner will lose the money invested in it. Also, the company that owns the mortgage may lose the money that is due it on the mortgage. Most mortgages contain a clause that requires the owner (mortgagor) of the property to carry enough insurance to protect the one lending the money (mortgagee). Figure 19-1 depicts the insurable interest of the mortgagor and the mortgagee.

In the case of property, the insurable interest ordinarily must exist at the time of the loss; otherwise, the contract is not enforceable. For example, you might carry insurance on property that you rent and occupy. If you move out of the property without canceling the insurance, you could not collect for a loss due to fire should the building burn after you move.

Figure 19-1
Two Parties With Insurable Interests in a Mortgaged Home

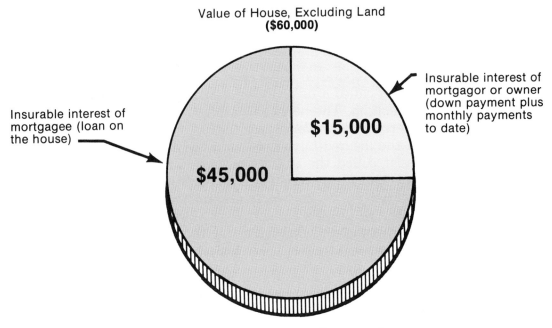

Value of House, Excluding Land
($60,000)

Insurable interest of mortgagee (loan on the house)

$45,000

$15,000

Insurable interest of mortgagor or owner (down payment plus monthly payments to date)

Types of Insurance Companies

All property and liability insurance companies set rates based on past experience and expected claims from their policyholders. Policyholders make periodic (usually semiannual or annual) premium payments to the insurance company. These premium payments are used by the insurance companies in somewhat the same manner as deposits are used by banks. In other words, insurance companies invest the funds paid by policyholders to earn income. This income helps lower the cost of the premiums. The insurance companies must, of course, keep a reasonable amount of cash available to pay the claims of policyholders.

There are two types of property and liability insurance companies: stock and mutual.

Stock Insurance Company. In a *stock insurance company*, the stockholders own the company and elect directors, who in turn hire executives to run the business. The stockholders may or may not be policyholders. A stock insurance company gets funds with which to begin operation from the sale of stock. Additional operating and reserve funds come from premiums and from income earned on investments. Profits of the stock insurance company may be paid to the stockholders in the form of dividends.

Stock insurance companies may issue *participating* or *nonparticipating policies*. Holders of participating policies may receive dividends that reduce the cost of insurance. Holders of nonparticipating policies do not receive dividends.

Mutual Insurance Company. A *mutual insurance company* is owned by its policyholders. There are no stockholders. Instead, each person who is insured in a mutual insurance company becomes a member of the company and is entitled to a share in the ownership and control of the company. These companies sell only participating policies.

Generally, mutual insurance companies set premium rates high enough to cover expected losses. If losses are not as high as expected, the excess of premium payments over loss payments can be returned to the policyholders. The return may be in the form of either dividends or lower premium rates. Some or all of the excess may be retained as a reserve for future losses.

State Regulation of Insurance Companies

The operations of insurance companies within a particular state are regulated by the state, usually through a department of insurance or an insurance commission. One of the important functions of the insurance commissioner is to make sure that insurance companies keep enough reserves to pay all claims as they are filed by policyholders.

State regulation also protects insurance buyers from fraud. Most states require reports from insurance companies, as well as inspection of the securities, accounting records, and business methods of the companies. In most states, the investments of insurance companies are confined to high-grade bonds of federal, state, and city governments, utilities, and high-grade real-estate mortgages. Although special bureaus provide information for setting rates for fire and casualty insurance, the state governments have the right to regulate these rates.

INSURANCE FOR THE HOME

The greatest risks of loss to a family or an individual are usually associated with ownership and operation of a home and an automobile. Therefore, we shall consider the different types of property and liability insurance as they relate to homes and automobiles.

Homeowners Policy

The homeowner must consider the possible loss of the home, its contents, and other personal property, as well as possible losses from lawsuits that result from personal injury to guests. While each of these risks can be insured against separately, insurance companies have developed policies that insure against groups of perils (dangers which lead to economic loss) which may befall a person's home, the contents of the home, and other personal property. These are called *homeowners policies*. Homeowners policies are also referred to as all-risk policies and are 20 to 30 percent less costly than insuring each peril separately.

COVERAGES AND LIMITS OF A SAMPLE HOMEOWNERS POLICY COVERING ALL RISKS

Coverage   A—Dwelling building, $75,000.

Coverage   B—Appurtenant (attached or accompanying) private structures, 10 percent of Coverage A.

Coverage   C—Personal property, 50 percent of Coverage A.

Coverage   D—Additional living expense, 20 percent of Coverage A.

Coverage   E—Comprehensive personal liability, $100,000 per occurrence.

Coverage   F—Medical payments, $5,000 per person.

Coverage   G—Physical damage to property, $500 per occurrence.

Property Insurance Under the Homeowners Policy

Figure 19-2 shows the three basic policy coverages (standard, broad, and comprehensive) that may be purchased to protect against certain perils to the house and appurtenant private structures.

Perils Covered. Under a homeowners policy, the house or dwelling is covered. Guest houses, sheds, garages, and other structures used in connection with and belonging to the home are known as *appurtenant private structures*. They usually are covered up to 10 percent of the amount of coverage carried on the house. Figure 19-2 shows the eleven perils covered under the standard form and the eighteen perils covered under the broad form. All perils are covered under the comprehensive form except those specifically excluded.

Figure 19-2
Perils Covered Under Different Types of Homeowners Policies

Homeowners Policy—Property Insurance
Summary of Coverage—Standard, Broad, and Comprehensive Forms

Policy Form	Perils Covered	
STANDARD	1. fire or lightning	6. aircraft
	2. loss of property removed from premises endangered by fire or other perils	7. vehicles
		8. smoke
	3. windstorm or hail	9. vandalism and malicious mischief
	4. explosion	10. theft
	5. riot or civil commotion	11. breakage of glass constituting a part of the building
BROAD	12. falling objects	16. accidental discharge, leakage or overflow of water or steam from within a plumbing, heating or air-conditioning system or domestic appliance
	13. weight of ice, snow, sleet	
	14. collapse of building(s) or any part thereof	
	15. sudden and accidental tearing asunder, cracking, burning, or bulging of a steam or hot water heating system or of appliances for heating water	17. freezing of plumbing, heating and air-conditioning systems and domestic appliances
		18. sudden and accidental injury from artificially generated currents to electrical appliances, devices, fixtures and wiring (TV and radio tubes not included)
COMPREHENSIVE	**All Perils Except:** earthquake, landslide, flood, surface water, waves, tidal water or tidal wave, the backing up of sewers, seepage, war, and nuclear radiation.	

Source: A Family Guide to Property and Liability Insurance, Insurance Information Institute.

Personal property is covered along with the house. *Personal property* includes household contents and other personal belongings used, owned, worn, or carried by the family. The protection applies both at home and away from home. Pets are not included as personal property. Automobiles and the property of roomers or boarders are not covered.

As an extension of the homeowners policy, it is possible to obtain a *personal article floater* or an *all perils policy* for a slight increase in the cost of insurance. The personal article floater or all perils policy insures all items of personal property that are listed, described, and assigned a definite dollar value. Property so listed in the policy is insured separately against almost all risks of loss or damage, with a few minor exceptions such as moths, vermin, and dampness.

The normal homeowners policy usually covers 10 percent of the total value of unlisted personal property or a maximum of $1,000 against loss that occurs off the premises. A personal article floater increases this amount to any sum desired. In addition, the personal article floater provides protection from loss due to *mysterious disappearance*, that is, personal property that disappears but no one is sure what happened to it. A camera missing from an unlocked car would be called a mysterious disappearance, and the loss would not be covered under a normal homeowners policy. The loss would be covered if the camera were listed as part of a personal article floater.

The homeowner is insured for additional living expenses incurred in the event that major damage to the home requires living elsewhere. Reimbursable expenses are limited to the period of time it takes (with due attention and speed) to repair the damaged property.

Perils Not Covered. Under the standard and broad forms, only those perils listed are covered. Under the comprehensive form, all perils are covered except those specifically excluded. Shrubs, trees, plants, and lawn are not covered against windstorms and hail in the homeowners policy. Damage from perils other than fire and lightning are usually subject to a *deductible clause*, a clause in an insurance policy that makes the insured responsible for a part of any loss covered by the insurance policy. For example, under a $250 deductible clause, the insurance company would pay the homeowner only $150 of a $400 loss. The homeowner is required to pay the first $250 of the loss.

Amount of Coverage. The amount of insurance that should be purchased is determined by the replacement cost of the home. Replacement costs are usually determined through an appraisal by a competent appraiser. Assume that the appraisal indicated that $75,000 of insurance should be carried on the house. This amount then determines the amount of other property coverages included in the homeowners policy. These coverages are shown below.

Dwelling	$75,000
Appurtenant private structures	
10 percent of dwelling	7,500
Personal property (not otherwise covered)	
50 percent of dwelling	37,500
Additional living expense	
20 percent of dwelling	15,000

Some insurance companies will, with the approval of the insured, automatically increase the coverage by 5 percent a year. This is done without an appraisal. Most real estate has appreciated (increased in market value) at least 5 to 7 percent a year during the last ten years. Inflation and a lack of good building sites are two reasons for this appreciation.

Need for an Inventory. An inventory of personal property is desirable in the event of loss. This inventory serves as the basis for making claims and prevents the need for depending on one's memory. Some homeowners photograph each room in the home. Of course, the inventory or photographs must be kept in a safe, fireproof place. The insurance company will often accept a sworn statement as to the loss of personal property. However, the safest practice is to keep some type of inventory record of the insured property. Figure 19-3 shows a portion of a household inventory record.

Liability Insurance Under the Homeowners Policy

People may injure themselves or suffer damage to their property while on the premises of a homeowner. In addition, the actions of the homeowner may result in injury to other persons or damage to the property of other persons either on the

Figure 19-3
Portion of a Household Inventory Record

Kitchen, Utility Room				
No.	Article	Year Purchased	Original Cost	Present Cash Value
	Chairs, Tables, Stools			
	Draperies, Rugs			
	Dishes, Glassware			
	Refrigerator			
	Range			
	Dishwasher			
	Washing Machine			
	Dryer			
	Waste Disposer			
	Electrical Appliances (Vacuum Cleaner, Toaster, Coffeemaker, Fry-Skillet, etc.)			
	Kitchen Equipment (Foodstuffs, Supplies, Cutlery, Utensils, etc.)			
	Kitchen Cabinets			

premises of the homeowner or away. The members of the family may become personally liable for claims arising as a result of these situations.

The liability insurance portion of a homeowners policy protects the family against claims in three areas:

1. comprehensive personal liability,
2. medical payments, and
3. physical damage to the property of others.

Comprehensive Personal Liability. Coverage under a comprehensive personal liability policy protects the homeowner against claims arising from bodily injury to others or damage to the property of others. No claim is paid by the insurance company under this provision unless it has been established that the insured is legally liable. A guest in the home might fall down a basement stairway, break a leg, and then file suit for damages. Under this provision, the insurance company would represent the homeowner in court. The company would pay the cost of defending the homeowner and would pay the

The homeowner must also consider possible loss due to lawsuits that
result from personal injury to guests.

damages, if any, up to the limits of the policy. Usually, the
basic coverage of this provision is $100,000 for each occur-
rence. Because of the size of some personal liability verdicts
(amounting to hundreds of thousands of dollars), many companies are selling personal liability umbrella policies that provide as much as $1,000,000 in protection against liability
claims.

Medical Payments. A medical payments provision protects
the homeowner from accidental injury claims of others arising
from actions of the homeowner, family members, or family
pets either on or off the homeowner's property. The insurance
company pays the claims of the injured party, regardless of
who is at fault. The claim would include the cost of medical
and surgical services incurred within one year of the accident.
The amount of coverage for each person usually is $5,000. This
coverage, however, does not apply to the homeowner or members of the homeowner's family.

Physical Damage to Property of Others. A clause providing coverage for physical damage to the property of others protects the homeowner and his or her family when any member of the family damages someone's property. For example, the homeowner's lawn mower might throw a stone through a neighbor's window. Such damages are paid up to the limit of the policy, usually $500 for each occurrence. Coverage is provided whether the act is committed on the property of the homeowner or off and whether the homeowner is at fault or not.

The Cost of Property and Liability Insurance

The cost of property and liability insurance varies according to geographical location, water supply available for fire fighting, efficiency of the local fire department, type of construction of the home, and other factors. Because of safety improvements in building materials and electrical wiring, some companies offer lower rates to owners of newer homes. Following are the comparative costs of three types of homeowner's policies based on the replacement value of a home worth $75,000.

Coverage	Cost each year based on $250 deductible
Standard form (11 perils)	$155.00
Broad form (18 perils)	$159.00
Comprehensive form (all risks)	$163.00

It is important for the buyer of property insurance to know the difference between the replacement cost and actual cash value of property. *Replacement cost* is the amount of money it would take to rebuild the same or similar item at prices existing during the time of loss. *Actual cash value* is the replacement cost minus depreciation. *Depreciation* is the amount an item has decreased in value due to normal wear and tear or obsolescence over a period of time. Most basic homeowners policies provide actual cash value on personal belongings, but make replacement cost available on buildings. Some insurers also market replacement value insurance for personal belongings. For a slight additional cost, the company will pay the full replacement cost of lost or damaged personal belongings and contents of the home.

INSURANCE FOR THE AUTOMOBILE

No automobile owner or driver should be without automobile insurance. In fact, some states require automobile owners and drivers to have certain types of insurance to protect others from loss. Other states may require an automobile owner or driver to show evidence of having insurance in the event of an accident. If unable to do this, the owner or driver may have to post a bond or go to jail.

Economic security is very uncertain unless the perils arising from automobile ownership are insured. The owner or operator of an automobile should consider the following types of coverage:

1. bodily injury liability,
2. property damage liability,
3. medical payments,
4. comprehensive physical damage,
5. collision, and
6. protection against uninsured and underinsured motorists.

These six coverages may be purchased separately; but, as in the case of the homeowners policy, it is more common to purchase the six coverages as a package. Each of the coverages will be discussed separately.

Bodily Injury Liability

Anyone who drives the insured's car with the insured's permission and all licensed members of the insured's family are protected by this insurance.

In addition, licensed members of the insured's family are covered while driving another person's car with the owner's permission. This insurance protects the insured against claims or suits of people injured or killed by the insured's car. It covers people in other cars, guests riding with you, and pedestrians.

State financial responsibility laws indicate the minimum amount of this coverage that must be carried. The minimum amount of coverage issued is often 10/20 ($10,000 for one person or $20,000 in total for more than one person injured in any one accident). Some automobile owners carry as much as $250,000 for one person or $500,000 in total for more than one person injured.

Illus. 19–3

Illus. 19–3
The owner or operator of an automobile may need insurance coverage for bodily injury, property damage, medical payments, comprehensive physical damage, collision, and protection from uninsured or underinsured motorists.

Car owners should consider carrying more than the minimum amount of 10/20. If a jury awarded an injured party $100,000 and the insured had only 10/20 coverage, the insurance company would pay $10,000 and the insured would be responsible for the rest.

Property Damage Liability

All members of the insured's family and all those driving the insured's car with permission are covered by this policy provision. Policyholders and family members are covered even while driving someone else's car as long as they have permission from the owner. The insured is covered whenever the insured's car damages the property of others. It does not cover damage to the insured's automobile, however. Property damage liability is usually available in amounts ranging from $5,000 to $100,000.

Both bodily injury and property damage coverage are vital for a car owner. The perils that face a car owner are too great to risk without adequate insurance coverage. In purchasing this coverage, the car owner should remember that large amounts of coverage cost relatively little more than smaller amounts. For example, if coverage of 25/50/5 ($25,000 bodily injury for one person, $50,000 bodily injury for more than one person, and $5,000 property damage) costs $100 a year, 50/100/10 might cost only $111. Thus, the insured may double the coverage with an increase of only 11 percent in premium costs.

Medical Payments Coverage

This coverage applies to the policyholder and family members while riding in anyone's car. It also covers the policyholder and family members if they are walking and are hit by a car. Guests riding in the policyholder's car are also covered. The insurance company agrees to pay all reasonable medical expenses incurred as a result of an accident within one year of the date of the accident. The coverage includes all necessary medical, surgical, X-ray, and dental services, up to the limits set in the policy. It may also include ambulance services, hospital services, nursing services, and funeral services. The insurance company pays regardless of who was at fault. The limits of coverage for each individual may range from $25,000 to $100,000.

Medical payments coverage is especially important for families with children and families who transport other children, as in a school car pool.

Comprehensive Physical Damage Insurance

This insurance coverage protects the insured against possible loss if the car is damaged or stolen. However, damage due to collision is not covered. Causes of damage covered include fire, lightning, flood, and windstorm. Glass breakage is covered under this insurance. Since this type of insurance is relatively inexpensive, most car owners include it in their coverage. The cost of replacing one windshield would very likely be greater than total premium payments on comprehensive insurance for two or three years.

Collision Insurance

Collision insurance coverage protects against loss arising from damage to the insured's own car as the result of collision. This is the most expensive insurance coverage among those discussed, mainly because of the many minor accidents that require costly body and paint work. The car owner can reduce the cost of collision insurance by increasing the amount deductible, often either $100 or $250 deductible. In the event of damage, the insurance company would pay only the amount of the loss in excess of $100 or $250. The policyholder pays the deductible amount. Since a new car represents a large investment, the car owner should carry collision insurance on it. As the car gets older and its value decreases, the owner should weigh the cost of this insurance coverage against the potential loss. For example, there would be little reason to carry $100 deductible collision insurance on a car valued at $250.

Costs for collision insurance vary widely from one geographic area to another. They also vary within an area according to driver classification. Unmarried male drivers under 21 years of age pay the highest rate.

Protection Against Uninsured and Underinsured Motorists

Uninsured motorist insurance coverage is designed to protect the insured against risks due to bodily injury by hit-and-run drivers and uninsured drivers. It provides coverage as though the uninsured driver had been insured or as though the hit-and-run driver had been identified. The insured cannot collect from the insurance company unless the uninsured motorist was legally liable. The coverage is limited to the amount of liability required under the financial responsibility laws of the various states. The cost of this coverage is very low. Underinsured motorist insurance pays when the damages owed for bodily injury are greater than the bodily injury limits of the legally liable other driver.

No-Fault Insurance

As you learned, bodily injury and property damage liability insurance are important to have should you be at fault in an auto accident. If you are at fault, your liability insurance protects you against lawsuits and pays the claims. In many cases, it is difficult to decide who is at fault. To go to court to try to prove who was at fault may be costly and time consuming. Because of our crowded courts, it often takes a year and a half or longer before a case is tried.

Therefore, some states have adopted a *no-fault insurance* plan. Under this plan, it is not necessary to decide who was at fault in an auto accident. Each insurance company will pay for property damages, medical bills, and wage losses of its own policyholders. Pedestrians and property owners would also be protected by a policyholder's insurance company. No-fault insurance can lower insurance rates because costly court trials are not needed. Caution: If your state has no-fault insurance but you drive in a state that does not have such insurance, you will still need liability insurance.

Factors Affecting the Cost of Automobile Insurance

Accidents involving automobiles are frequent, and the cost of repairs is quite high. Automobile insurance rates must reflect these costs. The insurance rates charged are based, for the most part, on what the companies have had to pay in claims over the last three-year period. State insurance departments or commissions regulate the insurance rates; however, this does not mean that all automobile insurance companies have the same rates. Some companies, by being very selective in choosing the owners and drivers that they will insure, can have lower costs and lower premium rates. Thus, insurance rates are affected by companies' practices of accepting risks.

A second factor affecting cost also relates to the experience of the company. More accidents occur in urban areas than in rural areas, with more occurring in some urban areas than in others. Therefore, comparable coverage in one city may cost more or less than in another.

A third factor is the cost of automobile repairs. Some cars are more expensive and more difficult to repair than others.

A fourth factor is the driver of the car. Statistics show that drivers of a certain age and sex have more or fewer accidents than others. Most insurance companies use a rating system that scales down the cost of insurance year by year. As seen in Figure 19–4, the highest rates are paid by unmarried male drivers who own or are the principal operators of automobiles.

Figure 19–4

Comparison of Insurance Rates by Age, Sex, and Marital Status

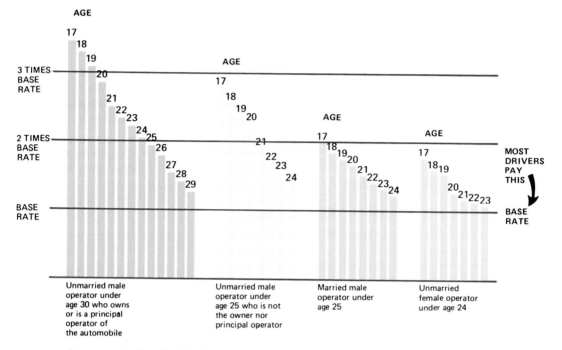

Source: A Family Guide to Property and Liability Insurance, Insurance Information Institute.

SELECTING A PROPERTY AND LIABILITY INSURANCE COMPANY

There are many good insurance companies. Since most of us are not expert enough to determine what is a good insurance company, we have to rely upon the companies' reputations.

The rates of some companies may be slightly lower than those of others, but rates are not the only basis for selecting an insurance company. Above all, you want an insurance company that will protect you and settle claims in a fair manner. An insurance company that will not pay honest claims promptly and without lawsuits is not one with which you would want to insure. One of the best ways to select a company is to inquire among your friends. They can help you learn the company's reputation and its methods of doing business and settling claims.

Many families rely on independent insurance agents rather than their own knowledge of insurance companies. By selecting an agent in whom they have complete trust, they are depending on the agent's judgment for the selection of the insurance company. A good agent will always act in behalf of the insured and will often render many extra services.

FACTS EVERYONE SHOULD KNOW ABOUT PROPERTY AND LIABILITY INSURANCE

1. Property and liability insurance is possible through small payments collected from many people to pay unexpected losses that may occur to any of the policyholders.
2. Property and liability insurance rates are determined primarily from past experience.
3. A homeowners policy is the most economical way of insuring the homeowner against the perils of home ownership.
4. It is vital for a driver to carry adequate automobile insurance.
5. A homeowner should buy property and liability insurance from a company she or he knows is reputable and fair or from an agent in whom the homeowner has complete confidence.

VOCABULARY BUILDER

actual cash value
deductible clause
face value
homeowners policy
insurable interest
insured
insurer

liability
no-fault insurance
premium
replacement cost
risk
underwriter

REVIEW QUESTIONS

1. How does an insurance company protect a policyholder (who pays small amounts periodically) against possible large losses?

2. What is the nature and purpose of property and liability insurance?

3. How does a stock insurance company differ from a mutual insurance company?

4. How does a participating policy differ from a nonparticipating policy?

5. How are insurance companies regulated? Why?

6. What are the coverages provided by a homeowners policy?

7. What are the names of each of the three forms of homeowners policies? Which gives the greatest protection? the least protection?

8. What steps should a policyholder take to make sure that proof of loss can be provided?

9. What are the types of insurance coverage for loss and for liability that are available to owners and drivers of automobiles?

10. How does bodily injury insurance protect the owner of an automobile insurance policy?

11. How does property damage insurance protect the owner of an automobile insurance policy?

12. What insurance is necessary to protect the driver and the driver's family against losses due to injury to the driver or the family as a result of an automobile accident?

13. How does automobile collision insurance protect the policyholder?

14. What type of insurance protection does a person have if he or she has 25/50/10 coverage?

15. What should one look for in selecting a property and liability insurance company?

DISCUSSION QUESTIONS

1. Are the following statements contradictory? Why or why not?
   a. Total losses for a given period of time in a given state due to fire can be predicted with reasonable accuracy.
   b. The locations and amounts of individual losses due to fire for a given period of time in a given state cannot be predicted with any degree of accuracy.

2. Insurance can be purchased for protection against almost any type of anticipated loss. Some insurance companies, for example, will insure the promoters of a baseball game or an outdoor play against possible financial loss due to rain.
    a. How could an insurance company determine rates for insurance against possible loss due to rain?
    b. Do you think that such rates would be high or low as compared with rates for fire insurance? Why?
3. Over a lifetime the amount of premiums on household insurance would amount to several thousand dollars. Why is it not advisable for a homeowner to save the money paid in insurance premiums for the purpose of replacing or repairing the house if it should be damaged by fire?
4. How would fire insurance rates in a city with strict building ordinances and strict inspection practices compare with rates in a city with weak ordinances and lax inspection practices?
5. What are some illustrations on the kinds of liability claims to which a homeowner might be subject?
6. What, in your opinion, represents the more serious risk to an automobile owner: the risk of property damage or the risk of injury to a person? Why?
7. If your automobile insurance policy provides $50,000 protection against bodily injury and a court awards damages of $60,000 to an injured person, how will the claim be settled?
8. Explain a situation in which one may have an insurable interest in property at the time the insurance is bought, but may not have an insurable interest in the property at the time it is destroyed.
9. Why do you or do you not have an insurable interest in
    a. your neighbor's house and
    b. a house on which you are holding a mortgage?
10. Why do you suppose certain automobile insurance companies provide a reduced rate for students who maintain a better-than-average scholastic record and also provide a reduced rate for persons who have completed a driver education course?

20

Protection Through Life and Health Insurance

Almost everyone needs to understand financial problems that result from a death in the family, an accident, or a disabling illness. This chapter is concerned with how life and health insurance may help solve those problems.

After studying this chapter, you will be able to:

1. state the purposes of life insurance,
2. identify different types of life insurance,
3. identify different features of life insurance policies,
4. explain how life insurance may be used as a part of a savings program,
5. identify different types of health insurance, and
6. identify different health care providers.

LIFE INSURANCE

Although life insurance can be used for many purposes, it is primarily purchased to provide an immediate income to replace the loss of income due to the death of the primary wage earner. People use this money for:

1. final expenses (burial expenses),
2. an income while the family adjusts to new conditions,
3. an income for the family while the children are growing, and
4. an income for the surviving parent after the children have left home.

Life insurance can also be used to provide funds for future expenses such as financing a college education, meeting financial emergencies, or providing income in retirement years. Some people pay regular premiums on life insurance as a means of forced savings.

HOW FAMILIES USE LIFE INSURANCE

If primary wage earner dies:
1. Cash—To pay last expenses, taxes, debts, and other costs. To pay off the family mortgage.
2. Readjustment income—Continuing primary wage earner's income while family makes necessary adjustments in living.
3. Family income—Monthly income for surviving parent while children are small.
4. Life income for surviving parent—Regular monthly income for life after children are grown.

If primary wage earner lives:
1. Money for future expenses—Financing a college education. Meeting family goals.
2. Money for emergencies—Cash to meet unexpected expenses.
3. Income for retirement—Monthly income for life for husband and wife.
4. Cash reserves—For use in meeting unexpected cash needs.

Life Insurance Defined

Life insurance is a voluntary financial agreement between an individual, called the *insured*, and an insurance company. The written contract of this agreement is called the *policy*. In this contract, the insured promises to pay the insurance company an annual fee or *premium*. (Premiums can also be paid as often as once a month at a slightly higher cost.) In return, the company promises to pay, at the time of death of the insured, a sum of money to the person or persons named in the policy as *beneficiaries*.

Life insurance may be bought only by persons having an *insurable interest*. Everyone has an insurable interest in his or her own life. Parents have an insurable interest in each other and in their children. Close kinship is often, but not always, enough to claim an insurable interest. Likewise, one need not be a relative of a person in order to have an insurable interest in that person. A person has an insurable interest in another if the person would be deprived of some benefit by the death of the other. For instance, a business organization may insure the life of one of its key employees.

Policyholders pay the same insurance rates under similar conditions. Most general forms of insurance require a physical examination to determine the condition of the insured's health. This is done so that the cost of the insurance and the protection to all members of the insured group will be fair. For instance, if no physical examination were required, a person in poor health and likely to die soon would not pay a higher rate than one in good health. Or a person 25 years of age would have to pay as high a rate as one 50 years of age. Thus, a physical examination determines eligibility; age and other conditions determine the rate. Many persons with poor health or in very dangerous occupations can obtain insurance but at higher rates than normal.

Illus. 20-1

Most general forms of insurance require a physical examination to determine the condition of the insured's health.

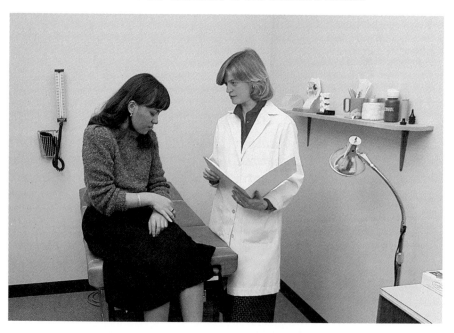

Life insurance premium rates are based on the experience of the life insurance company and on expected claims. Accurate estimates of expected claims are made from *mortality tables*. These tables show the percentage of a certain age group that will die from all causes each year. Although mathematicians cannot tell when a specific individual in the group will die, they can predict the approximate number of individuals who are likely to die each year until the generation is gone. With this information, it is possible for the insurance company to determine approximately how long a certain group of people will live. The company can then set up a schedule of premiums, spread out over time, so that everyone in the group can buy life insurance.

Forms of Life Insurance

Life insurance is generally bought in one of two ways: individually or as part of a group. Some people use both of these forms to establish their financial security. *Individual life insurance* is issued to a person after the individual has been approved for coverage by the insurance company. The applicant may be required to undergo a medical examination.

Group life insurance is generally issued without a medical examination to a group of persons under a single master policy. Group insurance is often purchased by an employer, who may pay all or part of the cost of the insurance for the benefit of the employees. The cost of group insurance is usually low in comparison with individual life insurance coverage. The cost is based on potential losses indicated by the ages, environment, occupation, and general health of the employees or members in the group.

Typically, group insurance ends when the worker leaves a job. If this happens, the worker can sometimes convert the group insurance to an individual policy without a medical examination. The rates for the individual policy would depend on the worker's age at the time the policy is converted.

Types of Life Insurance

There are many types of life insurance contracts or policies. Some of them are simple; others involve a combination of elements that cannot be explained without a great amount of detail. The basic types of life insurance are: term, straight life, limited-payment life, endowment, combination, and annuity.

Term Insurance. The least expensive type of life insurance is term insurance. As the name implies, *term insurance* provides protection for a stated period of time (a term). Term insurance offers the best means of obtaining the maximum amount of coverage. With term insurance a person pays only for coverage in case of death. Term insurance is often referred to as pure insurance because it provides protection only. One of the major advantages of term insurance is its low cost compared with other types of policies. Term insurance makes it possible for a person to buy a large amount of insurance coverage at the time protection is needed.

Common periods covered by term insurance are five years and ten years, but it may cover any period of years. Term insurance can be increased or decreased in amount of coverage or can be exchanged for other types of insurance. For instance, a family may wish a large amount of protection at a low cost while the children are of school or college age. After the children have been educated, the family may decrease the amount of protection or exchange the term insurance for some other type of insurance at a higher cost without a physical examination.

Term insurance is often used to cover special needs. For example, a person who has a debt that is to be paid over twenty years can buy a twenty-year term policy for the amount of the debt. If the person dies before paying the debt, the insurance will pay the debt. This type of insurance is called *credit life* or *mortgage insurance.*

Straight Life Insurance. A life insurance policy that provides protection over a long period of years is called *straight life insurance.* It is occasionally called ordinary or whole life insurance. These policies provide coverage in the event of death, and build up a cash value. These cash values may be borrowed against, or they may be withdrawn if the policy is terminated.

The premiums for straight life insurance are initially higher than the premiums for the same amount of term insurance. Because of the higher premiums, many people are not able to buy sufficient straight life coverage for the needs of a family. One should consider, however, that while the premiums for term insurance increase over the years, straight life insurance premiums stay constant. Most holders of straight life contracts do not continue to pay premiums until the policy matures (which may be at age 96 or 100). They stop paying premiums and take a reduced paid-up policy, which at age 65 can amount to 60 or 70 percent of the original policy's face amount (the amount that will be paid in case of death or at the maturity of the policy).

Limited-Payment Life Insurance. A *limited-payment life insurance* contract is the same as a straight life contract except that premiums are paid for a limited time. Payments may be for 10, 20, or 30 years instead of for life. Since premiums are paid only for a limited time, the rates are higher than for straight life insurance. When these premiums have been paid, the insurance policy is said to be fully paid. However, the face amount of a limited-payment policy will be paid only in the event of death. For example, a 10-year limited-payment policy for $10,000 will be fully paid after 10 years, but the insurance company will pay the $10,000 only when death occurs.

Endowment Insurance. The company that issues an *endowment policy* pays the face amount of the policy to the insured at a stated time. In the event of the insured's death before that stated time, the company pays the beneficiary. An endowment policy costs more than a limited-payment policy for an equal number of years. The face amount of an endowment policy, however, is available as cash at the end of the stated period as well as at the time of death.

An endowment policy is a way not only to save a definite amount for a future need but also to have protection while saving. Such future needs may be to educate children, to start a child in some particular profession or business, to purchase a home, or to pay a debt. Short-term endowments (from ten to twenty years) can provide for these needs. If future savings is an important goal, investing the amount ordinarily paid in premiums in some type of savings account or certificate for the same number of years as the endowment policy would yield a higher lump sum at maturity. This would be an important consideration during times of persistent and high inflation.

People today seldom buy endowment policies. The amount of insurance protection you get from an endowment policy is less than you could get from other types of insurance coverage.

Combination Life Insurance. Many contracts involve combinations of various types of life insurance. For example, one type of *combination policy* requires a low premium for the first four or five years and a higher premium in later years. This policy is, in effect, the same as buying a term insurance policy and then, after four or five years, exchanging it for another type of insurance. This type of policy would be good for a young graduate from college or technical school. Such a person could expect greater earnings in later years. With greater earnings, the person could afford higher premium payments.

Universal life is a combination of term insurance and a high-interest investment account. The policyholder is able to raise or lower insurance coverage without rewriting the policy. Unlike other cash-value policies which don't usually start to build any cash value until the second or third year, universal life begins building cash value with the first premium. The cash value is often invested by the insurance company in short-term government securities. The policyholder's return will vary, but it will be higher than the fixed return from a straight life policy.

With universal life, you can pay premiums when and in the amount you like, subject to certain minimums. You can withdraw money from the cash value and borrow against it without cancelling the policy.

Annuity Contracts. An *annuity* is a sum of money an insurance company agrees to pay at stated intervals to a person who has previously deposited money with the company. The money deposited may be in a single lump payment or in a series of payments. An annuity is designed to provide supplemental income (beyond private pension plans) during one's retirement years.

Monthly annuities may be guaranteed either for a specified number of years or for life. Some annuity contracts guarantee a minimum number of payments. Any payments not made to the owner of a policy before his or her death will be paid to a beneficiary.

Illus. 20-2

Term insurance is useful for a young family who wants to make sure a spouse and children would be taken care of if the primary wage earner dies.

Which Type is Best?

Buying life insurance, like other major purchases, should be based on the individual's particular needs. For a single person with no dependents or financial obligations to others, perhaps no life insurance, or at best a minimum amount, is needed. Term insurance is useful for a young family who wants to make sure a surviving spouse and children would be taken care of if the primary wage earner dies. For an older, more established family, a straight life policy with fixed premiums and a cash-value buildup may be more attractive. Table 20-1 summarizes the characteristics of term and cash-value policies.

Insurance companies have developed many variations and combinations of term and whole life insurance. Combination plans, such as universal life, are simply cash-value policies that combine term insurance and an investment fund in one contract. Combination insurance is probably the best way to obtain the advantages of each of the major types of insurance.

Table 20-1
Term v. Cash-Value Insurance

Term	Straight, Ordinary, Whole
1. Low initial premium allows for extensive coverage	1. Higher initial premium than term insurance
2. Protection for a specific period of time	2. Protection for as long as premium is paid
3. May be renewable at higher or lower amounts to meet changing needs	3. Growing cash value
	4. Fixed-level premium
4. Premium rises with each new term	

FEATURES OF LIFE INSURANCE POLICIES

There are many kinds of insurance contracts, as you have just learned. Some features are common to all policies; other features are found only in specific contracts.

Specific Features in Policies

All of the following features should be understood by anyone considering buying a life insurance policy.

Incontestable Clause. The buyer of life insurance should understand the meaning of the *incontestable clause* in the policy. This clause protects the insured against policy cancellation if information given by the insured in the application is later found to be false or incomplete. The insured may have made, purposely or not, misstatements of fact regarding age, health or other information. If the insurance company does not prove such information is false or incomplete within the time limit specified in the incontestable clause (usually one or two years), it cannot later cancel the contract.

Paying Premiums. Premiums are due on the date stated in the policy. They must be paid to the home office or to an authorized agent. Most companies do not give a receipt unless requested. A canceled check serves as a receipt.

Life insurance policies generally allow what is called a *grace period.* This is a period ranging from 28 to 31 days after the date the premium is due. If the premium is paid during this grace period, there is no penalty to the policyholder. If the premium is not paid during the grace period, the policy lapses. This means the ending of the contract and the loss of protection. If the policy has a cash value, that value will keep the insurance in force for a short time. If the policy lapses, you may reinstate your insurance if you have not exchanged your policy for a cash settlement. In order to reinstate it, you must meet all requirements of a person buying a new policy. You will be required to take a new physical examination and to pay all the overdue premiums with interest. Some policies have additional requirements for reinstatement.

Nonforfeiture Values. All life insurance companies provide a choice of *nonforfeiture values* to a policyholder who stops paying premiums on any policy except term insurance. These choices are cash value, extended term insurance, and paid-up insurance. The following is an explanation of these nonforfeiture values:

1. The policyholder may obtain the cash value (the amount of money that will be paid to the insured if the policy is canceled). The cash value is stated in the contract as required by law.
2. If the policyholder wishes to continue the full amount of insurance protection without paying premiums, one may accept extended term insurance. This continues the face value of the policy for as long as the cash value will pay the premium.
3. If the policyholder opts for the paid-up insurance plan, the cash value is used to buy a reduced amount of fully paid insurance.

Use of Dividends. Life insurance companies sell participating or nonparticipating policies as described in Chapter 19. Dividends paid to participating policyholders can be used in the following ways:

1. They may be obtained in cash.
2. They may be used to reduce the amount of the next premium payment.
3. They may be used to purchase more insurance.
4. They may be left with the company to earn interest at a rate set by the company. These dividends and interest

may be used later for any purpose, or they may be withdrawn in cash.

5. They may be left with the company to earn interest and
then used to pay up the policy faster than normal.

If the insured dies before using the dividends and any interest
accrued, these will be added to the face amount to be paid to
the beneficiary.

Changing the Beneficiary. If you do not name a beneficiary
when you buy insurance, the policy is paid to your estate
upon your death. *Estate* is the term used to describe the
money and other property left by a deceased person. The
estate is distributed according to a will or the laws of the
state. If you decide to change your beneficiary, you may do so
at any time by filling out forms furnished by the insurance
company.

Policy Limitations. All policies provide protection for travel
on a scheduled commercial airline or a nonscheduled private
plane with a licensed commercial pilot. Some life insurance
contracts limit coverage on travel in foreign countries that are
at war. Almost all policies provide protection in case of death
due to war, but there are still a few exceptions.

It is well to study the special clauses that provide such
limitations. These special clauses usually are placed at the end
of the policies and are called *riders*.

Death by suicide is usually not covered by an insurance
policy if the suicide occurs during the first year or two of the
contract. However, if suicide occurs during that time, the
insurance company usually will return to the beneficiary part
of the premiums that have been paid.

Extra Benefits. Some insurance policies have provisions that
waive the premium payments if the insured becomes permanently disabled. This provision is called a *premium waiver*.

Other policies provide twice the amount of death benefit if
the insured dies as the result of an accident instead of from
natural causes. This provision in an insurance policy is generally called the *double indemnity clause*.

Economics of Life Insurance

In considering life insurance as a form of saving, one must
compare it with other forms of saving. It must be remembered
that a part of every premium payment is used to pay for
insurance protection and does not go into savings. Also, life

insurance companies pay only moderate interest rates to policyholders.

Savings plans in banks and other financial institutions may pay interest rates greater than those of insurance companies. These plans range from the familiar passbook savings accounts to the higher-yielding certificates of deposit. A disadvantage of the higher-yielding savings plans is that the required minimum deposit may be larger than the insurance premium.

The advantage of using insurance as a form of saving is that it forces you to save. Policyholders will usually budget their incomes so they have money available for premiums; otherwise, they lose their insurance protection. People may not force themselves to budget regularly for savings, since they don't lose anything if they fail to save every payday.

Until insurance companies design more favorable insurance/savings plans, many financial advisers will not recommend insurance as a form of savings. Instead they recommend that people buy term insurance for needed protection and save by putting money in a savings account. After savings have built up over a few years, advisers then recommend investing part of the savings in municipal and corporation bonds, stocks, real estate, or collectibles.

FACTS EVERYONE SHOULD KNOW ABOUT LIFE INSURANCE

1. The primary purpose of life insurance is to replace lost income if the principal wage earner dies.
2. A life insurance policy is a contract.
3. Life insurance can be bought individually or as part of a group.
4. Group insurance generally does not require a physical examination.
5. Term insurance is the least expensive form of life insurance, but it does not build up a cash value.
6. Straight life insurance provides financial protection in the event of death and builds up a cash value (forced savings).
7. Universal life insurance combines the features of term insurance with an interest-bearing investment account.

HEALTH INSURANCE

The main purpose of health insurance is to protect the family against financial losses that might arise from illness or an accident involving any member of the family. Health insurance may provide one, a combination, or all of the following six coverages:

1. hospital expense insurance,
2. surgical expense insurance,
3. general medical expense insurance,
4. major medical insurance,
5. dental insurance, and
6. loss-of-income insurance.

Hospital Expense Insurance

Hospital expense insurance is the most widely used form of health insurance. This coverage provides benefits for hospitalization to cover daily room and board, regular nursing services while in the hospital, and certain hospital services and supplies such as X rays, lab tests, and medication. Hospital expense insurance policies often have certain limits built into them. For instance, a policy may have specific limits, such as $200 per day, for the cost of a hospital room. The patient will be obligated to pay any amount over the amount specified in the policy. Some insurance policies cover a lengthy hospital stay, such as 365 days, while others do not. Some policies provide full service benefits which pay reasonable and customary charges in full. It is important to check hospitalization policies for any limitations and the types of protection provided.

Surgical Expense Insurance

Surgical expense insurance provides payment for surgical costs according to a schedule of fees payable for each type of operation. The schedule of fees is based on the nature of the operation. For example, the surgeon's fee for a tonsillectomy may be $325; for an appendectomy, $450. If the doctor charges more than the established fee, the patient is obligated to pay the balance. Surgical expense insurance is the second most widely used form of health insurance.

General Medical Expense Insurance

This type of insurance pays part or all of the costs for doctors' calls at the hospital. It may also pay part of the costs for visits by the patient to the doctor's office. The number of calls of each type and the amount to be paid by the insurance company are stated in the policy.

Major Medical Insurance

This type of insurance is meant to cover the major portion of the costs incurred as the result of a serious illness or accident. Serious illness and accidents can result in expenses amounting to $20,000 or more. Most experts today believe that for a lifetime major medical maximum to be adequate, it should be $250,000 or more.

Major medical insurance is designed to begin where hospital, surgical, and general medical insurance leave off. Most major medical policies have a deductible clause and *coinsurance* provisions. A deductible clause may require the insured person to pay the first $200 of any cost not covered by the basic policies. The coinsurance provision may call for the insured to pay 10 to 20 percent of any amount above the deductible. For example, with a major medical plan that has a 15/85 coinsurance provision, the patient pays 15 percent and the insurance company pays 85 percent of the medical bills after the deductible. In other words, a medical care bill totaling $10,000 of eligible expenses would leave the patient paying $1,500 plus the deductible. For this reason, it is important to obtain a stop-loss provision. With a *stop-loss provision*, the patient pays up to a certain amount and no more. For example, after the insured pays $1,500 out of pocket, the insurer will pay 100 percent of all remaining covered medical expenses.

Dental Insurance

Dental insurance provides reimbursement for expenses of dental services and supplies and encourages preventive care. The coverage normally provides for oral examinations (including X rays and cleanings), fillings, extractions, inlays, bridgework, dentures, oral surgery, root canal therapy, and orthodontics.

Dental expense insurance provides reimbursement for expenses of dental services and supplies and encourages preventive care.

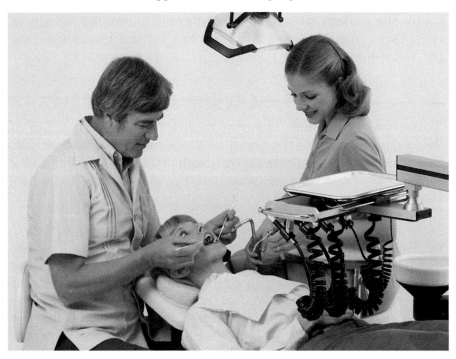

Dental coverage is generally available through insurance company group plans, prepayment plans, and dental service corporations. Dental insurance is growing in popularity as a way to help with dental costs.

Loss-of-Income Insurance

An illness or accident may cause you to lose your income. *Loss-of-income insurance*, also called disability insurance, provides for the partial replacement of income lost by employees as the result of an accident or illness. Generally, disability insurance policies are divided into two types: those that provide benefits for up to two years (short term) and those that provide benefits for a longer period ranging from five years to age 65 to life. Families with loss-of-income insurance are assured that they will have income in the event of an accident or prolonged illness.

The amount of the benefit from disability insurance may vary depending upon whether disability is total or partial. The duration of benefits may vary depending on whether the disability is the result of an accident or illness. Premiums are based on the amount of income that is to be replaced and the length of time for which payments will be made. One of the most important aspects of this type of insurance is the way disability is defined in the policy. If total disability is required, the policy may be of little value.

Usually, there is a waiting period of some days or weeks before benefits are payable. The expenses of a short illness can be met out of current income or savings, but the loss of income for an extended length of time can be disastrous. Whether a person or family should carry disability insurance depends on the sick-leave provisions of the wage earner's job, workers' compensation provisions, and other factors.

HEALTH CARE PROVIDERS

Dramatic changes have taken place in health care during the last decade. New professional groups have emerged for delivering health care. A multi-tiered health care system has evolved. As a result, there are many ways in which individuals or groups of individuals can obtain health care and many ways to pay for health care expenses.

Traditional Health Insurance Plans

More than 800 insurance companies in the United States write individual and/or group health insurance policies. Health insurance policies provide for payment directly to the insured or, if assigned by the insured, to the provider (doctor or hospital) of the health care services. The Blue Cross and Blue Shield plans are the most widely known health insurers in the United States. Blue Cross and Blue Shield plans pay medical care expenses directly to the hospital or doctor. Blue Cross provides hospital care benefits, while Blue Shield plans provide benefits for surgical and medical services performed by a physician. Blue Cross/Blue Shield is a nonprofit organization that operates much like profit-making health insurance companies.

Health Maintenance Organizations

Health care coverage is also available through *health maintenance organizations (HMOs)* which provide comprehensive health care services for their members for a regular fixed payment. In such plans a group of physicians, surgeons, dentists, or optometrists furnish the members with needed care as specified in the contract. After the fixed fee is paid there are few or no out-of-pocket expenses associated with an HMO. The emphasis in these plans is on preventive care and the treatment of disabling illnesses.

Many employers now offer their workers a choice between a traditional insurance plan and an HMO. From the early 1970s to 1985, the number of HMOs increased from 33 to 377 and the number of subscribers increased from 3.6 million to 16.7 million.

Self-Insurance

In recent years, some corporations, municipalities, and other organizations have turned to self-funded health plans. Because of the costs associated with employer-offered health insurance, some large organizations establish their own form of health insurance program. These self-insurance plans are designed to give workers medical benefits while allowing the company to economize. Usually a third party organization administers these plans, but does not assume any of the financial risks of paying benefits. It is important to remember that companies that self-insure must assume the financial burden if they encounter medical bills greater than the premium income.

Medicare

Medicare—a federal government program—provides medical care for people age 65 and over. Medicare provides hospital and physician insurance coverage that many older citizens would not otherwise be able to afford. Medicare was not designed to be a comprehensive health care program. In fact, it only covers about 40 percent of most older adults' individual medical expenses.

Medicaid

Medicaid helps pay medical bills for low-income Americans of all ages. Medicaid is basically administered by each state within certain broad federal requirements and guidelines. The program is financed jointly by state and federal funds and is designed to provide medical assistance to individuals eligible to receive payment under another assistance program, such as

Aid to Families with Dependent Children. In addition, states may provide Medicaid to the medically needy; that is, to persons who have enough income to pay for basic living expenses but not enough to pay for their medical care.

FACTS EVERYONE SHOULD KNOW ABOUT HEALTH INSURANCE

1. Health insurance protects a family or an individual against financial loss due to an accident or illness.
2. The most common types of health insurance are hospital, surgical, and general medical.
3. Many businesses provide hospital and surgical insurance coverage for their employees. This group insurance is paid fully or in part by the employer.
4. Major medical insurance insures against the major portion of the cost of a serious illness or accident.
5. There are numerous ways to provide for health care expense protection: traditional health insurance plans, HMOs, self-insurance, Medicare, and Medicaid.

VOCABULARY BUILDER

annuity
beneficiary
coinsurance
double indemnity clause
health maintenance
  organization

incontestable clause
life insurance
mortality tables
premium waiver
riders

REVIEW QUESTIONS

1. What does it mean to have an insurable interest in a person?
2. What are the two most common ways life insurance is purchased? Which way does not require a medical examination?

3. What type of insurance requires the smallest initial cash outlay?
4. What are the major characteristics of term insurance?
5. What are the major characteristics of cash-value insurance?
6. In what ways does a limited-payment life insurance policy differ from a straight life insurance policy?
7. What is universal life insurance?
8. Describe three types of nonforfeiture values.
9. What options regarding the use of policy dividends does a participating policyholder have?
10. What is the primary purpose of health insurance?
11. What are the six different types of health insurance coverages?
12. What expenses are covered by hospital expense insurance?
13. How does a coinsurance feature with major medical coverage work?
14. How is an HMO different from traditional health care insurance?
15. What is self-insurance? Explain the risk of self-insurance for the insurer.

DISCUSSION QUESTIONS

1. A widowed mother with limited funds is financing most of the college education for her son, although he is paying part of the cost from his own part-time work. Should she buy a life insurance policy on his life? If so, what kind? Should he buy a policy? Why?
2. Should a person whose income is to decrease sharply at some time in the future buy limited-payment life insurance?
3. Barbara Brown is single and has no dependents, but would like to have an insurance policy that forces her to save regularly. What type of insurance policy would serve as a forced savings plan?
4. What kind of policy should one buy in order to have a loan or cash value and to provide permanent protection but only pay premiums for a stated number of years?

5. Jack Carlson is married and has three children under the age of twelve. What type of insurance is likely to provide the fullest financial protection for the family?

6. Why is a premium waiver provision important in a life insurance contract?

7. Peg Reilly discovers that she is 60 days delinquent in paying a premium on her life insurance policy. What should she do?

8. Should a person with a well-planned life insurance program buy trip flight insurance when making trips by airplane?

9. Should the head of the family carry more than one health insurance policy?

10. Should all families carry loss-of-income insurance?

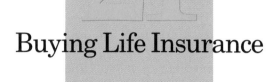

Buying Life Insurance

Life insurance is important to all members of the family. Planning a life insurance program that includes the whole family is most wise. To get proper coverage it is necessary to select a sound insurance company, a good agent, and the right policies. The problems that an individual or family must solve in planning a good insurance program are discussed and analyzed in this chapter.

After studying this chapter, you will be able to:

1. state how an insurance company should be selected,
2. explain how the rates of different insurance companies can be compared,
3. identify factors that should be considered in selecting an insurance agent, and
4. identify factors that should be considered in planning an insurance program.

SELECTING AN INSURANCE COMPANY AND AN AGENT

Selecting an insurance agent and an insurance company is an important step in planning a family's insurance program. A reliable agent can be very helpful in planning the program, and a reliable insurance company can assure the quality of protection.

Planning a life insurance program that includes the whole family is wise.

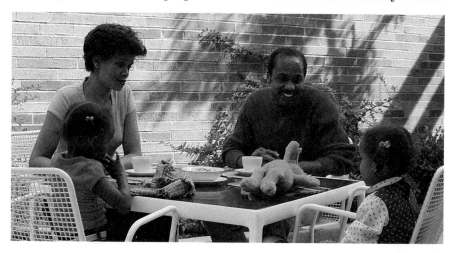

Guidelines for Selecting an Insurance Company

Reputation, operating success, and financial soundness should be carefully studied when selecting a life insurance company. Much of this information is available from your state insurance commission, since an insurance company must be licensed in the state in which it operates. Also, you can get a copy of a company's latest annual report from an agent or by writing to the home office of the company. Information on a company's reputation and financial standing may be obtained from people in your community—bankers, lawyers, business people, or friends who may have done business with the company. *Best's Insurance Reports,* a reference volume available in most libraries, is a good source for helping you determine the financial stability of an insurance company. Those companies with at least an "A" rating can usually be considered quite stable.

As is true with everything that we purchase, we should plan to buy insurance from the company that offers the best value. This means, therefore, that costs as well as provisions of policies should be thoroughly studied and considered.

Comparing Costs of Policies

The cost of life insurance varies with the type of policy being considered. Table 21-1 can be used to compare the approximate cost of the four different types of policies discussed in Chapter 20. From this table it is obvious that term insurance is the least expensive type of insurance available. As shown in

Table 21-1
Price Comparison of Four Types of Insurance

Bought at Age	Cash Value			Term
	Straight Life	Limited Payment 20-Payment	Endowment at age 65	5-Year Renewable-Convertible
15	$ 6.12	$14.05	$10.04	$ 3.96
20	7.10	15.70	11.90	3.96
25	8.40	17.45	14.23	3.96
30	10.25	19.55	17.35	4.08
40	15.50	25.30	27.75	5.62
50	24.25	33.85	52.32	10.28

Note: The figures shown here are approximate annual premium rates for $1,000 of each of four types of life insurance policies if the policies were purchased in units of $10,000. Rates shown are approximate premium rates for nonparticipating life insurance policies for men. Rates for women are somewhat lower because of women's somewhat lower mortality. Rates of participating policies would be slightly higher but the cost would be lowered by annual dividends.

Source: Policies for Protection, American Council of Life Insurance.

the table, the premium rates for term insurance increase as the insured's age increases. Because of its low cost, the buyer of term insurance can obtain sufficient amounts of coverage to provide for the financial security of a family or other dependents. With each of the cash-value policies above, the premium remains level or fixed at the rate shown when purchased. The fixed premium means paying more in the earlier years of the policy than the cost of protection at those ages and less in later years of the policy than the cost of protection at the older ages. The excess in the premium that the policyholder pays in the earlier years of the policy goes to building up the cash value that can be used in emergencies or at retirement. The major disadvantage of cash-value policies is the high cost of premiums. Because the cost is high, people often purchase insufficient amounts of cash-value insurance to assure the financial security of their family or dependents.

If your insurance needs are for protection only, you would want to consider and compare term policies. If your needs are for both protection and savings, you would want to consider and compare straight life, endowment, and limited-payment life policies. You must not forget, however, that the primary

SELECTING AN INSURANCE COMPANY

1. Compare premium rates among companies.
2. Select only a company that has a good reputation and is financially sound.
3. Deal only with an agent who has a good reputation.
4. In comparing the same or similar policies of different companies, do not compare cost alone. Be sure that the policies are the same in every respect. For example, some policies have a disability clause that relieves you from the responsibility of paying premiums in case of illness or other disability; others do not.
5. Buy life insurance only from a company licensed in your state.

purpose of life insurance is protection against loss of income you could earn while living. You should not count on life insurance to provide a major savings program. Instead, you should consider other savings plans discussed in Chapter 9.

In comparing different companies' policies, only compare policies that are equal. Policies that may appear to be the same often differ greatly in policy provisions. Some insurance companies offer participating policies which pay dividends to policyholders. Other insurance companies offer nonparticipating policies which do not pay dividends. Under a participating policy, a policyholder may receive an annual dividend based on the amount of premium paid. The amount of premium less the dividend received is the net cost of the premium on the policy. With a nonparticipating policy the amount of premium paid is the net cost of the policy per year.

Not only do the costs of various kinds of insurance differ, but the cost of similar policies differs among insurance companies. Over a twenty-year period the difference in cost for similar insurance can be several thousand dollars. To compare costs among similar policies, ask insurance agents to give you the interest-adjusted net-cost index for their policies. (*Best's Insurance Reports* also provides this index for a number of policies and companies.) This index takes into account what interest you would have earned on that portion of the premiums which increases cash value. The lower the index number, the less the insurance costs.

In some states insurance agents are required by law to provide the interest-adjusted net-cost index on request. Think twice about buying insurance from a company in which an agent refuses to provide this index, even if the company is in a state that does not require this disclosure. The honesty of the insurance agent who advises you is as important as the soundness of the company from which you buy insurance.

Selecting an Agent

As a general rule, insurance agents are honest and give careful attention to the insurance needs of clients. The buyer of insurance should bear in mind, however, that some insurance agents may be so eager to sell that they may not always make the best recommendations. The buyer should therefore be familiar with the basic types of insurance in order to judge the merits of an insurance agent's recommendations.

Many agents study life insurance by taking courses in schools. This study, which often takes several years, helps the agent learn the principles of life insurance. The agent also learns the nature of the various insurance policies and the principles of insurance program planning for an individual or a family.

After completing an extensive course of study (the equivalent of 30 credit hours typically taken over five years), an agent must take 10 examinations to qualify for the professional designation, *Chartered Life Underwriter.* The CLU is to the life insurance industry what the CPA (Certified Public Accountant) is to the accounting profession—the highest level of professional expertise. The letters CLU may be used after an agent's name. This means that the agent is well informed about insurance and is capable of giving sound advice about insurance planning.

How the Agent Can Help You

A reliable agent working for a reliable company will usually give sound advice to prospective insurance buyers. In applying for an insurance policy, the applicant is usually asked to state the amount of insurance already owned. This information helps the insurance agent decide if the applicant needs more insurance. If more insurance is needed and if the applicant can afford it, the insurance agent can help the applicant select the proper kind.

Total spending for insurance should be in keeping with a person's total income. A good agent should help fit an insurance program to the buyer's needs and financial ability. The agent can help you obtain the best use of your insurance dollar by:

1. planning insurance protection to fit your needs and those of your dependents,
2. building an insurance program that will include savings for your retirement and for specific purposes such as your children's college education,
3. fitting the purchasing of policies to your present and probable future income, and
4. revising your insurance program from time to time as your needs change.

DEVELOPING A LIFE INSURANCE PROGRAM

A life insurance program should fit the needs and financial ability of the buyer. These needs include protection from the loss of income of the primary wage earner and some form of savings plan. As needs and finances change, the insurance program should also change.

Planning the Initial Program

Every family should consider an insurance program at the time of marriage and then modify the program as changing conditions warrant. Three major problems are involved in insurance planning:

1. how much life insurance the family needs,
2. what kind of financial protection through insurance the family needs, and
3. how much insurance the family can afford.

Relationship Between Life Insurance Expenditures and Personal Income

Even when a family's income is small, insurance is needed to protect the dependents should the primary wage earner die. The amount that is set aside for insurance should be planned in the same way other expenditures are planned. As a person's salary increases, the amount spent for insurance may also increase.

Of course, a person without family responsibilities may not feel the need for much insurance. Such a person may prefer to invest the money in other ways. Single persons or married working couples who have no children may not need any life insurance. However, if a single person is supporting one or both parents, some type of life insurance would be advisable. Also, funeral costs, medical costs associated with an accident,

Illus. 21-2

Every family should consider an insurance program at the time of marriage and then modify the program as changing conditions warrant.

terminal illness, and debts (auto loan, for example) may make it advisable for a single person to have a modest amount of life insurance. A childless working couple who have a large home mortgage may find it wise to have each spouse covered by low-cost term insurance. The only people who do not need life insurance for protection purposes are those who have investments that provide enough income to support their dependents.

Each individual must determine, according to her or his unique circumstances, the amount of insurance to buy. It must be determined by considering income, necessary expenditures, amount of cash savings, and funds necessary for the care of dependents. Obviously, the amount expended in any particular case will depend upon:

1. one's level of living,
2. one's sense of responsibility,
3. cost of living,
4. number of dependents, and
5. type of insurance purchased.

Deciding the Amount of Life Insurance Needed

There is no simple answer to the question of how much life insurance is needed for a family. Some experts recommend that life insurance should equal five to eight times total annual take-home pay. Although this is a useful guideline, it may not be appropriate for everyone. The amount of life insurance a person needs depends largely on current family and financial circumstances. To determine the amount of life insurance needed, the buyer should carefully calculate his or her income, assets, expenses, and liabilities. By completing a financial statement similar to the one in Table 21-2, the buyer can determine the financial resources available to her or his dependents and the amount of income that would need to be replaced in the event of death.

In planning a life insurance program, the family's short-range and long-range financial needs should be determined and coverage should be provided for:

1. final expenses in case of death, such as medical care, funeral costs, and taxes;
2. mortgage payments and other debts;
3. survivors' living expenses (arranged so that payments are made monthly for a certain period of years or for an indefinite period of years;

Table 21-2
Insurance Protection Needed

Family Liabilities (Expenses to Be Paid)	Family Assets (Cash and Income)
1. Family living expenses fund $____	7. Life insurance............. $____
2. Mortgage debt.............. ____	8. Social security income .... ____
3. Education fund .... ____	9. Cash on hand............ ____
4. Emergency fund .... ____	10. Securities and investments ____
5. Final expenses fund .... ____	11. Other income .... ____
6. Total family liabilities........ $____	12. Total family assets .... $____
13. Amount to be made up with life insurance (difference between items 6 and 12) $____	

4. special needs, such as a fund of cash for the period of readjustment so the family can operate until it makes necessary changes in living style, a fund for emergencies and major illness, and a fund for children's education; and

5. retirement needs.

Life insurance programs should be planned mainly to replace income lost to the family when the primary wage earner dies. However, the other parent should also be covered by life insurance.

Except for certain sums that may be needed at the time of death, the proceeds of insurance should be paid regularly, under some prescribed plan, to the surviving family. Life insurance policies may provide monthly checks consisting of both principal and interest instead of a lump-sum payment.

Planning for the Readjustment Period

Accident, death, or disability of one of the chief wage earners of a family often results in financial emergencies. The reduction in or loss of a weekly or monthly wage presents a critical problem, especially where children are involved.

Many families are entitled to social security benefits, but these are seldom enough to take care of all needs. However, these benefits do add to the insurance program and should be taken into account. Unless an insurance program is planned, the family will have to depend upon its own earning power or upon income already saved.

At the time of death there are certain unusual expenses. Then comes the readjustment period when the family may

Illus. 21-3
Accident, death, or disability of one of the chief wage earners of a
family often results in financial emergencies.

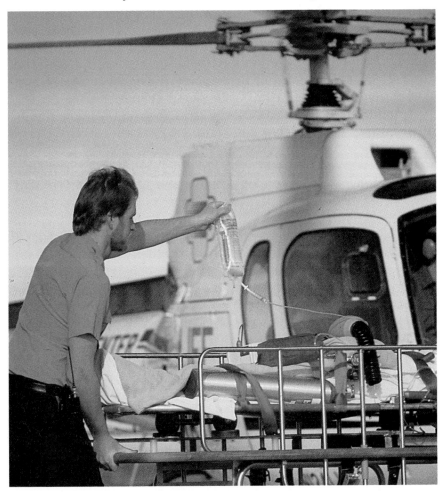

have to move into a smaller house and prepare for living on a
smaller income. In many families there is the problem of educating children until they are self-supporting and then providing an income for the surviving parent.

Insurance as a Factor in a Person's Estate

The proceeds from a life insurance policy may become due and
payable either because the policy has matured or because the
insured has died. If a beneficiary is named in the policy, the
life insurance proceeds are paid directly to that person upon
proof of death of the insured. If no beneficiary is named in the

policy, proceeds are paid to the estate of the deceased. The estate of a deceased person includes all property of value. All claims, such as debts, taxes, and legal costs of ending the business of the deceased, are filed against the estate for payment.

A person may prefer to make life insurance proceeds payable directly to the estate. Then, through a will, that person names the people who are to share in the estate after all expenses and claims have been paid. A *will* is a set of legal instructions for distributing a person's property after death.

A will may be changed at any time during the maker's life. A will may not deprive the wife or husband from either's rightful share in property according to the laws of the state.

When you make a will, you should select and name in the will an *executor* or *executrix*. This person prepares tax returns, pays taxes, investigates claims against the estate, pays outstanding debts, and determines the value of the property. The executor/executrix also distributes the property as instructed in the will and makes a report to the probate court where the validity of the will is proven. If a deceased person has not left a valid will or has not named an executor/executrix, the court will appoint an *administrator* or *administratrix*. The duties of the administrator/administratrix are the same as those of the executor/executrix.

Many people with a small amount of property feel that it is not necessary to make a will, especially if most of their savings are in life insurance that is payable to some member of the family. They feel that wills are only for rich people. However, even if you own only a small amount of property, your heirs will have less trouble and less expense if you make a will. And you are more likely to have your wishes carried out with a will than without it.

A close relationship exists between the provisions in one's life insurance policies and one's estate. Both are made up of one's property. Instructions for payments of the proceeds of life insurance are given in the policy. Instructions for the distribution of other property are given in a person's will. Thus, the provisions set up in life insurance policies should be considered when a will is drawn up.

In planning your life insurance program, you should have the advice of a competent insurance agent, preferably one who holds a CLU degree. In planning your estate and writing your will, you should have the advice of a competent lawyer.

FACTS EVERYONE SHOULD KNOW ABOUT BUYING LIFE INSURANCE

1. The reputation, success, and financial resources of insurance companies are important factors in selecting a company.
2. The insurance agent selected should represent a sound, successful company and should be able, through experience and training, to advise you about your insurance needs.
3. The honesty of the insurance agent who advises you is as important as the soundness of the company from which you buy insurance.
4. An insurance program is very important to individuals and families; many factors must be considered in planning such a program.
5. Total spending for insurance should be in keeping with a person's total income.
6. A person's life insurance, savings, and investment programs should be planned in conjunction with that person's will.

VOCABULARY BUILDER

administrator or
administratrix
Chartered Life Underwriter
   (CLU)

executor or executrix
will

REVIEW QUESTIONS

1. a. What are some sources from which one can obtain information to judge the standing and reputation of a life insurance company?
   b. What kinds of information can you obtain from these sources?

2. What is the main difference between a participating and a nonparticipating life insurance policy?
3. How can you determine the actual net rate that is charged for an insurance policy in a participating company?
4. Why is the interest-adjusted net-cost index important in comparison shopping for life insurance?
5. In planning an insurance program, what are some of the specific needs of survivors that should be taken into consideration?
6. What is meant by a readjustment period?

DISCUSSION QUESTIONS

1. Should a person with a family buy just one type of life insurance? Why?
2. If you start buying life insurance at age 30 and there is inflation (a general increase in prices and the cost of living), what happens to the value of the money that is paid to you in your old age or to a beneficiary on your death? In other words, what is the effect of inflation on insurance?
3. Give some reasons why you think it is very important to buy life insurance from a good agent and a reputable company.
4. a. When you apply for an insurance policy, why does the insurance agent ask how much insurance you already own?
    b. Why is it desirable for you to tell how much you own?
5. What kind of insurance program would you recommend for an unmarried person 17 years of age who expects to get a college education and then be self-employed?
6. a. Why is it undesirable for a person to carry too much insurance?
    b. How does one decide what is *too much* insurance?
7. Why should one avoid borrowing money to pay the first premium on a life insurance policy?
8. Many people feel that they do not have enough wealth to require the writing of a will. What do you think about this idea?

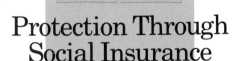

Protection Through Social Insurance

In the last three chapters you learned about insurance protection provided by private insurance companies. Most people in the United States also have economic protection through various federal and state social insurance programs. In this chapter you will study the protection provided to individuals and families by the federal Social Security Act and the state workers' compensation laws.

After studying this chapter, you will be able to:

1. state why federal and state social insurance programs are needed,
2. list the major provisions of the federal Social Security Act,
3. identify who is protected by unemployment insurance and by retirement insurance,
4. list the benefits that may be received under the federal retirement insurance program,
5. identify what special provisions are in the social security system for hospital insurance and for medical care for the aged,
6. describe how one applies for social security coverage, and
7. state how workers and their families are protected by state workers' compensation laws.

INCOME SECURITY

From the time we are born until the time we die, everyone is affected by the need for income security. Children are affected if their parents lose the ability to earn an income. Young adults are concerned about how they would exist if they were injured or disabled. Middle-aged people are concerned about how their children would be supported and educated if the parents died or became disabled. Older people often worry about living expenses because they cannot work and their incomes are considerably lower than those earned before retirement.

The Americans' Desire for Economic Independence

A characteristic of American pioneers was a strong will to be independent and economically self-supporting throughout one's lifetime. They carved out their own future by working and saving. Some pioneers worked for others as employees. Others acquired and developed land, mills, factories, stores, and other businesses. If they became disabled, they lived from their savings or their families took care of them. In some

Illus. 22-1

From the time we are born until the time we die, everyone is affected by the need for income security.

instances, they continued to receive some income for a short period of time from the businesses they had developed.

Gradually, Americans began to move to urban areas. They became employed in factories, stores, and other enterprises, which were owned primarily by others. Work was not always available; wage rates varied according to the demand for and supply of labor. The opportunity to draw income from an employer decreased greatly if one became disabled or old. For more and more people the desire to be independent and economically secure throughout life was not always possible. This was especially true for the many people who became disabled, for those unable to work because of old age, and for dependents who relied on someone else's income.

Legislation to protect and aid those who cannot help themselves is called *social legislation.* Some of the first social legislation provided for compensation of workers for loss due to accidents and illness. These laws, which now are common in all states, are known as workers' compensation laws. Next, the concern for old people who had no wealth or income was taken care of in old-age pension laws. Arizona was the first state to enact such laws. From these beginnings social legislation has been increased to include a wide range of benefits for larger and larger numbers of people.

In 1935, the United States government started a *social security system* to help protect its citizens from economic insecurity. Simply put, the social security system is insurance that is compulsory for most workers. The social security system provides a base on which individuals may build protection for themselves and for their dependents. The cost is paid by both the worker and the employer.

Since 1935, the details of social security legislation have been changed many times. Five major changes were made in the 1970s and major changes were again enacted in 1983. Therefore, any published information cannot be assumed to be up to date and accurate for more than a short time. However, the principles of providing social security will probably not be changed.

Income Protection Plans and Programs

Social security is not free. Someone must pay for it. The employee, the employer, and, in some instances, the self-employed individual pay social security taxes to the federal government. The government, in turn, places the taxes in a reserve fund from which social security benefits are paid to persons who qualify. The social security law was planned so that more than enough social security taxes would be collected to pay all claims. However, yearly cost-of-living increases in benefits called for by law, rising medical costs, and high unemployment during the 1980s forced the government to make adjustments in the law.

The Social Security Amendments of 1983 made major changes in the social security program in order to keep it financially sound into the 21st century. These changes include increasing taxes for employers, workers, and self-employed; making part of social security benefits subject to taxation for upper-income taxpayers; raising the age of eligibility for retirement benefits in the next century; and making new federal employees, members of Congress, the President, and other federal officials subject to social security taxes for the first time.

Social insurance programs do not provide complete economic security. For this reason, many forms of private insurance have been established. Some labor unions, employees of a particular business enterprise, and other groups and agencies have established privately sponsored and operated retirement programs. These programs are often financed by employers' contributions. In some instances, both employers and employees contribute to a reserve fund from which claims are paid.

Most families buy private insurance protection to add to the social insurance provided by government or private programs. Another way to provide protection is through an individual retirement account. An *individual retirement account (IRA)* is a tax-sheltered retirement plan that allows workers to deduct up to $2,000 a year from adjusted gross income when preparing a tax return. The deduction for a non-working spouse is $250. An IRA is not available to workers whose adjusted gross income before the IRA deduction exceeds $50,000 ($35,000 for singles) and who are covered by employers' pension plans. If a person is eligible for an IRA, the money deposited and invested and the interest earned on these accounts are tax free until the time of withdrawal (at age 59½ or later). A penalty is charged for early withdrawal. The investment choices for these accounts will vary according to the institution offering them. Some of the investment choices are money market certificates, stocks, bonds, certificates of deposit, mutual funds, Treasury bills, annuities, and real estate. Usually a fee is charged for maintaining these accounts.

It is possible to estimate what benefits to expect from social security if one is covered by that protection. If one is covered by a retirement plan sponsored by an employer or a union, the benefits from such a plan can also be determined fairly easily. All these benefits, plus the life and health insurance program of the individual family, will determine total retirement income or the benefits that are possible in case of sickness or accident. In addition, many people will receive benefits from state workers' compensation in case of a job-related injury or illness.

NATURE OF THE SOCIAL SECURITY TAX

Under the Social Security Act, employees, employers, and self-employed people pay social security contributions which are pooled in a special trust fund. Both employees and employers must regularly contribute a certain percentage of the employee's wages. Table 22-1 shows the current social security tax rates.

Nine out of ten workers in the United States are contributing to social security and are therefore earning protection under the social insurance program. For employees in occupations covered by social security, the tax is compulsory. In order for you or your family to get monthly benefits, you must earn the benefits by working for specified periods of time in

Table 22-1

Social Security Tax Rates

Year	Tax Rate*	Self-Employed Tax Rate
1985	7.05	11.8
1986	7.15	12.3
1987	7.15	12.3
1988	7.51	13.02
1989	7.51	13.02
1990	7.65	15.3

Note: These rates apply to yearly earnings subject to the tax, such as a maximum of $42,000 in 1985. The maximum covered earnings figure is adjusted each year in line with average wages.

occupations covered by social security. The amount of credit you earn is measured in quarters of coverage. Most employees get credit for one-quarter year of work if they are paid $50 or more in a 3-month calendar quarter. Four quarters are counted for any calendar year in which a person has $410 (1985) or more in wages. To qualify as fully insured, a worker must have ten years or forty quarters of work.

Benefits are computed on earnings over an entire working career. Congress has adopted an indexing formula which expresses prior years' earnings in terms of current dollar val-

Illus. 22–2

To qualify as fully insured under social security, a worker must have ten years or forty quarters of work.

ues. An employee's earnings will be indexed for use in computing the formula. After indexing the earnings over a person's working career, the government will eliminate several years (at least five) when earnings were lowest and average the rest. After the initial benefits level is determined, yearly cost-of-living adjustments are made to keep social security payments in step with inflation.

SOCIAL SECURITY BENEFITS

The federal Social Security Act involves two phases: benefits for unemployment and benefits for old age, death, disability, the needy aged, dependent children, and the blind. The first phase of this program is handled primarily through state agencies with federal assistance. The second phase is administered directly by the federal government from taxes collected by the federal government.

Unemployment Insurance

Under the Social Security Act, each state has set up its own law providing for an unemployment insurance system. This plan is operated in cooperation with the federal government. In most cases the tax is levied directly upon the employer. In a few states the employee also is required to pay a tax for disability or unemployment compensation.

The federal and state unemployment insurance that is operated under the social security laws applies to almost all classifications of workers. However, these laws do not cover students employed by a college or university under work-study programs, the clergy, or owners of a partnership or proprietorship.

Unemployed persons are entitled to compensation if they have been employed in occupations covered by the law for a certain length of time prior to unemployment. In order to get unemployment benefits, the worker must also meet the following qualifications:

1. be unemployed through no fault of the worker,
2. register at a public employment office for a job,
3. make a claim for benefits,
4. be able and available for work, and
5. be unemployed for the length of time specified by state law.

Retirement Insurance

Under the old-age insurance section of the Social Security Act, monthly social security payments may be made to a retired worker and to the worker's spouse. A fully insured retired worker is eligible for full monthly benefits at her or his normal retirement age of 65. She or he may begin receiving reduced retirement benefits as early as age 62. Starting in the year 2000, the full benefit retirement age will be gradually increased until it reaches 67 in 2027. For anyone born after 1960, the normal retirement age will be 67 years of age.

When a worker begins receiving social security payments, his or her spouse may also become eligible for benefits. The spouse, at age 65, is entitled to benefits equal to half of the retired worker's monthly amount. He or she may choose to begin collecting benefits at the age of 62, but the amount received will be permanently reduced to account for the additional years in which payments will be made.

For people who are receiving social security retirement benefits, there are limits to the amount of money they can earn. For example, in 1985, if a worker was between 65 and 70, she or he could earn up to $7,320 without losing any benefits. Annual exempt earnings increase automatically to keep pace with increases in average wages. At age 70, full benefits are payable regardless of the amount of earnings.

Survivors' Insurance

Upon the death of a worker covered by the Social Security Act, two types of payments may be made to eligible survivors: a single lump-sum death benefit and monthly benefit payments.

Single Lump-Sum Death Benefit. The surviving spouse or children of a covered worker are entitled to a lump-sum death benefit. This benefit of $255 will be paid regardless of other benefits that may go to the surviving spouse or children. Application for this payment must be filed within two years after the death of the insured person. If there were no surviving spouse or children of the worker eligible for monthly benefits, then no one would be eligible to receive the lump-sum death payment.

Monthly Benefit Payments. Monthly payments can be made to a deceased worker's:

1. unmarried children who are full-time elementary or secondary students and who have not attained the age of 19 (unmarried children 18 or older in post-secondary school are not eligible for benefits);
2. unmarried children 18 or over who were disabled before age 22 and who are still disabled;
3. widow or widower 60 or older;
4. widow, widower, or surviving divorced mother if caring for worker's child under 16;
5. widow or widower 50 or older who becomes disabled not later than 7 years after worker's death or within 7 years after she or he stops getting checks as a widow or widower caring for a worker's children; or
6. dependent parents 62 or older.

Disability Insurance

In 1954, disability insurance was added to the Social Security Act to give workers protection against loss of earnings due to disability. Such benefits are available to disabled workers and certain dependents. These include a child under 18 or disabled, a spouse caring for a child under 16 or disabled, or a spouse 62 or older.

Disability is defined as:

1. blindness or
2. a medically determinable physical or mental condition which has continued for 5 months and can be expected to result in death or to last for a continuous period of not less than twelve months, and that renders an individual unable to engage in any substantial gainful activity.

The worker's age, education, training, and work experience are considered in determining whether or not the individual is disabled. Payment of disability benefits begins only after the recipient has been disabled for five full months. The disability benefit paid is equal to the retirement benefit at age 65 or later.

Hospital and Medical Insurance for the Aged

In 1965, a major addition to the social security benefit program was made. This addition was a provision for hospital and medical care for the aged. The popular term given to this program is *Medicare*. Medicare, the program for hospital and medical care for people 65 and over, has two parts: hospital insurance (coverage is automatic) and medical insurance (coverage is voluntary).

Medicare's basic hospital insurance plan pays for some of the costs of hospitalization and some related medical expenses a person may incur after leaving the hospital. A supplementary medical insurance plan, for which beneficiaries pay a monthly amount if they choose to enroll, defrays a share of the doctor bills and other medical costs not covered under the basic hospital insurance plan. In addition, many people pay for health insurance policies to cover expenses not reimbursed by Medicare's hospital and medical insurance. These are known as Medicare supplemental policies.

The two Medicare programs are not designed to pay all hospital and doctors' bills. They will, however, cover most of the major charges. Each program includes a deductible provision under which the recipient pays an initial portion of the bill and Medicare helps pay the remainder. Medicare is financed by payroll taxes paid by the worker and the employer into a separate trust fund from which benefits are paid. Eligibility for Medicare is tied to eligibility for social security.

Other Social Security Programs

The earlier discussion on social security dealt with the benefits that are paid as a result of deductions from wages and on the basis of previous earnings. Under the Social Security Act, however, the federal government has made provisions for assistance to other needy groups. In general, the plan provides funds for:

1. needy aged,
2. needy dependent children,
3. needy blind,
4. welfare of infants and mothers,
5. crippled children,
6. child welfare,
7. vocational rehabilitation, and
8. public health.

If a state has a plan satisfactory to the federal government, that state may obtain from the federal government a contribution of up to 50 percent of the state expenditures.

The federal government also shares with state governments the cost of providing health benefits to low-income families. This form of aid to medically needy families is known as *Medicaid*. A *medically needy family* is defined as one whose income provides for basic necessities but not for adequate medical care or large medical bills.

Applying for Social Security Coverage

Since so many occupations are covered by social security, you should fill out Form SS-5, "Application for Social Security Number Card," early in life. This form, shown in Figure 22-1 on page 380, can be obtained from the local social security office or an employer. When applying for a social security card you will need two documents: one showing evidence of age and citizenship (a birth certificate or a baptismal certificate), and one showing evidence of identity (an insurance policy, a school I.D. card, a driver's license, a school record or report card, or a vaccination certificate).

You can apply for a social security card in person at any social security office or by mail. If you apply by mail, the social security office will return the two documents you submitted as proof of age and citizenship and as evidence of identity. The number assigned to you is yours for your lifetime even if you change your name. Figure 22-2 is an example of a social security card.

Figure 22-2
Social Security Card

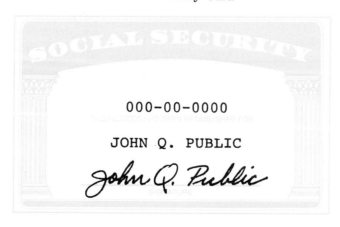

Figure 22-1
Application for Social Security Number

DEPARTMENT OF HEALTH AND HUMAN SERVICES	Form Approved
SOCIAL SECURITY ADMINISTRATION	OMB No. 0960-0066

FORM SS-5 – APPLICATION FOR A SOCIAL SECURITY NUMBER CARD (Original, Replacement or Correction)

Unless the requested information is provided, we may not be able to issue a Social Security Number (20 CFR 422-103(b))

INSTRUCTIONS TO APPLICANT — Before completing this form, please read the instructions on the opposite page. Type or print, using pen with dark blue or black ink. Do not use pencil. SEE PAGE 1 FOR REQUIRED EVIDENCE.

1

NAA NAME TO BE SHOWN ON CARD — First: *Judith* Middle: *Ann* Last: *Smith*

NAB FULL NAME AT BIRTH (IF OTHER THAN ABOVE) — First / Middle / Last

ONA OTHER NAME(S) USED

2

STT MAILING ADDRESS (Street/Apt. No., P.O. Box, Rural Route No.) — *6080 Broadway*

CTY CITY (Do not abbreviate) *Mabana* **STE** STATE *Washington* **ZIP** ZIP CODE *98110-1524*

3 CSP CITIZENSHIP (Check only one)
- ☐ a U S citizen
- ☐ b Legal alien allowed to work
- ☐ c Legal alien not allowed to work
- ☐ d Other (See instructions on Page 2)

4 SEX
- ☐ MALE
- ☒ FEMALE

5 ETB RACE/ETHNIC DESCRIPTION (Check one only) (Voluntary)
- ☐ a Asian, Asian-American or Pacific Islander (Includes persons of Chinese, Filipino, Japanese, Korean, Samoan, etc., ancestry or descent)
- ☐ b Hispanic (Includes persons of Chicano, Cuban, Mexican or Mexican-American, Puerto Rican, South or Central American, or other Spanish ancestry or descent)
- ☐ c Negro or Black (not Hispanic)
- ☐ d Northern American Indian or Alaskan Native
- ☒ e White (not Hispanic)

6 DOB DATE OF BIRTH — MONTH *10* DAY *3* YEAR *72*   **7 AGE** PRESENT AGE *16*   **8 PLB** PLACE OF BIRTH — CITY (Do not abbreviate) *Columbus* STATE OR FOREIGN COUNTRY (Do not abbreviate) *Ohio* **FCI** ☐

9 MNA MOTHER'S NAME AT HER BIRTH — First: *Jane* Middle: *Amy* Last (Her maiden name): *Wray*

FNA FATHER'S NAME — First: *Harry* Middle: *Leroy* Last: *Smith*

10 PNO
a. Has a Social Security number card ever been requested for the person listed in item 1? ☐ YES(2) ☒ NO(1) ☐ Don't know(1)

b. Was a card received for the person listed in item 1? ☐ YES(3) ☐ NO(1) ☐ Don't know(1)

▶ IF YOU CHECKED YES TO A OR B, COMPLETE ITEMS C THROUGH E; OTHERWISE GO TO ITEM 11.

SSN c. Enter the Social Security number assigned to the person listed in item 1. ☐☐☐ — ☐☐ — ☐☐☐☐

NLC d. Enter the name shown on the most recent Social Security card issued for the person listed in item 1.

PDB e. Date of birth correction (See Instruction 10 on page 2) — MONTH / DAY / YEAR

11 DON TODAY'S DATE — MONTH *10* DAY *17* YEAR *1988*

12 Telephone number where we can reach you during the day. Please include the area code. — HOME *555-9413* OTHER

ASD WARNING: Deliberately furnishing (or causing to be furnished) false information on this application is a crime punishable by fine or imprisonment, or both.

IMPORTANT REMINDER: WE CANNOT PROCESS THIS APPLICATION WITHOUT THE REQUIRED EVIDENCE. SEE PAGE 1.

13 YOUR SIGNATURE *Judith Ann Smith*

14 YOUR RELATIONSHIP TO PERSON IN ITEM 1 — ☒ Self ☐ Other (Specify) _____

WITNESS (Needed only if signed by mark "X")   WITNESS (Needed only if signed by mark "X")

DO NOT WRITE BELOW THIS LINE (FOR SSA USE ONLY)		
DTC (SSA RECEIPT DATE)	NPN	DOC
NTC CAN	BIC IDN ITV ☐ MANDATORY IN PERSON INTERVIEW CONDUCTED	
TYPE(S) OF EVIDENCE SUBMITTED	SIGNATURE AND TITLE OF EMPLOYEE(S) REVIEWING EVIDENCE AND/OR CONDUCTING INTERVIEW	
		DATE
	DCL	DATE

Form SS-5 (8-85)
5/84 and 1/85 editions may be used until supply is exhausted

3

The federal government keeps a separate account for each person registered. This account is credited for all social security payments made by the employer and for all deductions from the employee's wages.

Keeping a Record of Deductions. You should keep a record of your wages and the amount of social security taxes paid. The employer is required by law to furnish regularly to each employee a written statement or statements showing the wages paid to the employee during the year. Each statement must be suitable for permanent keeping. The usual form used is the W-2 wage and tax statement, illustrated in Figure 22-3.

Whenever you change employment, you should see that your new employer has your correct social security number. In this way you will be sure to receive credit for any wages that you earn. It is your responsibility to see that your employer uses the right number.

Verifying Your Social Security Account. Mistakes may be made in one's social security account. The regulations provide that any insured person may check his or her account for accuracy. However, any mistake more than three years old will not be corrected, except the complete omission of a wage

Figure 22-3
W-2 Wage and Tax Statement

1 Control number		OMB No. 1545-0008			
2 Employer's name, address, and ZIP code			3 Employer's identification number	4 Employer's state I.D. number	
Hartford Insurance Co. 400 Court Street Hartford, CT 06102-7633			5 Statutory employee □ Deceased □ Pension plan □ Legal rep. □	942 emp. □ Subtotal □ Deferred compensation □ Void □	
			6 Allocated tips	7 Advance EIC payment	
8 Employee's social security number 251-30-7427	9 Federal income tax withheld 3,032.70		10 Wages, tips, other compensation 18,575.00	11 Social security tax withheld 1,235.24	
12 Employee's name, address, and ZIP code			13 Social security wages 18,575.00	14 Social security tips	
Julia P. Rowe 127 Holly Road Hartford, CT 06102-7633			16	16a Fringe benefits incl. in Box 10	
			17 State income tax	18 State wages, tips, etc.	19 Name of state
			20 Local income tax	21 Local wages, tips, etc.	22 Name of locality

Form **W-2 Wage and Tax Statement   1987**
This information is being furnished to the Internal Revenue Service.   Copy C For EMPLOYEE'S RECORDS   Dept. of the Treasury—IRS

item by a particular employer. Thus, any person with a social security account should check it for accuracy and compare it with one's own records at least once every three years. A convenient card, usually obtainable at the post office, is provided for this purpose. Figure 22-4 is an example of this card.

Figure 22-4

Card for Checking the Accuracy of Social Security Contributions

REQUEST FOR STATEMENT OF EARNINGS

SOCIAL SECURITY NUMBER: 400 | 56 | 5532

DATE OF BIRTH: MONTH 1 | DAY 21 | YEAR 1950

Please send a statement of the amount of earnings recorded in my social security account to:

NAME (MISS / MRS. / MR.) Eva May Kelly

STREET & NUMBER 6789 Kildare Drive

CITY & STATE Cincinnati, Ohio ZIP CODE 45238-2290

Print Name and Address In Ink Or Use Type-Writer

SIGN YOUR NAME AS YOU USUALLY WRITE IT Eva May Kelly

Sign your own name only. Under the law, information in your social security record is confidential and anyone who signs someone elses's name can be prosecuted.
If your name has been changed from that shown on your social security account number card, please copy your name below exactly as it appears on that card.

WORKERS' COMPENSATION

As was mentioned in the first part of this chapter, workers' compensation, sponsored by all states, is another form of social security. The laws providing protection against loss of income due to accidents and sickness differ from state to state. You should become familiar with the plan in operation in your state. These laws have no connection with the federal Social Security Act.

Workers' compensation provides financial protection from job related injuries and diseases due to the nature of the work. The worker is not covered for any injury that occurs away from the normal place of employment. Under most of these laws, the employee receives compensation for an accident whether the employer or the employee is at fault. Exceptions to this law are cases of intoxication or recklessness.

All states have workers' compensation laws. In some states employers are required to pay into a fund for the protection of the workers. In other states these payments are optional. If the employer is not insured, an employee can sue for compensation as a result of an accident and can receive compensation. If intoxicated on the job or reckless in ignoring danger when injured, the worker cannot sue the employer.

The laws of all states provide that all medical and hospital bills will be paid regardless of the amount. If injured, the worker will also receive compensation each week while disabled. In most states this compensation will be paid for life if the worker is permanently disabled. In the case of death of the worker resulting from an injury at work, the spouse and children will receive weekly compensation.

ECONOMICS OF SOCIAL INSURANCE

The problems of old age and disability are both social and economic problems. They are problems of the individual and of society in general. Some people can save money and plan for the future; others either cannot or will not. If they cannot or will not provide for themselves, they will be burdens on society at some time.

Some people argue that because social insurance is compulsory, one of our economic freedoms (the right to spend our income the way we choose) has been taken away. Others argue that in a democratic country the welfare of each member is important. If no social insurance were available, millions of aged, orphaned, and widowed people would be homeless and without food and clothing in a short time. If there were no friends or relatives to take care of these needy people, the government would have to take care of them. The government then would have to raise taxes to pay for this added cost. At least under some form of compulsory insurance, the argument continues, these individuals have already paid for their benefits. Therefore, they do not have to become dependents of the government and they can maintain a sense of personal dignity and economic independence.

FACTS EVERYONE SHOULD KNOW ABOUT SOCIAL SECURITY INSURANCE

1. Most workers are covered by retirement and unemployment insurance.
2. Retirement benefits are generally determined by the average yearly income during the time of employment.
3. Spouses, widows, widowers, children, parents, and survivors of insured workers are entitled to certain benefits under social security.
4. Social security does not replace the need for life insurance and other retirement income.
5. Workers' compensation is a form of social security.

VOCABULARY BUILDER

individual retirement
   account (IRA)
Medicaid

Medicare
social legislation
workers' compensation

REVIEW QUESTIONS

1. Why was the federal social security plan developed?
2. How does social security differ from private insurance protection?
3. Who pays social security premiums?
4. Does social security provide complete economic security?
5. What are the two phases of the Social Security Act?
6. How is the unemployment insurance system operated?
7. Are all unemployed workers in covered occupations eligible for unemployment insurance?
8. To receive retirement benefits under social security, what is the minimum number of calendar quarters a person must have worked?
9. What is meant by the term *single lump-sum death benefit?*

Paul Schott
12/12/05
Economics
Per. 4

Vocabulary Builder.

- individual retirement account - an account in which deposits are made and invested over a period of years to provide retirement income; earnings on these accounts are tax free until time of with - drawal. (IRA)

- Medicaid. - a federal program which provides health benefits to low-income families.

- Medicare. - a federal program of hospital and medical care for people 65 and over.

- Social legislation - legislation to protect and aid those who cannot help themselves.

- workers' compensation - laws providing for

work-related accidents and illnesses.

Review Questions.

1. To give the elderly people a retirement income after working for years.

2. Social Security is just like the IRA each check you get there is money taken out for the income in your future of not working. A private insurance protection is what you have to take money aside to put in it.

3. You the worker pays for the social security premiums.

4. Social Security provides enough money for one month and every other month of the year.

5.

10. To what benefits is a disabled worker entitled?
11. How does one apply for social security coverage? When?
12. Does the federal government maintain a separate account for each person covered under social security? May one check the accuracy of one's account?
13. What is the purpose of workers' compensation?
14. What do workers' compensation laws provide regarding medical and hospital bills?
15. What would be the effect on local, state, and federal government spending if social security insurance programs were discontinued?

DISCUSSION QUESTIONS

1. Why do you suppose that social security, unlike private insurance, is not voluntary on the part of many workers?
2. How do the provisions for retirement benefits under social security eliminate certain economic risks?
3. What should be the relationship between one's life insurance program and the benefits one may be entitled to under social security?
4. In your opinion, are the requirements for obtaining unemployment compensation in your state reasonable?
5. Should social security benefits be increased as the cost of living increases?
6. If a worker gets lead poisoning from handling materials at the job site and becomes ill, do you think that worker can obtain benefits under workers' compensation? Explain your answer.

CLASS PROJECTS

1. A $100 deductible collision insurance policy on an automobile has cost Ms. Hulbert an average of $75 a year for five years. At the end of the fifth year she had a wreck costing $650 in repairs to the car.
    a. How much has she saved or lost by carrying the insurance as compared with assuming her own risk and paying all her own damages?
    b. If she would save by carrying her own insurance, is it wise for her to do so?
2. Using the chart below, indicate to which party or parties each of the automobile liability insurance coverages apply.

Liability Insurance Coverage

Type of Insurance Coverage	Applies to		
	Policy-holder	Policy-holder's Family	Other Persons
AUTOMOBILE INSURANCE COVERAGE:			
Bodily injury coverage:			
Bodily injury liability	yes no	yes no	yes no
Medical payments	yes no	yes no	yes no
Protection against uninsured motorists	yes no	yes no	yes no
Property damage coverage:			
Property damage liability	yes no	yes no	yes no
Comprehensive physical damage	yes no	yes no	yes no
Collision	yes no	yes no	yes no
No-fault	yes no	yes no	yes no

3. Paula Resznik has a $20,000 straight life insurance policy which has a cash value of $3,500. She recently borrowed $2,000 on this policy.
   a. If Paula dies before making any payments on the loan, how much would her beneficiary receive?
   b. When a person borrows on life insurance, in essence, from whom is that person borrowing?
4. Raul Martinez, age 20, collided with another car, swerved, and knocked down a traffic signal. Martinez and the occupant of the other car were both taken to the hospital and treated for minor injuries.
   a. Which expenses will Raul be responsible for paying?
   b. Which types of insurance coverage will Raul need?
5. Conduct a class survey to find out from the students' parents what type of health insurance protection they have. What type of policy: HMO, basic policy, major medical, or catastrophic coverage? Do they have individual or group insurance policy membership? deductibles? other limits? co-insurance?
6. As a class, gather rate information from several insurance companies for:
   a. $200 deductible collision insurance for an '87 Ford Mustang owned by a 19-year old male,
   b. term and whole life insurance for a 25-year old, and
   c. medical insurance that covers doctors' bills, hospital costs, and extended illnesses.
   Report the findings to the class. Draw conclusions about the advantages and disadvantages of different policies.

COMMUNITY PROJECTS

1. Write to the insurance commissioner of your state (your city or county library can give you the correct name and address) to find out what state regulations are imposed on mail-order insurance companies. Report your findings to the class.
2. From a local insurance agent, collect information regarding unusual or unexpected insurance claims involving personal liability in connection with homes, pets, and places of business. In addition find out the approximate cost of liability insurance for a homeowners policy. What conclusions can you draw from this investigation?

3. From a local life insurance agent find out what kinds of questions would be asked of three prospective life insurance policyholders to help plan a life insurance program for them. The prospective life insurance policyholders are:
    a. an 18-year-old high school graduate who plans to attend college for the next 4 years,
    b. a 20-year-old married factory worker with one child who plans to rent housing for the next 5 years, and
    c. a married working couple (ages 19 and 21) who have a mortgage on a mobile home but have no children.
    Report your findings to the class.

4. Check with an official in your school to learn of the features of the health and accident policy covering each student in your school (in some schools only those students participating in contact sports are insured). Report to the class what the coverages are and how much the insurance costs for each student. You might also report on the total number of claims filed by students in your school for the past year.

5. Make an investigation of the laws in your state affecting workers' compensation. These laws usually cover industrial accidents and sometimes sickness and death benefits. Write a report on the important features of these laws and list the occupations covered.

Glossary

absolute advantage: a nation's production advantage when it produces a product more efficiently than another nation

abstract of title: a report of the information taken from the recorded history of a piece of property

actual cash value: a type of insurance coverage that includes replacement cost minus depreciation

add-on costs: the costs that are added to the price of a raw commodity as it goes through the processing and marketing steps in the channel of distribution

adjustable-rate mortgage: a loan with an interest rate that can go up or down an agreed upon number of times during the length of the loan

administrator (administratrix): a person appointed by the court to settle the estate of the deceased according to the laws of the state

advertising: any form of public announcement that makes known the existence of a good or service for the purpose of stimulating a desire for that good or service

age of majority: the minimum legal age at which a person can make a contract

aggregate economic analysis: the study of the relationships that exist among the major components (parts) of the total economy

aggregate income: the combined total income earned in the country

aggregate supply: the combined total production of all goods by all the people and all the business firms in a country

annuity: a sum of money an insurance company agrees to pay at stated intervals to a person who has previously deposited money with the company

arbitration: the process of a third-party resolution when labor disputes cannot be settled by mutual agreement

as is: the seller has no further responsibility for the car or product once the sale is completed; if there are problems with the car or product after it is purchased, the owner must pay for any needed repairs

assets: all valuable items owned by a family, individual, or business

automation: continuous manufacturing or production achieved through the use of automatic equipment

backing: an item of real value (such as silver or gold) available to exchange for money in case one doesn't want to buy goods and services

bailment lease: a legal arrangement whereby the buyer rents an article and, after payment of sufficient rent to equal the purchase price, has the option to take title of the article

bait and switch: a type of deceptive advertising in which the seller advertises a product at a cut-rate price in order to lure customers into the store and then persuades them to switch to another higher priced item

balance of payments: the difference between total payments to and total receipts from foreign nations

balance of trade: the balance between a nation's exports and its imports

bank discount: interest on a loan deducted in advance by a bank

base period: the period, usually a year, assigned an index number of 100 and against which current data about prices or production is compared

beneficiary: the person named in an insurance policy to receive the insurance benefits upon the death of the insured

Better Business Bureau: a nonprofit, business-supported organization that is concerned with problems that arise from false advertising or misrepresented products or services

bill of sale: a written contract which provides evidence of ownership

boycott: a mass effort to withdraw, and to influence others to withdraw, from business relations with an employer

brand name: a trade name placed on a product to encourage people to keep buying that particular product

business: any organized activity conducted by either a person or a group of people that in any way helps to satisfy the wants and needs of people for economic goods and services

business cycle: alternating periods of expansion and contraction in production, employment, income, and other economic activities

business organization: a company that produces and makes available the economic goods and services we want and need

buying on margin: purchasing stock with a cash down payment and owing the brokerage firm the remainder

C

capacity: one's ability to earn money and to pay obligations when they become due

capital: any buildings, equipment, or other physical property (other than raw materials) used in a business

cashier's check: a check that a financial institution draws on itself

certificate of deposit (CD): a deposit which is made for a specified period of time, at the end of which time the deposit plus interest may be withdrawn

certified check: an ordinary personal check drawn by a depositor on which the financial institution stamps or writes a certification that guarantees its payment

Chartered Life Underwriter (CLU): a certificate awarded after a person successfully passes an exam measuring an agent's knowledge of life insurance and insurance program planning

character: a person's conduct, attitudes, and achievements

charter: a license issued by the state in which the corporation is organized authorizing the formation and operation of a corporation

chattel mortgage: a claim against goods that are usually moveable, such as a piano or an automobile

check: a written order by which a depositor directs the financial institution to pay a certain amount of money to another person

civilian labor force: the portion of the total labor force which includes self-employed persons but does not include students while in school, unpaid family workers, those in the armed services, retired persons, or those not able to work because of physical or mental problems

coinsurance: an insurance provision by which a person agrees to pay a percentage of the medical expenses

collateral: negotiable paper (bonds or notes) or property used by a borrower to guarantee the payment of a loan when it is due

collective bargaining: the negotiation between employer and union members over wages and working conditions

commercial bank: a financial institution owned by its stockholders that is authorized to accept money for deposit and to perform a variety of financial services

comparative advantage: a nation's productive advantage when it can produce one good more efficiently than another country

competition: the effort among sellers of goods and services to attract buyers

complements: two products that are related or used together

compound interest: interest added to the total invested before interest is calculated

⸺conditional sales contract: a security contract whereby the seller retains title to goods sold until the buyer has made all payments for the goods purchased

condominium: an individually owned unit of an apartment-like building or complex

consideration: what both parties to a contract agree to do in return for what each promised the other

consumer advertising: advertising addressed to or intended for the public

consumer credit: debt incurred by a consumer for goods or services needed for personal and family use

consumer finance company: a company that makes loans directly to consumers with weak credit ratings

consumer goods: those goods consumed directly and not used in the production of additional goods

consumer movement: a drive to achieve greater consumer protection through heightened consumer awareness of common problems

Consumer Price Index (CPI): an index of the average change in prices of a fixed group of goods and services

Consumer Product Safety Commission (CPSC): a federal agency responsible for setting safety standards for household and recreational products

consumers: people who purchase and use goods and services

Consumers' Union, Inc.: a nonprofit corporation which tests and rates the efficiency of consumer products

consumption: the act of using goods and services to satisfy our wants

contract: an agreement between two or more parties that creates an obligation enforceable by law

cooperative: a group owned and operated business that provides goods and services for its owner-members

cooperative apartment: a building in which each apartment is individually owned

cosigner (comaker): a person who signs a note with the borrower and promises to repay the loan if the borrower fails to do so

cost-push inflation: a relationship between wage increases and price increases

craft (or trade) union: union of workers in a single occupation or trade such as carpenters, airline pilots, plumbers

credit: an advance or loan of money with which to buy goods and services or an advance of goods and services in exchange for a promise to pay at a later date

⸺credit life insurance: short-term life insurance which pays off any remaining debt of the buyer should the buyer die before the installment contract has been paid in full

credit rating: an indication of a person's reputation for paying financial obligations on time

credit union: a nonprofit association operating as a savings and a lending institution for the benefit of its members

d

daily cash record: a form on which to record actual income received and actual expenditures made on a daily basis

debit card: an identification card that enables authorized users to instantly transfer funds electronically from their accounts to retailers' accounts

deductible clause: a clause in most major medical, homeowners, or automobile insurance policies which states that the insured person has to pay the first $50, $100, or $250 and the insurance company will pay the remainder

defective agreement: an agreement which is not enforceable because of a defect such as misrepresentation or concealment of vital facts

deficiency judgment: the right of a mortgagee to collect the difference between the amount due on the mortgage and the foreclosure sales price

deflation: the situation which occurs when the average level of prices falls

demand: the amount of a good or service that buyers are willing and able to purchase at different prices during a given time

demand deposits: money held in a checking account

demand-pull inflation: inflation caused by an excess of demand for goods and services over aggregate supply

depository institution: any financial institution that accepts deposits such as a commercial bank, savings and loan association, mutual savings bank, savings bank, or credit union

depreciation: the loss in value of capital (buildings, equipment, vehicles, etc.) due to wear and tear, passage of time, and obsolescence

derived demand: the demand for a resource (land, labor, capital, management) that is determined by the demand for the final good produced by the resource

direct marketing: any process by which the producer sells a product to the consumer directly

discount houses: stores that are able to give customers considerable price reductions by selecting low-cost locations, offering few special services, operating on a cash-and-carry basis, and keeping overhead expenses to a minimum

discounting: the act of financial institutions buying installment contracts from merchants at prices lower than the prices appearing on the contracts

discouraged worker: individuals who are not working and have given up seeking employment

discretionary funds: money a person has left after spending for necessities

disposable personal income (DPI): the amount of income left after all local, state, and federal income taxes are paid

double indemnity clause: a special benefit of life insurance whereby the insurance company will pay twice the amount of the death benefits if the insured dies from an accident instead of natural causes

double taxation: when the government taxes corporate profits and the dividends distributed to shareholders

drawee: the financial institution on which a check is written

durable goods: long lasting goods, such as appliances, automobiles, etc.

e

economic good: any material (tangible) object that people use to satisfy their wants or needs *economic needs:* basics such as food, clothing, and shelter

economic rent: that portion of income derived solely from the land without buildings and other improvements

economic scarcity: the inability to have all the goods and services desired

economic service: any intangible products that people use to satisfy their wants or needs

economic vote: the economic choice whereby consumer spending for goods and services determines the kinds of goods and services available in the marketplace

economic wants: goods or services we buy for pleasure or comfort

economizing: the choice making that people do in an attempt to get the most satisfaction from goods and services purchased

effective demand: a condition in which a person is willing and able to buy

—elastic demand: the demand for a product which is affected considerably by a change in the price of the product

emotional appeals: advertising that involves the emotions and excites people to buy even if the decision to buy is not a logical one

Environmental Protection Agency (EPA): a federal agency responsible for developing programs to protect and improve the quality of our environment

estate tax: a tax on the total amount of property left by a person who dies

executor (executrix): the person selected to settle the estate and to carry out the instructions set forth in the will of the deceased

expenditures: amounts of money spent for goods and services

extended service contract: added coverage that, for a fee, provides the buyer protection for a period of time beyond the normal warranty period

f

face value: 1. the amount of insurance stated in the contract; 2. the dollar amount printed on the front of a bond

factors of production: the resources which are needed in order to produce goods and services—land (natural resources), labor (human resources), capital (tools and machinery), and management (entrepreneurship)

Federal Reserve Note: the currency issued by the Federal Reserve System

Federal Trade Commission (FTC): a federal agency responsible for preserving healthy competition between businesses in our free enterprise system

fiscal policy: government decisions affecting spending and taxation for the purpose of increasing or decreasing production, income, and employment in the economy

fixed-rate mortgage: a loan with an interest rate and the monthly payment remaining the same during the length of the loan

float: the time it takes from writing and mailing a check to the time it is cashed at the bank

franchise: the right to operate a business in a given area

fringe benefits: employee compensation other than wages, such as life insurance, vacation time, and pensions

full employment: maximum use of all productive resources, particularly labor

g

garnishment: a legal procedure by which a creditor may require an employer to deduct a specified sum from an employee's wages until a debt has been paid

generic labeling: labeling characterized by plain white wrapping, single-colored printing, and a lack of a company name

gift tax: a tax levied by the government on large amounts of property given away

grade: a term applied to standards of quality when more than one quality of a particular food is available

grading: the process of separating the supply of a commodity into classes according to established standards

gross national product (GNP): the total dollar value of all final goods and services produced in the economy in a given year

h

health maintenance organization: an organization which provides complete health care to its members for a fixed regular payment

holder in due course: the purchaser of an installment loan or contract

homeowners policy: an insurance policy that insures against groups of perils which may befall a person's home, the contents of the home, and other personal property

human capital: the productive capacity of people

i

impulse buying: buying a good or service on a sudden whim or urge without first considering cost, need, alternatives, and ability to pay

impulse item: a good or service that a consumer buys on the spur of the moment

incontestable clause: a clause that protects the insured against cancellation of the policy in the event that false or incomplete information is given by the insured

indirect marketing: any process by which the products pass through several hands in going from a producer to a consumer

individual retirement account (IRA): an account in which deposits are made and invested over a period of years to provide retirement income; earnings on these accounts are tax free until time of withdrawal

industrial union: union of all classes of workers in an industry, such as automobile workers or mine workers

inelastic demand: the demand for a product which is not affected much by a change in the price of the commodity

inflation: the situation which occurs when total demand for goods and services is greater than the supply available at a given time; this results in an increase in the general price level

inheritance tax: a tax levied on the share of an estate received by an heir

injunction: an order from a court commanding an individual or group to do or refrain from doing an act or acts

insurable interest: a financial interest in property or the life of another person

insured: the person for whom risk is assumed by an insurance company; the buyer of an insurance policy

insurer: the company from which the insured buys the policy

interest: the amount paid for the use of money borrowed

intermediate goods: products used in the production of final goods and services

international trade: the buying, selling, and exchanging of goods and services by individuals and businesses of different nations

investment funds: savings available to buy an interest in a business

j

joint tenancy: co-ownership that features the right of survivorship

l

label: a written statement attached to an article or a product describing its main characteristics

labor: all forms of mental and physical effort directed toward the production of goods and services; a factor of production

labor force: all those 16 years old or older who are willing and able to work and who are employed (including self-employed) or seeking employment

labor union: an organization of workers formed to give workers greater bargaining power in their dealing with management

land: natural resources from which all of the goods that we use originate

landlord (landlady): the owner of a house or an apartment building which is, by agreement, occupied by others

lease: a rental agreement between the owner and the tenant

legal aid society: a society which handles legal cases for persons who cannot afford to obtain legal assistance

legal tender: any kind of money that by law must be acceptable in paying debts and taxes

lemon laws: legislation at the state level that helps new-car owners who cannot get a car fixed in a reasonable length of time

lessee: the tenant; the one that holds real property under a lease

lessor: the owner of the property; one that conveys real property by lease

level of living: the quantity of goods and services that we are able to buy

liabilities: debts owed by a family or individual

life insurance: a financial plan that pools or shifts the probable risks of loss of life among a group

loanable funds: savings made available for loans to businesses

lockout: a temporary stoppage of the operation of a business by an employer in an attempt to win a labor dispute with employees

m

maker: one who issues a promissory note

manufacturer's suggested retail list price: the maximum price which manufacturers believe should be paid for a car, sometimes called the *sticker price*. This is a suggested maximum price; most new cars are sold at a negotiated price.

market clearing price: the price at which the quantity demanded and the quantity supplied are equal; there is no shortage and no surplus

marketing: the business activities that direct the flow of goods and services from producer to consumer or user

marketing channel: the route goods for sale take from producer to middleman to consumer

mass production: the making of products in large quantities rather than in small quantities, which makes for greater efficiency in business operations

mechanics lien: a claim filed against the real property of a debtor for the unpaid value of labor or materials

Medicaid: a federal program which provides health benefits to low-income families

Medicare: a federal program of hospital and medical care for people 65 and over

merchandising: the process of actually filling demand for products

monetary policy: a plan to promote economic growth and to maintain a stable economy through control of the supply of money and bank credit

money: anything that is generally accepted in exchange for goods and services or in payment of debts

money order: a written order to pay a certain sum that is guaranteed by the financial institution issuing it

money supply: the total amount of money (coins and currency and demand deposits) in circulation in the economy

monopoly: complete control of a market by a single manufacturer or seller

mortality tables: tables showing the percentage of certain age groups that will die from all causes each year

mortgage: a legal paper pledging property to secure the repayment of a loan if principal, interest, or both are not paid as agreed

municipal bonds: bonds issued by city and state governments and special districts

mutual assent: the arrangement in which one person makes an offer and another person accepts the offer

mutual fund: a corporation that sells its own shares to the public and buys stocks and bonds of many other corporations

n

national debt: the amount of money that the federal government has borrowed from individuals and business firms

national income (NI): the total income received in a given year by all the people who contributed to the production of goods and services

national income accounting: the system used by the government for recording statistical information about the total economic activity of all people, business firms, and government

net national product (NNP): the result obtained after subtracting depreciation from the gross national product

no-fault insurance: a type of automobile insurance for which it is not necessary to decide who was the cause of an accident; each insurance company will pay for property damage, medical bills, and wage losses of its policyholders

nondurable goods: goods that are consumed quickly, such as food, clothing, gasoline, etc.

NOW account: an interest-bearing checking account (negotiable order of withdrawal)

o

odometer: a mechanical device on a car that records the number of miles driven

operating costs: variable expenses that increase as a car is operated

opportunity (real) cost: the value of the economic want that one gives up when choosing another economic want

over-the-counter securities: securities not listed on a stock exchange

ownership costs: the expenses, usually fixed, associated with owning a car; these expenses are not likely to change with the amount of miles driven

p

payee: the person to whom a check is made payable

personal economic analysis: a study of how an individual earns and uses income while functioning as a worker, a consumer, and a citizen

personal income: the total annual income received by all persons in a country from all sources, whether earned or not

picketing: the union practice of stationing a person near the entrance of a place of employment during a labor dispute

preferred stock: certificates representing ownership in a corporation entitling the holder to dividends at a stated percentage rate before dividends are paid to common stockholders

✛ ***premium:*** the amount paid for insurance

premium waiver: a provision whereby it is not necessary to continue to pay premiums if the insured becomes permanently disabled

private property: the portion of personal income that people can keep in the form of money, securities, or material assets

producer (capital) goods: anything manufactured that is used in the production of other goods

Producer Price Index (PPI): an index of farm products, processed foods and feeds, and industrial commodities

producers: people who create economic goods or services

production: the output of economic activity; a quantity of goods or services created

productivity: a ratio of output to input

profit: the portion of income left over after all business expenses or costs of production have been paid

progressive tax: a tax in which the rate of taxation increases as income increases, such as federal income tax

promissory note: an unconditional written promise to pay a certain sum in money at a certain date

property tax: a tax levied on real estate or any personal property that has value and can be bought and sold

public goods: goods and services produced by the government rather than by businesses and used by people collectively; individuals cannot be excluded from use of public goods

purchasing power: the quantity of goods that a given amount of money will buy

q

quota: a limit imposed on the quantity of an imported good allowed into a domestic market

r

rational appeals: advertising appeals that supposedly center on logic by providing basic facts and information

real (opportunity) cost: the value of the economic want that one gives up when choosing another economic want

regressive tax: a tax in which the rate of taxation decreases as income increases, such as a sales tax

rent: the price received from a tenant for the temporary use of land including buildings and other improvements

✛ ***replacement cost:*** the amount of money it would take to rebuild the same or similar item at prices existing at the time of loss

required reserve: the percentage of customer deposits that a depository institution must deposit with the Federal Reserve Bank

retailer: a business that sells directly to consumers

revolving charge account: a credit plan which stipulates a maximum amount that may be owed at one time and a minimum part of the debt that must be paid each month

riders: attachments to an insured's policy that change or add to the terms of the policy

risk: a predictable and insurable chance of economic loss

Rule of 78s: a prepayment plan which charges more interest in the early life of an installment contract than it does near the maturity of the contract

s

sales finance company: a company that deals only in installment notes arising from sales by business firms

sales tax: a tax on consumer purchases

savings and loan association: a financial institution organized for the purpose of accepting savings deposits from individuals and making loans primarily for purchases of homes

secured loan: a loan in which the borrower pledges or turns over to the lender some kind of property called collateral

share drafts: checks offered by credit unions

shortage: the condition that exists when demand is greater than supply at a given price

social legislation: legislation to protect and aid those who cannot help themselves

specialization: the assigning of an employee to a particular task rather than to the performance of all tasks pertaining to an operation (also called division of labor)

spending plan: a guide for spending and saving income

standard: a measure of quantity, weight, size, performance, and sometimes quality

standardizing: the process of preparing a definition or description of the various qualities of a commodity

standard of living: the way a person wants to live

statement of assets and liabilities: a statement which lists how much a family or individual owns, how much is owed, and the net worth of the family or individual

stockholder: a person who has a share in the ownership of a corporation

stock plans: housing plans which you can buy from a catalog

strike: a temporary stoppage of work by a group of employees for the purpose of compelling an employer to agree to their demands

subsidy: a grant of public money to private businesses to encourage production

subsidized: to be financially helped by the federal government

substitute: a good that may be used in place of another good

supply: the amount of a good or service that sellers are willing and able to offer for sale at different prices at a given time

surplus: the condition that exists when supply is greater than demand at a given price

sweat equity: the work and effort a homeowner puts into a home, which may make the house worth more money if sold

t

take-home pay: the amount of earnings available after the employer has withheld taxes and other deductions

tariff: a tax levied on imports and sometimes on exports

technology: the invention of machines and the discovery of new processes in industry which enables workers to produce more per day with less effort

tenant: a renter; one who occupies the property

title: the proof of ownership of property

Torrens System: a special system for registration of land ownership

trade puff: a general claim which should not be relied upon by the buyer of merchandise

transfer payment: income received by individuals from government, business, or other individuals for which no goods or services were produced or exchanged

u

underemployment: condition existing when workers have part-time jobs but prefer full-time work or have jobs that require less skill than they possess

underwriter: the party, usually the insurance company, from whom one buys insurance and who agrees to pay the loss

unemployed: those persons 16 years old and older who are willing and able to work but who are unable to get jobs

unemployment: the condition that exists when people are not working and are obviously not producing goods and services

unemployment rate: the percentage of the civilian labor force that is unemployed though actively seeking employment

unit pricing: the cost of a standard unit of an item given for the comparison of brands and sizes

unsecured loan: a loan in which the borrower merely signs a contract binding the borrower to the terms of the contract; no collateral is pledged

U.S. Office of Consumer Affairs (OCA): this office analyzes and coordinates all federal government activities in the area of consumer protection

utility: the ability of goods and services to satisfy human wants

w

wages: the prices that are paid for labor

waiver of lien: a legal form that releases the homeowner from claims against the contractor of work in the event that the contractor fails to pay suppliers for materials used in construction

warranty: a promise made that an article will operate in a specific way and that it has certain qualities

wealth: the total money value of the things we own at a given time

wholesaler: a business that buys large quantities of goods and sells to retailers or other middlemen

will: a set of legal instructions for distributing a person's property after death

workers' compensation: laws providing for compensation to workers for loss due to work-related accidents and illnesses

working capital: money for day-to-day business operations such as wages, materials, and other expenses

Index

PHOTO CREDITS